T0352689

BACK TO THE SHOPS

BACK TO THE SHOPS

SHOPS

The High Street in History and the Future

RACHEL BOWLBY

OXFORD
UNIVERSITY PRESS

OXFORD
UNIVERSITY PRESS

Great Clarendon Street, Oxford, OX2 6DP,
United Kingdom

Oxford University Press is a department of the University of Oxford.
It furthers the University's objective of excellence in research, scholarship,
and education by publishing worldwide. Oxford is a registered trade mark of
Oxford University Press in the UK and in certain other countries

First Edition published in 2022

Impression: 1

Published in the United States of America by Oxford University Press
198 Madison Avenue, New York, NY 10016, United States of America

British Library Cataloguing in Publication Data
Data available

Library of Congress Control Number: 2021944967

ISBN 978–0–19–881591–4

Printed and bound in Great Britain by
Clays Ltd, Elcograf S.p.A.

CONTENTS

III SPECIALITIES

LIST OF ILLUSTRATIONS

Introduction

O ver the past decade, news of the failure of one more familiar high street name has become so familiar as to seem part of a sad new shopping normality. With the growth of online retail, shopping in shops is seen and said to be coming to an end. And if the screens in front of our eyes and the keys at the tip of our fingers can supply the same pleasures or practical needs as the places you have to leave home for, then what, in the long term, would really be lost if they were? Or, to put this positively, what might be gained by continuing, still, in a digital age, to seek to be shopkeepers and shop customers?

Quite a lot, I think; and this book tries to show how and why, by going back to the shops—the many shops—that there have been. On the high street—that is, in the main shopping centres of towns—but also, and numerously, in side streets and housing estates, in cities and in villages, and in all sorts of temporary forms, from weekly markets to charity bazaars, and from the milkman's delivery float to the pedlar with his pack. The aim is to give some sense of the many kinds of business and building and human relationship that shops, in all their variety, have sustained and suggested.

The book is mainly set in one place—the UK—and with most attention to the past two hundred years, which is the time of most shops, most shopping, and most evidence of what they have been—by far. Most of this period is distant enough to have been almost forgotten, beyond living memories; but it is also close enough to be comprehensible as both preceding and contrasting with later developments. These past but not ancient times are striking now because they show a world in which daily shopping (for food) was fundamental, and shops were far more numerous. In the later part of the twentieth century it was also taken for granted by everyone—by the customers, the shopworkers, and the planners of public policy—that both shops and shopping were essential to the lives of communities and to the futures of towns and cities.

In outline, the long-term contours of shopping history can be set out with utmost simplicity, in five stages. First, there were pedlars, markets, and fairs. Second, there were small shops. Third, there were chains and some very big shops. Fourth, there was self-service and supermarkets. And fifth, there is online shopping. But while changing developments can be marked out in retrospective summary, in reality the history was anything but one of straightforward linear development: there was never a clear direction, inexorably moving from markets to supermarkets, or from pedlars to Primark. For most of the time it is a matter of long years and centuries of little variation; certainly of little 'growth' in the sense that the word is used now to mean an expectation of ever more economic activity. There were all sorts of differences between regions, or parts of regions, as well as by concentration of population or class or local resources and habits. Elements of the several stages are always present at the same time in different places, with different degrees of importance. And at every point, older practices survive, or come back, or mutate, sometimes unacknowledged, into what will then seem like quite different, more modern phenomena. Long derelict forms of trading—to put this the other way round—will have modern-day reinventions. Online shopping, for instance, that seems so twenty-first century, has a complex history of partial analogues. Mail order is one of these, in that it is shopping at a distance. Home delivery, which used to be standard for many types of food purchase, is another. This too is a case of customers not going to the shop themselves; but unlike most online deliveries, or mail order, it was based on local shops and custom.

As with other aspects of the history of everyday life, for shopping the evidence available for the period since about 1800 is overwhelmingly greater than for earlier times. Before the nineteenth century, the ever less evidenced past reaches back to mainly non-shopping medieval times: when most of the little that was consumed was produced or gathered at home or nearby, and little of that was bought. Food, the eternal single-use product, is the perpetual necessity. But in a culture where most people worked on the land, much was home-produced or neighbour-traded. A few basic items of furniture and kitchen equipment would be owned, and kept for as long as they lasted. But in general, the paucity of evidence and the uncertainty of its meaning make it difficult to know about the limited consuming and selling lives of most people before more modern times. As Dorothy Davis put it in the 1960s, in the first long-term history of shopping in Britain: 'No customs or taxation yields, no family papers or court records, will enable us to reconstruct in modern economic terms the business of the medieval butcher or baker or candlestick-maker, still less the turnover of market or fair.'[1]

In post-medieval centuries, information about what kinds of goods were purchased can sometimes be gleaned from the inventories of shop and house contents taken as part of probate.[2] Even so, it is hard to infer from a valuation if and when and where an item in a private dwelling had been purchased (rather than, say, inherited, or received as a gift, or in exchange for something else). And in order to have an inventory made at all, the person needed to have reached a certain level of wealth. There is some indication that in the course of the sixteenth and seventeenth centuries, ordinary people began to want or be able to acquire more or better furniture and clothing than previously. Very occasionally there are glimpses of the scope of local shopping, thanks to the rare survival of records from village shops from before the nineteenth century.[3]

In these earlier epochs, and on into much later periods, there is commonly no clear line between the shop as a place of purchase and as a place for manufacture or repair or alteration. A carpenter or cobbler naturally sold where they made. The shop as purely a selling place is only slowly separated off from what would now be known as a workshop. Shops were also commonly part of the house where the shopkeeper lived; most had accommodation attached to them. In the nineteenth and twentieth centuries there were many 'house shops' in residential areas, trading from a street-facing front room. 'Living over the shop' is still common, with the shopkeeping family occupying the same building as the selling and storage areas of the business.

The history of the consumption of the wealthy in early times is another kind of story from that of ordinary people. It is more—it has always been more, almost by definition. And there is far more surviving evidence about what things were bought, and more documentation of purchases and sales. In several instances, lists and receipts survive that show what was purchased for aristocratic households at the fairs. The great medieval fairs, most of all those at Stourbridge in Cambridgeshire and St Giles outside Winchester, were huge events, lasting up to two weeks and drawing customers and traders from far and wide. There, noble households sold the products of their estates and obtained supplies for the coming year from traders who came from all over the country. And from abroad: foreign goods of all kinds, from spices to wine to fabrics to jewellery, were exchanged. Some of these unusual things made their way into pedlars' packs to be carried around from village to village or to smaller, more local fairs and weekly markets; this was where you might find and buy pretty little things to give or be given as presents, the 'fairings' for a sweetheart. At the fairs there were travelling entertainers as well as merchants and other sellers; the goods and the people came long distances, on journeys lasting a long time, to be there.

Local markets provided different goods, and an outlet for selling them; but equally important, as with fairs, was their social function. Markets were normally weekly—'market day'. Most people, even if they were farming for others—farming being the default occupation—were also growing food or tending livestock on their own behalf, often on common land. Almost everywhere was within travelling distance of a weekly market, meaning that it was possible to get there and back on foot at either end of the day. This distance was understood to be about seven miles; regulations laid it down that the site of a new market might not intrude on the catchment area of an existing one. Markets were subject to detailed rules, and as a mark of their formal significance in a local polity, they were granted charters directly by the Crown. As a result, this aspect of early shopping history is better documented, often through court cases dealing with violations. It was illegal, for instance, to trade before the official opening time; this was to prevent the buying up of stock to resell at a profit.

Fixed shops, trading in their own buildings and open most days, are a feature of cities and towns from the Middle Ages; but towns are relatively small and far between until the period of the industrial revolution. With occasional exceptions, such shops were not set up with attention to their appearance as buildings, or to how they showed their merchandise. But from around the eighteenth century, luxury shopping became a regular feature of city centres, and some kinds of shop begin to put on a display not only of what they sold but of their attentive service, to customers who were now being given something like a shopping 'experience'. That is to say, the visit to the shop was becoming more than a means to a purchasing end; it was also intended to gratify the customer with a sense of privilege and favour in special surroundings. The word *shopping* itself dates from this time, and is noted (by women themselves) as a distinctly feminine preoccupation and occupation. Now for the first time urban shops were becoming, architecturally, a category clearly distinguishable from other types of building.[4] That aesthetic enterprise reached a high point much later in the 1920s and 1930s, when even ordinary food stores—the grocer, the butcher, the baker, and so on—were expected to renovate their interiors in line with new 'modern' principles of both style and hygiene.

Those decorative eighteenth-century inventions were signs of things to come, but did not in their time impinge on many places or many people's lives. A large-scale expansion of ordinary shops began with the industrial revolution and the movement of people into newly expanding towns, or large villages adjoining factories and pits. Unlike older settlements, there were no established markets or shops in these places, and people did not have access to adequate land (or time) to grow or rear food for themselves. At the same time, the supplying of goods from elsewhere became simpler and swifter. From the middle of the nineteenth century the developing railway network could deliver perishable goods to most parts of the country at speeds that were far ahead of what had been possible with horse-drawn traffic. Food shops could be restocked every day. Orders of almost anything could be dispatched from the metropolis or the ports, without delay, to almost anywhere. By the end of the nineteenth century—as early as that—there were chains or 'multiples' across the country, some with dozens of branches and a few with hundreds. Most were grocers, dairies, or butchers, and most were regional. But there were also non-food chains, and some chains were national. The growth of railway travel had prompted the development of WHSmith as a great chain of station newsagents and booksellers. Equally successful, and equally everywhere, was an enterprisingly expansive chemist's called Boots.

Other nineteenth-century changes involved a different kind of activity from the daily purchasing of necessities. Large city centres, as opposed to smaller towns, whether old or new, drew visitors who came in for the day by train to go to the shops. To London, and to other cities too, came middle-class women who began to spend enjoyable time on that pleasant activity called shopping. Shopping in this leisurely sense was not primarily a matter of supplying the needs of a household, its food, and other predictable requirements. Instead, it was more to do with occasional or unfamiliar prospects: looking at more various things than those to be found in the shops near home. And apart from whatever was purchased, the trip into town was an outing, a change from the routine. This is the implicit distinction, still resonant today, between 'going shopping'—a chosen and open-ended activity, to be enjoyed—and 'doing the shopping', an essential and regular task, most often associated with the buying of food.

The struggle of on-the-ground stores to resist the arrival of new ones is hardly a novelty in itself: the battle of new big stores versus older little stores goes back to the nineteenth century, when the first types of discounting megastore appeared in large towns. Independent traders, at the start of a long retail story, complained of the chains undercutting them because they could buy cheaply in bulk and sell with lower profit margins. The department stores that formed in the city centres from the late nineteenth century onwards offered their particular kind of special shopping experience; this was the glamorous, front-of-house face of what was at the same time a highly efficient economic set-up, based in the same way on low profit margins supported by high sales volume and fast turnover. In the later part of the twentieth century, supermarkets operated on exactly the same model, but with the opposite selling point: not fashion and luxury, but regular food at minimal prices. As supermarkets developed, they began to reverse the nineteenth-century movement that had brought people into the centre of towns to shop. The superstores of the very end of the twentieth century were built outside the towns, as newly built shopping 'centres' (the centres of nowhere) started to take the shops—and the customers—out of the actual centres altogether.

Alongside these larger changes of shopping direction, there were also constantly altering micro-types of specialized shops in the small and larger towns where most retail activity took place. Pre-war shops included many that were branches of larger 'multiple' organizations, and many more that were not—with the majority of both types occupying small units only. But in most ways, and certainly in the most visible ways, the long development of shopping has been a story of more and more, with shopping coming to be a daily activity, and with ever-increasing quantities and types of goods bought and sold, all the time. In another way, though, the story can be said to have come back to its point of origin. In the beginning, the not-yet shop was the pedlar's pack; inside it the rare small things that came to the customer once in a while. And at the end, the no-longer shop is the smartphone, offering all the commodities that money can buy. Both items, the pack and the phone, are carried around on the person, the seller in one case and the buyer in the other. In the long centuries that separate them is the fixed, located space of the shop that a customer comes to and a shopkeeper keeps. It is the semi-public space that sells what is needed or what is wished for: what customers don't (or no longer) produce for themselves, or else what is new and what they will start to want when they see it or know it is there.

There is a temptation, when making a narrative of shopping history, to romanticize the world before buying and selling took over as a dominant part of most people's lives. Life really was slower and simpler than it is today. But it was also, for the great majority, much poorer in every sense. For most people, in most places, what would later come to be called the standard of living was well below any recognizable modern threshold before the twentieth century. Little choice of food, few purchases of household goods or clothes; none of what used to be known as 'modern conveniences', from fridges to flushing toilets to just being attached to the gas or electricity mains.

An appealing example of such historical idealization turns up in an otherwise plain work of economic history from a century ago. The author, L.C.A. Knowles, presents a vignette from the bygone world before the industrialization of food production and selling:

> In a town of over 10,000 people, direct trading between producer and consumer becomes more and more difficult. The picturesque days are practically over when the farmer's wife or daughter drove in to market with her butter and poultry and exposed them for sale and dealt with the housewife who knew her personally. Butter merchants, egg merchants, poultry merchants, wholesale butchers and milk companies, either supplying smaller shops or trading themselves, have taken the place of the old 'market day.' Even in the market halls the sellers to-day are middlemen and not producers.[5]

Knowles is conscious that the pretty description of the horse and cart and the friendly interaction is 'picturesque', but lets it appear all the same in the middle of long tracts of prose about industrial developments in the nineteenth century. Especially striking in the idyllic image is that the participants on both sides are women: the farmer's 'wife or daughter' and, in the town, 'the housewife'. This happy imagining of a female world of pre-industrial rural trading becomes all the more interesting when we learn that the author was a woman herself (as well as the first professor of economic history at the London School of Economics).

Knowles' sketch of the post-rural world of town shops illustrates a further feature of shopping history. She describes a recent division of commodities into separate specializations of butter or milk or poultry, each with their own operations; and contrasts this with the all-in-one world of the market day, when everything was traded in the same place at the same time. When supermarkets began to appear in Britain in the later decades of the twentieth century, they concentrated initially on the packaged, non-perishable goods that were simple to stock long term and simple for the new 'self-service' customer to pick up and put in her basket. But then, increasingly, supermarkets also began to engage in the selling of all the farm products in Knowles' list of different types. By the 1980s they were selling it all, and the move that Knowles describes had reversed itself. It is a notable example of the way that one large and identifiable shift in a way of doing things may have the effect of obliterating all the differences and the earlier forms that preceded it. In the late twentieth century, it was the small shops with their individual categories that were taken over by the all-encompassing, all-assimilating big new stores that were the supermarkets. But when Knowles, whose vantage point is the early twentieth century, describes what has happened to weekly food markets, what she sees is that separated trading has superseded what used to be the market selling everything in one place. That earlier state of things, in both cases, appears as an unchanging time that was ruptured, for worse or better, by radical new developments in the means of shopping.

For as long as there has been talk of a high street, of 'the' high street and the town centre, there has been talk of its past and its likely or actual futures, whether commercial, aesthetic, or social—and of possible remedies for present challenges. In present-day laments for the decline of the high street, the fear is that the shops will close down altogether. But between the wars, a common complaint was the opposite. Too many shops! So many, and most of them so small that—with a Darwinian logic transferred as if naturally to businesses—they cannot all survive.

Often, though not always, the perceived danger to the high street has come—as with internet shopping—from some identifiably new external challenge that seems to be reducing existing shops to oblivion or irrelevance. In the 1980s and 1990s, it was that edge-of-town or out-of-town shopping centre or superstore, with acres of free parking, taking the shoppers away. Real destruction has also been a spur. In the wake of the war, there were bombed town centres that needed to be rebuilt, and reimagined. New towns and new housing estates were also being constructed at this time—with multiple levels of planning, including questions about the desirable or appropriate type of shop provision, which had become a major topic for formal planning discussion. More than this, it is striking that provision for shops was treated as a matter of public interest and investment, on both national and local scales. For the first time, imagining the likely or desirable shops of the future was itself a part of their ongoing development.

In what follows, the focus on British shopping history enables particular kinds of difference and variation to emerge, not only by period but also by region and locality: smaller and larger towns and their suburbs, as well as cities, or villages. But there are also comparisons and counterexamples from elsewhere, especially France and the United States. The short chapters are designed to bring out points of connection and contrast between different times and types of shopping and shops; they are not chronological and can be read in any sequence. Each is self-contained, but many topics appear across more than one. The first group is about particular selling and buying set-ups, with some related to the design and layout of shops as spaces and buildings. The second group looks at the roles of the people on both sides of the counter as described by themselves and others. The third group is primarily to do with types of shop, classified according to what they sell.

The book draws on literary narratives that have featured shop settings and scenes of shopping, or described what occurs in the minds of shoppers or vendors. But other kinds of author, from economists to architects to textbook writers, think about shops in similarly creative and analytical ways: as involving distinctive locations and situations, with certain kinds of likely behaviours that follow from them. How shops and the people in them have been imagined, inside and outside literature, is part of their history, too. And it is one way to think about possible shopping futures.

Notes

1. Dorothy Davis, *A History of Shopping* (London: Routledge & Kegan Paul Ltd., 1966), 35.
2. See Margaret Spufford, *The Great Reclothing of Rural England: Petty Chapmen and Their Wares in the Seventeenth Century* (London: Hambledon Press, 1984); Lorna Weatherill, *Consumer Behaviour and Material Culture in Britain 1660–1760* (1988; 2nd edn London: Routledge, 1996).
3. See Jon Stobart, *Sugar and Spice: Grocers and Groceries in Provincial England, 1650–1830* (Oxford: Oxford University Press, 2013); David Vaisey (ed.), *The Diary of Thomas Turner 1754–1765* (Oxford: Oxford University Press, 1984); T.S. Willan, *Abraham Dent of Kirkby Stephen: An Eighteenth-Century Shopkeeper* (Manchester: Manchester University Press, 1970).
4. See Davis, *A History of Shopping*; Kathryn A. Morrison, *English Shops and Shopping* (New Haven: Yale University Press, 2003); Claire Walsh, 'Shop Design and the Display of Goods in Eighteenth-Century London', *Journal of Design History* 8:3 (1995), 157–76.
5. L.C.A. Knowles, *The Industrial and Commercial Revolutions in Great Britain during the Nineteenth Century* (London: George Routledge, 1921), 222.

PART I

SETTINGS

1

Chains

Figure 1. A branch of the Nottingham Hosiery Co. in Upper Norwood, south London. Photograph taken by Emile Zola, 1898 or 1899
© Association du Musée Emile Zola

For more than a century, shops have been shackled with the misleading metaphor of the chain. A (non-metaphorical) chain has no centre: it is a line of links. But separate chain store shops are known instead as 'branches', and the tree would be a more useful metaphor for their dependent relationship to the central, supporting company to which they are attached, and which is also, reciprocally, extended by their growth. Whether the scope is vast (all the way to the global) or much more local, and whether the number of branches is two or three or two thousand, the structure implied is one of spreading out from a primary point of beginning.

The term *chain store* is American in origin, used from the beginning of the twentieth century. Britain had a perfectly good technical word of its own at that time to refer to the same development (which was not an American invention), and that was *multiples*. For some reason that useful term was gradually taken out of service, in favour of the clanking alternative. Chains themselves, meanwhile, were continuing to multiply and add on—as they had been prolifically doing in several areas of British retail, from grocers to chemists to newsagents, since the second half of the nineteenth century.

Remaining still from the first phase of multiples (or chains), Boots and WHSmith are today more like old institutions. There was a branch of Smith's selling newspapers on every railway station of any size almost as soon as there were railway stations at all.[1] Jesse Boot, whose Nottingham chemist's branched out rapidly in the 1880s, was committed to making medicines available at a reasonable cost to working-class customers. Prices were cut by such means as offering no credit ('Boots Cash Chemists') and promoting own-brand products, locally prepared; staff received a commission on sales of these, but not on the much more expensive proprietary brands made by other manufacturers. Unlike most chains, Boots and Smith's both grew mainly on their own, not by merger or takeover of other companies (Boots did however buy up a couple of small chains in the south of England, to gain swift access to areas where it was not yet represented). Smith's had around eight hundred branches by the turn of the century, on high streets as well as in stations. Boots had not far short of two hundred, and continued to extend its reach: the thousandth branch was opened in 1933 in the small Scottish town of Galashiels.

Numbers of branches give some sense of the scale and speed of expansion for these two firms, but a more common-sense point about

Boots and Smith's is that throughout the twentieth century they were the two chains of which a branch could be found in all but the smallest of towns in Britain. Marks & Spencer, with fewer but larger shops, and in larger towns, had the same sort of comfortable familiarity. Dependable own-brand goods were part of the appeal for Boots and Marks & Spencer in particular. These chains were in competition with independent chemists and newsagents and clothing shops—and with smaller chains. In an attempt to limit its growing success at the expense of other shops, Boots was challenged in its early years of expansion on a technicality: the right of a company, as opposed to an individual with their own business, to dispense prescriptions. This was settled for good by a court judgment (on appeal) in 1880, after which it was clear that as long as the pharmacist making up the prescription had the proper qualification themselves—and at Boots, they always had—they could do so under the auspices of a company.[2]

When it comes to food shops, the history of chains is equally surprising from a later perspective. At the turn of the twentieth century, just like the supermarkets a hundred years later, there was already a dominant group of companies that had hundreds of branches, with much publicized takeovers or amalgamations taking place from time to time in the years that followed. The blankly named consortium of Allied Groceries was formed at the end of the 1920s out of several of these big businesses, which continued thereafter to trade under their own more idiosyncratic and at the time household names: Home and Colonial, Lipton's, Maypole Dairy (already owned by Home and Colonial), Meadow Dairy, and Pearks Dairies Home and Colonial had over three thousand branches across Britain in the early 1930s. International Stores was also huge, as were the different Co-operative societies, each regional group often having hundreds of branches. There were also numerous smaller regional chains of food stores.

Most food chain stores concentrated on a few basic commodities, with a preference for the non-perishable and the pre-packable as the simplest to deal with—from ordering to transport to storage. As with later supermarket practices, typically there were long-standing arrangements with wholesalers and manufacturers, and own-brand labels. Tea, for instance, was one of several standard commodities behind the rise of especially multiple multiples in the last decades of the nineteenth century and of these, Lipton's was the best known and ultimately the most strongly identified with that item, which was packed and branded under that name and even grown on Lipton's own plantations in Ceylon (they were not alone: the Co-op did this too). But Lipton's did not specialize in tea from the outset; that came at the end of two decades of phenomenal expansion, in Scotland and then around every part of the rest of Britain, beginning with a first shop opened in Glasgow by a very young Thomas Lipton in 1871. Already at the end of the first decade, Lipton was sourcing dairy products from an Irish agency in County Mayo; in 1878 he called his first non-Glasgow shop, in Dundee, an 'Irish market'. The expansion of the 1880s is a triumphant southern progress, beginning with Leeds in early 1881. 'Then followed Liverpool (1883)...Birmingham, Sunderland and Manchester (1885), Bristol (1886), Cardiff (1887); London (1888), Swansea, Belfast and a second London shop in 1889.'[3] It was at this point, and only then, that Lipton turned to tea: the tea that would make the most enduring fame of the man, the chain, and the accompanying brand.

Of the dominant multiples of the time, Lipton's was the one with the most strongly presented legend of its own history, in which the hero-founder played a diverting role. There is a barrow-boy-to-superstore-billionaire tale of the rise of Tesco's founder, Jack Cohen; but it is nothing compared with the Lipton story of early adventures in foreign parts. Lipton's own gifts for self-publicity surely equalled those of Gordon Selfridge, the American arrival whose launch of his London department store in 1909 was brilliantly orchestrated as a major media event.[4] Lipton's parents had been Irish peasant farmers who emigrated to Glasgow, where they started a small provisions shop. As a teenager, in the mid-1860s, Thomas went to America for four years, where he gained all sorts of work experience. He was a labourer on a Virginia tobacco plantation and had a desk job at a rice plantation in South

Carolina. He also had a job for a time in an upmarket grocery store in New York. On his return to Scotland, such was the rare combination of prudence with enterprise, he had saved up enough to open his own first shop. Twenty years later, in 1891, the head office moved to London in the wake of the instant success of the newly embarked on tea trade. So prominent was the company in its city of origin by that time that the move, it was claimed, entailed the loss of £1,000 a week in business for the Glasgow post office.[5]

In 1844 the 'Rochdale Pioneers' founded the first successful Co-operative consumer organization for the collective purchase and resale of food, with their own staffed shops and (later) warehouses and factories. Profits not reinvested in the company went to members, not shareholders. The Co-op was a radical force for social and economic change, especially in the northern industrial towns where it had its roots, and where the provision of shops was often limited, sometimes virtually monopolistic. Where workers' houses were built near a factory or mine, and there was no pre-existing town, there might be just a single shop controlled by the owner of the works, with the power to charge any price, or deduct purchase costs from wages.

In the period of its Victorian and early twentieth-century expansion, the Co-operative movement became hugely influential as a model of a non-capitalist means of distribution. There was a distinctive philosophy of how to do business differently, for the common good. There were local and national sections, and conferences whose purpose was not only to manage the business of food distribution and the other Co-operative trades but also to engage the membership in the broader politics of the movement. Especially significant was a separate women's organization, with miners' wives prominent in it.[6] Like the Labour movement, with which it had close connections, the Co-operative movement was seen as principally northern and working-class—though it also had southern branches and middle-class sympathizers and activists, including (in the first part of the twentieth century) intellectuals such as Beatrice and Sidney Webb, and Leonard and Virginia Woolf.

The Co-ops extended their range of goods beyond food to most other items of likely household expenditure: clothing, boots and shoes, chemists' goods, furniture, travel, and funeral services. They ran one of the largest milk delivery services in the country (there was also a coal delivery service). The funeral services and some travel agencies are still in business, with surviving high street branches, but apart from general food stores of every size, including supermarkets, the other shops had gradually passed away by the start of the present century, including over a hundred department stores.

In addition to the experiment with an egalitarian model of trading, the Co-operative movement pioneered two other significant innovations in the wider field of retailing history, both of which are now so much part of the fabric of everyday shopping that it is hard to see back to a moment when they might have been tried out as new. The first was the branch structure as a feature of food retailing. By the early 1880s there were over a thousand separate societies and over half a million individual members. (At the start of the 1950s there were twenty-five thousand shop units.[7]) These societies, each with their own branches, were self-governing but connected to the broader movement.

The second innovation was the self-service store, with goods no longer asked for at a counter but laid out for open customer access. This new arrangement was not invented by the Co-op; the honour of that accident goes to some American discount outlets of the 1930s which quickly evolved into fixed stores known by the name of super-markets.[8] But the Co-op did consciously take up the novel American practice right after the war, transferring it to a diminished British scale, and operating planned 'conversions' of its existing shops with military efficiency. Unique in so many ways, the Co-op is also the only one of the first generation of national food chains to have maintained a strong presence throughout the subsequent supermarket period. Nor did its stores follow the swings of size and location enacted by Tesco and Sainsbury's, their largest rivals: the Co-op never had super-stores outside the towns. As a result, though it may have been criticized, often affectionately, for failing to move with the times, or for doing so in the wrong ways, the Co-op has for the most part remained staunchly local and community-based.

Numerous and ubiquitous as their branches were, complaints about the multiples of the nineteenth and earlier twentieth centuries were not normally of the commonest twenty-first century type: that ubiquitous 'high street chains' are detrimental to local environments, detracting from the distinctive identity of any town large enough to attract their presence. That may have been partly because their physical presence in the same streets as other shops did not take customers away from that particular shopping area—as out-of-town stores would do at the later time. But here, from the late 1920s, is a striking exception to that broader absence of general condemnation. In a long linkage of writerly relays, an economist writing about British multiples quotes at length a writer in an architectural journal, whose own thoughts had been triggered by a speaker at a recent congress in Rome, in 1929. That speaker had drawn attention to 'the serious danger to the amenities of our old towns by what are now known as multiple shops':

> The evolution of society is obviously in the direction of bigger combines, and if this develops to extremes we shall see one combine owning all of the tea shops, another the clothiers, another the tobacconists, another the shoe shops, and so on. About a dozen or so firms will conduct all the shopkeeping throughout the country; each of these combines will have its own special design of shop-front, and these few designs will arrange themselves along our streets in all our cities, towns, and villages. It is a horrible thought. Consider the plight of the motorist, who would not know what town they were passing through, or the awkward dilemma of some absent-minded person who forgot the name of the town he was in. Of course, we know he could find out the name by going to the railway station (or would it be the air port [sic]?). But something ought to be done about it before it is too late.[9]

Imagining the clone town, a hundred years ago: strangely familiar.

Notes

1. James B. Jefferys, *Retail Trading in Britain 1850–1950* (Cambridge: Cambridge University Press, 1954), 285.
2. For the history of Boots see Stanley Chapman, *Jesse Boot of Boots the Chemists: A Study in Business History* (London: Hodder and Stoughton, 1974).
3. Peter Mathias, *Retailing Revolution: A History of Multiple Retailing in the Food Trades based upon the Allied Suppliers Group of Companies* (London: Longmans, 1967), 98.
4. See Lindy Woodhead, *Shopping, Seduction, and Mr Selfridge* (2007; London: Profile, 2012).
5. See Mathias, *Retailing Revolution*, 41–2. The most recent of many histories of Tesco is Sarah Ryle, *The Making of Tesco: A Story of British Shopping* (London: Bantam, 2013).
6. See Gillian Scott, *Feminism and the Politics of Working Women: The Women's Co-operative Guild, 1880s to the Second World War* (London: Routledge, 1998).
7. See Jefferys, *Retail Trading in Britain*, 16, 471.
8. See Rachel Bowlby, *Carried Away: The Invention of Modern Shopping* (London: Faber, 2000), 134–51.
9. Quoted from the journal *Building*, in A. Edward Hammond, *Multiple Shop Organization* (London: Sir Isaac Pitman & Sons, 1930), 45.

2

Convenience

In relation to shopping, the word *convenience* is about stable demands for predictable things. Marketing theory stresses that a great deal of purchasing is tied to an idea of regularity, whereby particular items are sought and bought over and over again. They are known technically as 'convenience goods', as opposed to the 'shopping goods', which are out of the ordinary purchases, taking time and significant outlay. Convenience goods are relatively cheap: there is no specific decision to buy them on any one occasion, and not much variety in what they are. In the middle of the twentieth century, for instance, they meant basic food—plus tobacco, newspapers, and confectionery.

The American *convenience store*, small and self-service, goes back many decades, but in Britain the term and the place have been adopted alongside the homelier *corner shop*, which is a small general store in a mainly residential street. Unlike corner shops, British convenience stores are generally urban. They are small branches of big chains, and they have proliferated in the past two decades. As in the early days of self-service, convenience stores utilize baskets as opposed to trolleys; often it is a matter of what can be physically carried, as opposed to the seemingly limitless amounts that are shoved into the back of a car. At a considerable historical distance from the housewife who was the original British self-service customer in the 1950s, however, the paradigm convenience store consumers today are individuals on their way home or to work, seeking a certain amount of choice, but not much (which takes time). As a species, they do not allot time to food preparation and are open to buying the qualitatively superior versions of the ready meals that used to be called *convenience foods.*

Convenience has more of a history, with more variations, than these present uses of the word might suggest. In the middle of the twentieth century '*All mod. cons.*' was a standard abbreviation in classified advertisements for modest lodgings or holiday accommodation. That 'modern conveniences' referred—depending on the precise period—to such features as flushing toilets, hot and cold running water, or small fridges; these amenities had not yet reached the level of obviousness that would make it redundant to point them out. The *cons* and the *mod* have appeared in similar residential connections since the eighteenth century, when writers would regularly remark on a house having being 'modernized' or 'improved', along with the various 'conveniences' now supplied. These later included plugged-in or networked facilities (gas, electricity, water, phone); outside the home, the phrase *public conveniences* also suggests the provision of plumbing for basic bodily functions. *Conveniences* require no effort on the part of the present user; they are simply there where you are when you need or want them. But whereas *modern* implies a degree of innovation, at least in the sense of leaving behind an old-fashioned and likely dysfunctional past, with 'convenience' the emphasis is rather on the straightforwardly practical: what is basic and used all the time. The same, much later, was true of convenience goods and the convenience store.

Long before it was a technical term for particular kinds of product or shop, the notion of convenience had established a commercial value. George Eliot's short novel of 1858, *Janet's Repentance,* takes place in a small Midlands town. The arrival of a new clergyman generates passionate doctrinal arguments which lead, in the course of the story, to defections not just from churches but also from solicitors or doctors when their clients have different religious allegiances. Amid all this local ferment there is, though, one field of activity that remains untouched by the controversy, and that is shopping. At a point when one of the tradesmen, Mr Dunn, is worrying about customers leaving him, Eliot gives a gleeful description of how, when it comes to commercial rather than theological loyalties, trade trumps religion every time. And the word used to name this distinction is *convenience*:

> It is probable that no speculative or theological hatred would be ultimately strong enough to resist the persuasive power of convenience: that a latitudinarian baker, whose bread was honourably free from alum, would command the custom of any dyspeptic Puseyite; that an Arminian with the toothache would prefer a skilful Calvinistic dentist to a bungler stanch against the doctrines of Election and Final Perseverance, who would be likely to break the tooth in his head; and that a Plymouth Brother, who had a well-furnished grocery shop in a favourable vicinage, would occasionally have the pleasure of furnishing sugar or vinegar to orthodox families that found themselves unexpectedly 'out of' those indispensable commodities. In this persuasive power of convenience lay Mr Dunn's ultimate security from martyrdom. His drapery was the best in Milby.[1]

Never mind what religious denomination the grocer or draper belongs to; the bottom line is the service he offers right now. When a customer needs something at 'a moment's notice', or because they have run out of it, they are not going to worry about the affiliations of the shopkeeper who can provide it—and a quality product into the bargain. The dental analogy gives a pseudo-medical seriousness to these minor buying emergencies of everyday life, just as the best baker, never mind his church, supplies bread free of additives. Certain secular services have to be always available when you might need them, and immediate accessibility of this kind surpasses any other considerations that might influence choosing to buy from one provider or another. Convenience, in this logic, comes first.

Convenience generally takes its meaning not only in relation to practical access and regular purchase but also through a distinction from brighter qualities such as novelty or sophistication. In William Cowper's popular poem of the late eighteenth century, *The Task*, it is allotted a precise place in an order of qualities to be assigned to different forms of seating. The poem begins with something like a mock celebration of modern reclining: 'I sing the sofa'. Suitably sung, this charming item is honoured as the culmination of a clearly demarcated evolution of furniture for sitting on:

> Thus first necessity invented stools,
> Convenience next suggested elbow chairs,
> And luxury th'accomplish'd Sofa last.[2]

Necessity and luxury are usually contrasted as opposite terms in this period, but here convenience enters the picture to occupy the intermediate phase in a three-part story. Like an also-ran, or an also-sat, it is found in a blankly middle position, as though with no particular qualities of its own. Appropriately, perhaps, in light of current convenience-store shopping trends, the armchair or 'elbow chair', as opposed to the sofa, accommodates just one body: it is designed for individual rather than collective use. And while it may not attain to the luxurious perfections of the sofa, it does offer more comforts than the basic stool, which is single-seating but portable and unsoft (the 'easy' chair, so called, was a familiar object by this time). Cowper's necessity, convenience, and luxury are all three given as inventors of successive stages of sitting development; there is no indication of the process of how the seats get beneath the bums, or in other words by what means they are commissioned or constructed or distributed or paid for. But the presentation of a line of progress in this way—a three-piece suite—suggests that furniture and other domestic items are beginning to become the sort of commodity that a middle-class household might seek or plan to acquire by purchase.

The Task may be the first or the only poem to give pride of place to sedentary convenience—or to convenience of any sort. And given that convenience is about routine behaviours, the same goods bought and the same things done each day, it is delightful to note that the same poem is also the source of a line that is like a familiar jingle against the blandness or repetitions of convenience: a line so well known and so often repeated that it has lost any link to its origin in this work at all. 'Variety is the spice of life' is such a familiar phrase that it tends to get

cited in short form, without the last two words being needed. It is
repeated so automatically that it goes against its own suggestion,
providing no variation in the recommendation of variety. In fact the
original line from *The Task* is a tiny bit different, since it includes a little
alliterative *very*. Cowper is protesting at the seasonal pattern whereby
clothes 'Just please us while the fashion is at full,/But change with ev'ry
moon.'[3] An ingratiating tailor, who wants a new order, trashes what is
still being worn for any number of reasons:

> The sycophant
> That waits to dress us, arbitrates their date,
> Surveys his fair reversion with keen eye;
> Finds one ill made, another obsolete,
> This fits not nicely, that is ill conceived,
> And making a prize of all that he condemns,
> With our expenditure defrays his own.[4]

By announcing his objections to the non-new things, the tailor creates
the obsoleteness or poor workmanship or lack of fit that will ensure
that something else is commissioned, and thus also, 'with our expenditure', ensure his own continuing income. It is this bitter analysis of the
selling technique of the person who will profit from the purchase of new
outfits which leads to the piquant line that has never gone out of use:

> Variety's the very spice of life
> That gives it all its flavor. We have run
> Through ev'ry change that fancy at the loom
> Exhausted, has had genius to supply,
> And studious of mutation still, discard
> A real elegance a little used,
> For monstrous novelty and strange disguise.
> We sacrifice to dress, till houshold joys
> And comforts cease. Dress drains our cellar dry,
> And keeps our larder lean.[5]

Perfectly good clothes, in other words, are thrown out when barely worn; artificial 'novelty' is strenuously invented when the genuinely stylish is only 'a little used'. Variety is the very spice of life, adding flavour to the food we eat. But why do we think we have to be changing and discarding all the time for the sake of a 'monstrous novelty'? Worse—and here the spice metaphor starts to approach its literal meaning—the amount that we spend on clothes then means that there is less to spend on food. If we spend too much on attire, Cowper says, there will be nothing left for domestic consumption. Unexpectedly, given the general moral drift of the lines, Cowper does not refer to primary needs not being met; instead, it is the dependable 'houshold joys / And comforts', on top of the plain essentials; which will be lost. These small extras are not unlike what spices provide.

As Cowper's use of the word implies, in his time, real as well as metaphorical spices are in common use. Spices as such are not a novelty, whether in literature or in life—although some, as now, will be rarer. They are regularly mentioned as part of what grocers need to know how to purchase and store. Thomas Turner, who kept the village store in East Hoathly, a Sussex village, at the same time as Cowper was writing, and who also kept a journal, refers to his brother picking up 'a parcel of spices' ordered by their mother at a cost of two pounds and sixpence, a substantial sum, and received both 'in cash' and 'in full'. Tantalizingly, there is no detail about just what spices went into the package.[6]

Cowper's condemnation of the needlessness of making things appear 'obsolete' is as relentless as the hypothetical sycophant's many objections—'all he condemns'—to clothes that have supposedly passed their wear-by date. Looking now from a perspective more than two centuries on, the lines sound like an early repudiation of the insistence of the fashion cycle, with novelty the constant demand and datedness a reason for discarding. And that really is what they say. But this is not yet the world of fast fashion—or not with a speed that would be identifiable as such in the twenty-first century, and not with the much wider participation that was developing towards the end of the nineteenth century, once mechanized production of clothing had greatly increased the rate of production, and lowered costs. This was the unprecedented development enabled by sewing machines and factories, and the large city stores that sold their products. In *Au Bonheur des Dames*, his novel about a Paris department store, Emile Zola described all the ways that the new shops were 'democratizing luxury', *démocratisant le luxe*.[7] But Cowper's community is much more exclusive, just as his fashion seasons are surely slower to go round and to trickle down from one social circle to another. With garments that have been little worn but are no longer the latest, 'We' will probably pass them on to servants and they in their turn, eventually, to second-hand outlets. Or else—and in the course of these movements—the clothing may well be reworked; but discarding, letting go, and replacing in this way are not the same as binning. In the poem there is no suggestion of waste, only forced expenditure; nor is there any indication that the producers are being exploited. It is rather they, the tailors—working individually for themselves—who are said to be exploiting 'us' by pressing us to get something new.

Ultimately, though, the convenience of convenience is always and only in the perception and practice of the buyer. And it is rare to find commentators on this most perennial and spiceless of shopping subjects offering any variation on the usual routine about the usual routine: convenience is a subject that is taken for granted, serving as background for the discussion of more various and enticing shopping questions. But consider the following extract, from a 1930s economist's argument about distribution. He is commenting on that distinction in marketing theory between 'shopping goods' (requiring forethought and comparison across a range) and 'convenience goods' (when buying them is automatic):

> It is necessary to note, however, that the difference between them lies not in the nature of the goods themselves but in the attitude of the 'normal'

purchaser to them. To a certain type of housewife all goods are shopping goods, while to a certain type of bachelor it is probably no exaggeration to suggest that all goods are convenience goods.[8]

Notes

1. George Eliot, *Janet's Repentance*, in *Scenes of Clerical Life* (1858), ed. Thomas A. Noble (Oxford: Oxford University Press, World's Classics, 1988), 225–6.
2. William Cowper, *The Task* (1785), in Cowper, *Verse and Letters*, ed. Brian Spiller (London: Rupert Hart-Davis, 1968), 398.
3. Cowper, *The Task*, 434.
4. Cowper, *The Task*, 434.
5. Cowper, *The Task*, 434.
6. *The Diary of Thomas Turner, 1754–1765*, ed. David Vaisey (1984; Oxford: Oxford University Press, 1985), 166.
7. Emile Zola, *Au Bonheur des Dames* (1883; Paris: Garnier Flammarion, 1971), 110.
8. Henry Smith, *Retail Distribution: A Critical Analysis* (London: Oxford University Press, 1937), 18.

3

Fixed Prices

One of the innovations of nineteenth-century department stores and the big bazaars that preceded them was their setting and showing of prices for the goods on sale. The department stores were associated with an accessible form of luxury: not just the (really) rich, but anyone who chose to could come in and look around, without the obligation to make a purchase. Thus, aspirations of upward mobility were enabled and fostered by the downwards invitation which welcomed visitors not as definite customers, as with the traditional shop, but as open prospects (if not today, they might be able to buy in the future). A crucial element of this shift in the atmosphere was the policy of visibly, readably, marking the prices. There was now no need for a customer to ask; the cost ceased to be an object of either uncertainty or negotiation.

In food shops, fixed prices had been widespread and often standard since the early eighteenth century. Grocers advertised their prices for commonly ordered goods, like tea or biscuits (there were many types of each). In a local setting, and with customers generally known to the shop in the same way that the shop was known to them, prices would informally be adjusted for regular patronage, or as a reward for a large order.[1] Market trading, on the other hand, remained a more open matter of negotiation—otherwise known as bargaining, or higgling, or haggling. This verbal transaction, preliminary to the exchange of the goods and the cash, was expected and often enjoyable, both parties consciously taking part in a game.

There was also, in the middle of the twentieth century, a tenacious issue around fixed prices of another order. Resale price maintenance was the rule that allowed manufacturers to set the minimum price for their branded goods. This was beneficial to small shops struggling against the growing number of chains, then supermarkets, with their faster turnover accommodating lower profit margins: these bigger businesses were unable to undercut them. But the law was also represented as an unjustifiable refusal of fair competition, as well as a violation of consumers' right to the lowest possible price. In 1964, after Tesco had brought the matter to a head by effectively disregarding it, RPM was officially abolished.

The fixed price also developed into another shopping scenario altogether. With discount stores, not only was the price predetermined (non-negotiable and clearly stated), as in the first transformation, but everything in the store cost exactly the same, or else no more than a certain amount. The original American Woolworth's five-and-dime store—where everything cost either five or ten cents—was translated across the Atlantic to become the sterling iteration of this, with all items priced at either threepence or sixpence. F.W. Woolworth opened the first British branch of his firm in Liverpool in 1909—the same year that another American, Gordon Selfridge, launched the grand new Oxford Street department store. Branches of Woolworth's, small and large, were soon an expected fixture in every town, as with Boots, or WHSmith, or Marks & Spencer—whose own beginnings, with Michael Marks' store in one of the Leeds covered markets, had involved a similar one-price tag: 'Don't Ask the Price, It's a Penny.' For a long time later, too, and now with more varied and valuable merchandise, Marks & Spencer used the slogan 'Nothing over 5s.'[2] But unlike those other familiar chains, each with their specialist type of merchandise even if they also sold other things too, what Woolworth's offered was a bit of everything or anything.

A book of the early 1930s lays out a version of this miscellany, evoking a typical Woolworth's experience: 'Here, while passing from counter to counter to buy cheap crockery, strings of beads, lamp-shades, and toffee, toys, soap, and flower-bulbs...the customer is beguiled into patronising literature.'[3] Except that the writer is a literary critic and being sarcastic, it sounds almost utopian: everything, and books into the bargain! Then, as if to make a witty response to the prevailing assimilation of low price and low quality, Penguin Books, which was launched in 1935, set its own standard price at the consecrated sixpence. This was not only the same as for articles bought at Woolworth's but also, at that time, the cost of a packet of ten cigarettes. The minimal outlay now vindicated the paperback book as a new kind of affordable, everyday pleasure—with the quality of the contents bearing no relation to the small price. Thus cheapness along with the single, set pricing could be put together as part of a different kind of value and offer. The initiative was beautifully validated when Woolworth's itself placed a big order in the first months of Penguin's precarious existence.

Nor was Woolworth's the only or the first chain of fixed-price variety stores. H.G. Wells's novel *The History of Mr Polly* names a 'sixpenny-halfpenny bazaar' as one of the shops on a provincial high street.[4] It isn't a fiction: the Domestic Bazaar Co., which began in Southampton in 1895, was a chain with some two hundred branches at its peak; on their window frontages appeared the words 'D.B.C. Any Article 6½D': that is, sixpence halfpenny. Perhaps Woolworth's fixed price of sixpence, when those stores entered the country, was calculated as a targeted halfpenny undercutting of the D.B.C.

In the twenty-first century, the one-price store has come back. While high street shops were closing all around it, even Woolworth's itself eventually (in 2009), there rose again the fighting entrepreneurial force of the discount store, now (after a century's inflation) with a price tag of a pound, and operating as an outlet for unsold stocks of branded goods—often with the original identifying label cut off. The stores are laid out like small supermarkets, with aisles and checkouts. Some food and drink is sold, almost all of it—as in the first days of self-service—being packaged, non-perishable staples, such as packets of biscuits or instant coffee. As with any store of some size, there are themed seasonal variations, with Hallowe'en outfits in the autumn, or gardening gloves in the spring; but the availability or return to stock of any given product or even category is never assured. The stores sell whatever they happen to have been able to acquire; when it's there, it's there.

As the low-down prices declare, recent British one-price stores have been, without exception, one-*small*–price stores. Almost by definition, the primary concern for those seeking or able to buy the most expensive goods is not the money, even if the pleasure of purchase may include, as at any other level, the sense of getting a good deal. But while there have never been one-price shops for luxury items, in the first decades of the mass production of ready-made clothing there was the related phenomenon of, as it were, downmarket upmarket products. Men's suits and men's hats, in particular, were produced in quantity and at pre-set low prices. In the fictional *Diary of a Nobody*, from the early 1890s, a character by the name of Murray Posh turns out to be part of the family behind a well-known product called 'Posh's-three-shilling-hats': the price is in the name.[5] The firm's pretensions to becoming a global brand are worthy of the early twenty-first century, with plans to open up branches in Calcutta and Kimberley and Adelaide, among other far-reaching outposts; Kimberley, at the time, was world famous as the centre of South African diamond mining.[6]

Not quite all first-generation one-price shops had the varied and free-for-all atmosphere of Woolworth's. In the memoir of her time as a counter assistant in a smart Brighton milliner's in the 1930s, Marjorie Gardiner says that 'some of my friends did used to buy patterns to make clothes, and those who were better off even bought their own for under a guinea a time at the "Guinea Shop" on Western Road— where nothing was allowed to cost more.'[7] This was a major expenditure. The wages were 'a few shillings a week for the younger ones', so not that much more for the others; a guinea was twenty-one shillings.

Another unlikely recent return takes customers and vendors back before the days of shops at all, to a mode of price-setting before fixed pricing was even in the offing. Who would have imagined that haggling, that properly old-time word for bargaining over a price, would have had a comeback in the midst of an ever more online world—and in an official capacity at that? Yet that is exactly what purchasers of domestic fuels or broadband 'packages' are pressed to do today, via real one-on-one conversations, over the phone. The respected consumer organization *Which?* has advice headed 'Haggling' ('Here's how to haggle successfully...'), and the popular website MoneySavingExpert also has a prominent section on the topic, under that name. It is a new form of repetitive work, both for those employed at call centres to negotiate in pre-set ways and for customers, who pay more if they do not expend this talking time to obtain the cheapest available rate.

Notes

1. See Jon Stobart, *Sugar and Spice: Grocers and Groceries in Provincial England, 1650–1830* (Oxford: Oxford University Press, 2013), 211–12.
2. Nicholas A.H. Stacey and Aubrey Wilson, *The Changing Pattern of Distribution* (Oxford: Pergamon Press, 1958), 45.
3. Q.D. Leavis, *Fiction and the Reading Public* (1932; London: Chatto & Windus, 1968), 17; ellipsis mine.
4. H.G. Wells, *The History of Mr Polly* (1910), ed. Norman Mackenzie (London: J.M. Dent, 1993), 110.
5. George and Weedon Grossmith, *The Diary of a Nobody* (1891), ed. Kate Flint (Oxford: Oxford University Press, 1995), 96.
6. See Grossmith, *The Diary of a Nobody*, 132–3.
7. Marjorie Gardiner, *The Other Side of the Counter* (Brighton: QueenSpark Books, 1985), 10.

4

Local Shops

Concern today for the climate emergency targets the survival and preservation of the planet. Only quite recently has 'the planet' come to be conceptualized as one single object of care, the victim of destructive human actions almost all inflicted over the past two centuries. Among the big interconnected issues being taken up is that of overconsumption: too much, too often, and with too much waste. Four letters capture that issue: the *fast* of fast food and fast fashion. These urgent concerns played a strong role in the environmental and countercultural movements of the 1960s—only to be largely forgotten in the intervening years.[1] Today they are sparking calls for changes in production as well as consumption. For the fashion industry in particular, this starts with the countries of origin, where working conditions as well as wages fall far short of those in the countries of consumption.[2]

Sometimes, the rhetoric makes it sound as if the planet is really the nearest thing that we have to a familiar home to be cherished and protected: our local habitation. But closer to where we really know one corner or side street from another, there is also a growing concern for the small shopping cultures of daily purchasing life. As vital as the global arguments that spur them are the buying choices that are on the doorstep, involving households or individuals in their relation to the shops down the road or down the town. As a British expression, 'the local' usually just means the pub—with a sense of community and attachment, and also with the assumption, no longer so nearly valid as it used to be, that everywhere and everyone is bound to have such a place within walkable distance. But shops are shared local spaces in the same way as pubs ('public' houses), and equally need to be used to be kept.

Advocacy on behalf of local shops, whether promotional or ethical, has a long history, with wide variations in the scale of the difference and distance imagined as separating any particular local spot from a centre elsewhere. Take the firm of Rabnett's, glossing itself as 'The Shrewsbury Warehouse', which in 1899 took out a full-page advertisement in the Wilding's local trade directory for that town (see Figure 2). The headline was 'Private Enterprise versus London Stores'.[3] Rabnett's lists *sixty-six* 'departments' to be found within its establishment; their headings range improbably from trays to croquet to step ladders, but also include more familiar general categories such as jewellery and lamps and corsets. The sales pitch of this establishment is based on three different elements: payment by cash only (no credit); fixed pricing ('No two prices'); and no middleman ('Buys direct First Cost, and Sells Retail at Wholesale Prices'). Essentially, this is the same trading ethos and structure as that of present-day discount stores. What is distinctive about this one is its emphatic foregrounding of the local: this is all here in your home town, the things you would think you could only get in London. And cheaply, too: the low price is the nub of the pitch: 'If any left over will continue same price till all sold, but a good thing is soon snatched up.'

At the other extreme from the big local emporium with metropolitan pretensions is the cosiness of the friendly shop just a few steps away. The feel of 'the corner shop' is nostalgic and old-fashioned, all nooks and grannies. Warm and timeless, as if it had always been there and always will be, this place is an imaginary source of old stories and old people's stories—to the point that English corner shop memoirs and novels have lately become what amounts to a micro-genre of their own.[4] No matter that a grandmother in the 2020s may well have grown up in a family whose food was bought from a supermarket in the town centre, still the name, if not the real place, retains its nostalgic

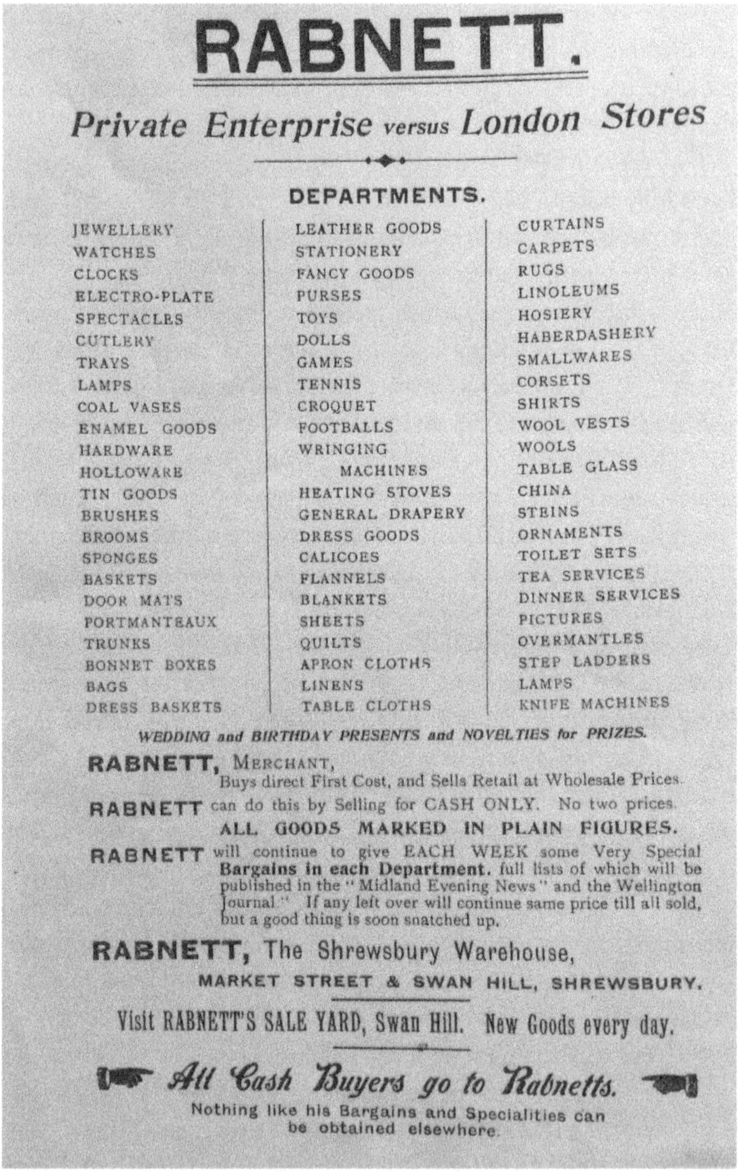

Figure 2. Advertisement for Rabnett's, Shrewsbury, 1899
Image courtesy of Shropshire Archives

resonance. As it has done since almost beyond living memory: in 1932, already, the economist and retailer Lawrence Neal could speak of 'the public's innate desire for its "shop around the corner"'—a desire he regards as unjustified but understandable.[5] And as Neal's phrase implies, the corner shop is not necessarily at the point where two roads meet. It is really any shop so close to home that to go to it is not to go anywhere; it is just, as it were, to pop out with a momentary purpose. As Jenny Shaw neatly puts it in a sociological study of the early 2000s, 'not only were not all "corners shops" on corners, not all shops on corners counted as "corner shops".[6] Wilfred Burns, a town planner writing in the late 1950s, defines the corner shop as 'a term used to describe not only the shop physically on the corner of a street but also the isolated individual shop which is "round the corner".[7] Typically, today, the corner shop is a general food store that also sells other goods in the 'frequently needed' or 'convenience' category. This includes standard small luxuries: confectionery, newspapers, scratch cards, lottery tickets, cigarettes.

Shops fitting the broad definition of a small shop in a residential area used to encompass many more varieties, as the economist Gertrude Williams makes clear in a book published shortly after the war. What Williams describes is now an unfamiliar picture: 'In a street of about a hundred houses (a usual size in most towns) we find that there is nearly always a grocer and a clothing shop; for every two streets there is a butcher; for every three, a sweet shop, a paper shop and a greengrocer.'[8] This is a combination, in Williams' own terms, of 'ubiquitousness' and 'convenience'. And the shops are not fall-backs for extra or forgotten items: 'Even if we realize that we can get a larger variety of greens and groceries at a big store we prefer to buy from the shop at the corner and save a long walk or a bus ride.'[9] Naturally, no cars are yet parked in front of the hundred shops and houses.

Most estimates conclude that there were probably half a million separate retail outlets in Britain for most of the first half of the twentieth century (they are only estimates, since there was no actual 'census of distribution' providing real statistics until 1951). It is an extraordinarily high number, more than one shop for every hundred people. But the figures are misleading on their own, since the units are barely comparable: a tiny wool shop is duly counted as one, but so is the largest city department store, with hundreds of employees. And even as seen along Williams' typical working-class street, shops are far less like one another than the non-shop houses. Residential buildings are either lived in or not, whereas a shop can subsist indefinitely in a nebulous state—on the verge of non-viability, but still technically a functioning business. Also, by no means all shopkeepers sought to make a living from their trade. Between the wars, many 'house shops' were opened out of the front rooms of terraced houses as a way of providing small supplementary incomes.

In her memoir about English corner shops in the last part of the twentieth century, Babita Sharma emphasizes their utility through an unexpected analogy:

> Mum was more comforted by the repeated 'ker-ching' ringing out from the till and the influx of customers who seemed undaunted by the shop's dilapidated shell. Perhaps it was like a public toilet in that respect: unappealing as it might appear, when you needed to go, you needed to go, and so despite its state of neglect, the corner shop continued to hold its own.[10]

It is probably not advisable to give too much attention to this comparison, suggesting a new twist to *spending a penny*, that friendly old euphemism now all but defunct. (Public toilets today are generally accessed by other means than a coin in the slot—and if paid for, they cost rather more than a penny, new or old.) But Sharma's shop-as-toilet does rather grotesquely bring up the affinity if not identity between the two kinds of facility as conveniences: the point being not only that (as in her suggestion) you might *need* to go but also that thanks to them being there, you can. In the last part of the nineteenth century, ladies campaigned for the provision of toilets in city centres; the new department stores were beginning to provide that facility within their own buildings.[11] Toilet facilities meant that women could spend far more time (as well as more money, more pennies) in the city, and away from home—whether that home was a short way away, or whether they came in by bus or tram or train. For those who had the leisure and the means, it was a new kind of freedom.

Local shops tend to be singled out as providing a social service which goes far beyond—and may even take precedence over—customers' need or wish for whatever they came in to buy. This is implicit in Neal's reference to the desire of 'the public' for its 'shop around the corner'—where that desire relates to the place itself and its closeness to home, not (as is usually expected in relation to shopping) to what you might want to buy. In the 1960s, when it could be seen that supermarkets were pulling custom away from other food stores, W.G. McClelland stated the issue in the form of a clear either/or decision about the future: 'On the one hand we are attracted—by the low prices, the brightness and cleanliness, the variety, and the convenience of one-stop shopping. On the other hand we suspect sharp practice, and regret the loss of the personal touch and the impending demise of the corner shop.'[12] That personal touch is not only the conversations across the counter but also to do with customers talking to each other while waiting to be served, and afterwards. This talk may ultimately take in everyone who is there:

> there are shops—small, working-class, North of England, village and dying out now perhaps as slum clearance work proceeds—where the conversation is a general one, embracing all the staff and the customers present up to a dozen or so, with the implicit invitation to any to interject their own badinage or other comment.[13]

In this case it is not so much the superseding supermarket as the actual destruction of a neighbourhood that is causing the death of the small shop and the silencing of the small shop talk. But the effect is the same (and noted by McClelland—who runs a small chain of supermarkets—with an as if ethnographic neutrality).

The sounds of shared talk in the local shop are echoed in the sociologist Ruth Glass's planning study of Middlesbrough from the late 1940s:

> The use of the smaller shops as meeting places is more often combined with a trade transaction, but many customers make a small purchase the excuse for a long gossip. In the poorer areas, they often buy goods in the smallest possible quantities to the annoyance of the shopkeeper, and visit the same shop three or four times a day. Once in the shop, they are sometimes joined by neighbours passing by, who come in merely to chat. At all hours, one can see little groups standing talking round the counter or at the doorway. Some even come and go without buying anything.[14]

Here, as with going to the shop to get out of the house for a moment, the local convenience to the customer is primarily, not secondarily, as a conversational space: a talking shop.

Historian Avram Taylor's study of credit in twentieth-century working-class households in the north-east of England documents in some detail the nuances of class difference between shop owners and customers living on the same street.[15] In many regions of England that picture shifted in the decades beyond Taylor's study, as local shops, now losing out to the supermarkets, started to be taken on by Asian immigrants who were willing to keep them open till late in the evening; at this time, in the 1970s and 1980s, supermarkets were not, and were further away. These new owners restored or maintained the twofold local convenience of the neighbourhood shop: more time, and no distance. This connection between immigrant enterprise and the little local shop was not new to this particular time and place. In Olive Schreiner's novel of the 1880s, *The Story of an African Farm*, a tale is told in which a mother in Cape Town asks her little boy to 'go and buy sixpence of "meiboss" from the Malay round the corner.'[16]

In the new century, the small local store looks different again, in two ways that were unforeseen in the previous phase. First, in some areas new immigrant groups from eastern European countries have opened stores of their own, selling the Polish or Czech foods not found in other shops in a British town. And second, several big supermarket chains have gone in the other direction from their end-of-century relocations out of town, with the trend at that time being for big stores of ever-increasing size. Instead, as if shifting into reverse, they have returned to the centres of towns and cities to open much smaller stores, with long opening hours that match those of the local corner shops. In some ways the change is not as radical as it looks at first sight. The lesser outlets remain offshoots of very big businesses, controlling their stock, employing their managers, taking their profits. And some of these seemingly little stores are in fact no smaller than the high street supermarkets that seemed so vast in their initial 1960s time: three tills! Also, if out-of-town weekly shopping has ceased to appeal to most twenty-first-century customers, that may be less the result of a green change of hearts and minds—small and local are beautiful—than because they are doing an online food shop instead. But still, there has to be more—and less—to it than that: or it is hopeful to think so. New generations of customers think differently—including, in some cases, those who fifteen or twenty years ago were driving to distant superstores every weekend to do their 'big shop'. Also, demographics are different, with smaller living spaces, and more one-person households in all generations. But for those who wish to do it that way, it is possible in many localities to pick up what is needed every day, and on foot. This kind of daily shopping is not so removed from the pattern of many decades ago. At the same time it is also different, because then there were typically housewives at home, and no car, and no fridge or freezer or microwave.

Notes

1. Two profoundly influential books of this period were Rachel Carson, *Silent Spring* (1962; London: Penguin, 2000) and E.F. Schumacher, *Small is Beautiful* (1973; London: Abacus, 1988).
2. See Elizabeth L. Cline, *Overdressed: The Shockingly High Cost of Cheap Fashion* (New York: Portfolio/Penguin, 2012); Dana Thomas, *Fashionopolis: The Price of Fast Fashion and the Future of Clothes* (London: Head of Zeus, 2019).

3. *Wilding's Directory of Shrewsbury 1899* (Shrewsbury: Longworth Wilding's, 1898), 195.

4. See for instance Kathleen Hey, *The View from the Corner Shop: The Diary of a Wartime Shop Assistant*, ed. Patricia and Robert Malcolmson (London: Simon & Schuster, 2016); Alrene Hughes, *The Girl from the Corner Shop* (London: Head of Zeus, 2019); Babita Sharma, *The Corner Shop: Shopkeepers, the Sharmas and the Making of Modern Britain* (London: John Murray, Two Roads, 2019).

5. Lawrence E. Neal, *Retailing and the Public* (London: George Allen & Unwin Ltd, 1932), 143.

6. Jenny Shaw, *Shopping: Social and Cultural Perspectives* (London; Polity Press, 2010), 64.

7. Wilfred Burns, *British Shopping Centres* (London: Leonard Hill, 1959), 17.

8. Gertrude Williams, *The Economics of Everyday Life* (1950; Harmondsworth: Penguin, 1953), 100.

9. Williams, *The Economics of Everyday Life*, 100.

10. Sharma, *The Corner Shop*, 95.

11. See further Erika Diane Rappaport, *Shopping for Pleasure: Women in the Making of London's West End* (Princeton: Princeton University Press, 2000), 79–85.

12. W.G. McClelland, *Studies in Retailing* (Oxford: Basil Blackwell, 1963), 176.

13. McClelland, *Studies in Retailing*, 42.

14. Ruth Glass (ed.), *The Social Background of a Plan: A Study of Middlesbrough* (London: Routledge & Kegan Paul, 1948), 177.

15. See Avram Taylor, *Working Class Credit and Community since 1918* (London: Palgrave Macmillan, 2002), 77–99.

16. Olive Schreiner, *The Story of an African Farm* (1883), ed. Dan Jacobson (London: Penguin, 1995), 71.

5

Mail Order

It is usual to think of online shopping as the great new retail upheaval at the start of the twenty-first century. It is, and it isn't. It is, because it has taken trade away from physical shops. Online shopping for clothes or for food usually involves sending for goods that will come from miles away, via companies that are likely to be national if not international. It isn't, because previously—in the twentieth century, especially its third quarter—there was another successful retailing form that involved, in the same way as online shopping, choosing from a pictured stocklist, and then awaiting a home delivery from a supplier who might well be many miles away.

Mail order, like online shopping, had powerful advocates who believed in its progressive potential. It was said to result in a relative equalization of regional shopping conditions. Some sense of a liberation from geographical limitations comes over in a book about British industrial and commercial history published in the early 1920s, including (which is rare for the type) some material on retail. In the course of otherwise general and large-scale descriptions of major economic changes, the writer suddenly homes in on an evocative vignette of one aspect of a middle-class life in one part of England:

> The effects of railways and steamships on the small shopkeeper and independent artisan class was to make his position more difficult. The growth of great giant stores which could despatch goods by post or rail after reaching its customers by illustrated catalogue tended to concentrate business still further in large urban areas to the detriment of local

industry. The local draper with his limited range of patterns or styles, or the small grocer whose new stock is being 'expected in every day' and which fails to arrive for weeks or even months, is seriously affected by the despatch, often carriage free, of the great distributing stores. It is possible for a woman in an outlying country district of Cornwall to shop by catalogue with ease in either Manchester, London or Paris. Shopping by post is a feature of the distributing business in Germany, the United States and Great Britain.[1]

And there you have it. The shopper may be down in the most remote corner of England, but with the help of a catalogue she can now be metropolitan or cosmopolitan, northern or southern, as the mood takes her. (There is perhaps more personal context here than meets the reading eye: the author, L.C.A. Knowles, had been a pupil at Truro Grammar School in Cornwall.) The language used to describe her buying opportunities—'the growth of great giant stores'—is exactly the same as would soon be applied across the Atlantic to the vast discount food stores called supermarkets that developed there from the 1930s. With the catalogue in front of her, and no salesperson in the vicinity, the mail order customer is in the same position as the slow self-service shopper: considering the goods at her leisure, and making her choices without persuasive interference.

In Knowles' picture of the fashion-happy remote customer, what mail order makes possible is for her to be where she isn't: *in* 'Manchester, London or Paris'. The catalogue takes you there, and gets you what is on sale there; the distinctiveness of where it comes from, as both a place of origin and a place to shop, is still a vital element in the description. This contrasts with a quite different representation of the appeal of mail order twenty years later, this time from a report by the Liberal Party about the challenges faced by small-scale shopkeepers, competition from mail order being one of them. Mail order's attractiveness to the customer, according to this account, is twofold. First there is the saving of money through the direct sale, called 'maker-to-wearer': the shop's intermediate profit is taken off the price. And second, there is the pleasure of the parcel. This otherwise plain-style text speaks of 'The fascination to many people of buying from a catalogue, a technique which invests the most ordinary purchase with an element of surprise and excitement.'[2]

American mail order, it is worth pointing out, served a practical geographical purpose that did not apply in the same way in most parts of most European countries. The vast land area of the continent, much more sparsely populated, meant that even with cars, when cars came along, those in the most distant rural areas were never going to get into the cities to buy the new consumer goods. Here mail order—with the famous catalogues of the Chicago companies Sears, Roebuck and Montgomery Ward—did not compete with the high street (or main street); instead, it fulfilled a parallel function. But in Britain, in spite of the glamorous Cornish connections evoked by Knowles, the principal dividing line was not so much between city and country as between social classes. If there were geographical differences, they followed the north/south industrial divide in England, with companies like Grattans and Empire Stores, both based in Bradford. Kay's was a Worcester firm, GUS (Great Universal Stores) was from Manchester, and Littlewoods from Liverpool; of the large mail order houses only Freemans, with its centre in London, was not northern. And the use of mail order in northern towns was intensely community-based, not (as in the United States) because the shops were too far away.

Local agents of mail order firms lent out catalogues that were distributed by hand ('the book') to friends and neighbours. It was the agents who placed the orders, took customers' weekly payments, and for the most part took round the parcels when they arrived. They also dealt with returns, which were allowed (goods were sent 'on approval') but were less likely to happen, it was thought, in the set-up whereby they would cause extra work for the agent who was your neighbour. This same agent, as much as a shopkeeper, also had every reason to affirm a customer's choice: it saved the labour of the return, and the loss of the commission, typically 10 per cent and sometimes more. Considerable paperwork was involved. Agents were recruited from among customers themselves, and also had a key role in making their own decisions about the creditworthiness of those who became the customers in their group. This British form of mail order was anything but impersonal; on the contrary, as with local shops, it depended on (and also developed) the mutual obligations and benefits of small community cultures.[3] The mail order companies also succeeded in cultivating a community ethos of their own, often with in-house magazines for agents, or personal visits from central office staff. Patrick Beaver, in his history of Empire Stores, describes the meetings held every day with senior management to discuss and respond to that morning's correspondence from local agents.[4]

From the late 1970s, the function of credit assessment was increasingly shifted away from the informality of an agent's neighbourly knowledge, and over to computer-administered points-based systems; this change coincided with a decline in the community role of the agent, as mail order shopping, more and more, became a matter of customers ordering on their own behalf. Slightly later, in keeping with these changes in the buying pattern, there were successful launches of more upmarket catalogues, as established national brands or chains introduced a mail order string to their selling bow, sometimes utilizing the resources of one of the mainstream catalogue companies. In the mid-1980s, the designer Jeff Banks was associated with a successful catalogue version of the fashion store Warehouse, dispatched via the mail order company Freemans; while the high street store Next launched its own glossy 'Directory' in 1988. These initiatives pushed against the dominant class and regional associations of mail order at the time. In the words of a newspaper write-up, 'With the doing away of the need for the agent, a concept alien to the middle classes, there is the possibility of offering stress-free convenience shopping with no more bother attached than flipping through a brochure, picking up a phone and quoting a credit card number.'[5]

Acting as a part-time mail order agent was astonishingly widespread. According to a survey conducted in 1980, almost half the female population (46 per cent of those over 16 years old) were or had been agents.[6] Some, though, were agents just for their family and perhaps a neighbour or two: the commission was in effect like a permanent discount on their own purchases. The other side of this is that normal mail order prices, with the long-term weekly instalment payments (typically for twenty weeks, 'rolling over' to further extension when other purchases were made), had the cost of their credit built in. The proportion of larger local agencies declined as personal shopping, so called—buying on your own behalf—became the norm, thanks to the growing use by all classes of customer of that combination of the credit card and the telephone (meaning the landline, by now installed in most homes).

Illustrations in Beaver's book show uniformly male managers seated round an imposing table, and rows of uniformly female operatives at work in front of their individual VDUs (visual display units) in the period after computerization came in. In the later decades of the twentieth century, the local agents that remained were almost all female too, as were the rest of the purchasers. But the early history of mail order, and especially of the firm from which Empire Stores developed, was a story about men in the customer roles as well. Mail order developed in the late nineteenth century out of a sociable local practice. A group of men would form a 'watch club' that met regularly at the pub—watches being, at the time, a desirable major purchase. Each person paid in the same small sum each week, adding up to the cost of one watch, which went to whoever drew lots for it that week. At the end of however many months the process took, every man owned a watch. Later, other items apart from timepieces were added, especially as groups that had done their time often chose to continue as a meeting organization, repeating the process whenever a given commodity had been bought for every member.

Fattorini's was the Bradford shop that sold the goods for these first watch clubs. From these beginnings there developed a catalogue and ultimately the larger form of organization that became the Fattorini family's Empire Stores; Grattan's was a breakaway offshoot, also based in Bradford, which had been founded by a member of the same family at the beginning of the twentieth century. For many years, for the various mail order firms, even after they began to deal via catalogues rather than clubs, it remained the case that men were the agents, officially at least, because married women did not have independent financial liability (so could not take financial responsibility). It is likely, though, that in practice it was mainly women who were doing the work and spending the time when the role of the agent began to be based in the home rather than the pub. In general, the history of mail order might be said to recapitulate some of the leading features of the history of class and gender over the past hundred and fifty years, moving as it does from a masculine pub culture and collective endeavour, through the street culture of women at home with pin-money part-time jobs, and on to the time of every shopping woman acting individually, credit card and phone at the ready.

In areas where shops were readily available and sometimes cheaper for the same or equivalent goods, the popularity of mail order has often seemed hard to explain. A statement of this puzzlement many years ago can be found in the incredulity of a question asked in the *Director* trade journal in 1963: 'Why does the housewife buy something, often quite a major item in her year's budget, from a picture book, when in nine cases out of ten she could see a similar range of items in a shop or shops not unduly far from her home?'[7] With the slight alteration, today, of picture book to screen images (and the less slight alteration of the housewife to just about anyone), that remains the great unanswered online question. *Why?*

The peak moment of mail order shopping was around 1980, when it represented approximately 5 per cent of total retail sales in the UK. (This estimated percentage had been constant for a while, but the total volume of sales had been steadily increasing.) There is some overlap, too, with the period of home food deliveries across the whole social range, with the butcher, the baker, the greengrocer, and the milkman all operating through local rounds, as well as from shops. Thus many of the elements of online shopping were there already at this time, and the further question to the *Director*'s 'Why?' is then, Why not? Yet commentators during mail order's boom years, the 1960s and 1970s, never wonder whether it might eventually come to supersede regular shopping from shops, not even in its primary categories, which by then are clothes of all kinds, as well as household and 'fancy' goods. From today's perspective, it looks almost as if the subsequent decade or two of the weekly supermarket shop and the out-of-town mall—with the customer's own delivery vehicle saving the retailer from making the trip—might have been just a short interlude or diversion, before the full-on home delivery of online shopping took over.

A government inquiry into shop opening hours in the mid-1980s was prescient about the future:

> People have long been able to shop by mail order; now, for some of their purchases they can take advantage of telephone shopping. The increasing use of computers will make such 'long distance' shopping easier, quicker, and, therefore, more attractive.[8]

How right they were, we might think. But in late 1984, the computers referred to are not the Amstrads that people had just that year begun to buy for use in the home (no internet yet); they are the business systems that the big mail order houses had begun to instal, at great expense, to improve their operational efficiency.[9]

Notes

1. L.C.A. Knowles, *Industrial and Commercial Revolutions* (London: George Routledge & Sons, 1921), 223.
2. *Fair Play for the Small Man: The Report of the Liberal Independent Trader Committee*, 6; this pamphlet of fifty pages, printed in Manchester, was published in the wake of the committee's recommendations being passed at the Liberal Party's Annual Assembly in July, 1943. It was priced at sixpence.
3. See Avram Taylor, *Working Class Credit and Community since 1918* (London: Palgrave Macmillan, 2002), 108–78; Richard Coopey, Sean O'Connell, and Dilwyn Porter, *Mail Order Retailing in Britain: A Business and Social History* (Oxford: Oxford University Press, 2005); Coopey and Porter, 'Agency mail order in Britain c. 1900–2000: spare-time agents and their customers', in John Benson and Laura Ugolini (eds), *A Nation of Shopkeepers: Five Centuries of British Retailing* (London: I.B. Tauris, 2003), 226–48.

4. Patrick Beaver, *A Pedlar's Legacy: The Origins and History of Empire Stores 1831–1981* (London: Henry Melland, 1981), 107.
5. Sarah Mower, 'Now you traipse round smart shops with your feet up', *Guardian*, Thursday 10 July 1986, 11.
6. Coopey, O'Connell, and Porter, *Mail Order Retailing*, 134.
7. Quoted in Coopey, O'Connell, and Porter, *Mail Order Retailing*, 129.
8. Home Office, *The Shops Acts: Late-Night and Sunday Opening*, Report of the Committee of Inquiry into Proposals to Amend the Shops Acts (London: Her Majesty's Stationery Office, 1984), 11.
9. See Coopey, O'Connell, and Porter, *Mail Order Retailing*, 173–202.

6

Markets

Each stage of the history of shopping is marked, to differing degrees in different places, by the continuation or return of elements of previous ones; or by anticipations, as they turn out, of things to come. But the elements that reappear, or have stayed beyond their moment, will look quite different from when they are part of normality. This is especially true of markets, the earliest form of organized shopping and for many centuries the only one, other than in towns large enough to have shops. Markets have been around in settled human cultures in all times, and they are still present, in various forms, in cultures where other modes of exchange have largely superseded them. But in industrialized countries they have long ceased to be prominent or dominant in the way they once were, so that even where their places and forms are unchanged, they are not what they were. Thus Dorothy Davis, writing in the 1960s, points out the anomalous appearance of pure continuity in one feature of a long-standing urban market:

> When we see the farmer's wife, as we still do today in York and many other north-country towns, sitting on an upturned box at the edge of the Saturday market with her home-made butter, her few chickens and fresh eggs, or the independent small-town butcher bidding for a beast from the side of the cattle pen, we are seeing something as old as English civilization. But these accidental survivals do not mean that present day markets bear any resemblance to their medieval forerunners.[1]

In the same way, a monthly farmers' market held in a supermarket car park may have many likenesses to a market in rural Italy in the first century CE—the goods piled high, the makeshift stalls—but its social meaning is radically different. This present-day market enables the environmentally conscious to buy against the dominant grain of big business—supermarket business in particular. To look at, it may be the same. But in practice, as with the ethical purpose, it is not. There may be an ad hoc markdown for buying a large quantity, but trading will probably involve a muted and orderly sequence of polite purchases, rather than any kind of bargaining game, as in the older set-up.

On a much larger scale than the current initiatives to set up occasional open-air markets, there was a striking resurgence of ambition during the nineteenth century, with local authorities sponsoring the construction of spectacular new market halls, especially in northern industrial towns (see Figure 3). These vast vaulted buildings, often neoclassical on the outside, were as grand as the new railway stations of the same period. Many had glazed roofs for light and ventilation. They were forerunners of the enclosed shopping malls of the late twentieth century—with the difference that most of the selling space took the form of stalls rather than separate, enclosed shops. Most sold food, with separate areas for meat and vegetables and fish. Newcastle's Grainger Market, built in 1835, had almost two hundred butchers' units, and over fifty for greengrocers. Its opening was celebrated with a grand civic dinner for two thousand men—and three hundred women watching from a gallery. At Swansea the hall constructed in the 1890s had space for eighty butchers' stalls. Most markets provided table space for informal vendors, mainly those farm women depicted by Davis, coming in with their dairy products and fruit: there was room set aside for up to four hundred of them at Bolton's market; five hundred at Liverpool's.[2]

It is worth noting too that long before shop design or advertising, markets were always places of display, with the fruit and vegetables laid out in blocks of bright colour. And they were showplaces for the performances of stallholders and shoppers alike. This is the cultural critic Stuart Hall, who lived most of his life in Britain, recalling the markets of his childhood in Jamaica in the 1940s:

Figure 3. Kirkgate Market, Leeds, 1885

One potent memory is the spread of foods you can still find at the Saturday morning markets. I recall how the higglers brought their produce down from the hills in straw baskets carried on their heads. Setting up the market, they created an atmosphere of bustle and hilarity as they greeted one another, reviewed the week in stories and anecdotes, recycling gossip and scandalous tales or rehearsing grievances. This was a very Jamaican scene with its high drama, loud contention, joshing and jostling, taste for exaggeration and caricature, its (often manufactured) sense of outrage—performances which Jamaicans manage to stage on even the most chance encounter. In fact nothing escaped these ladies' eagle eyes. However relaxed they seemed, they were always proprietorially on guard behind their improvised stalls, keeping a sharp lookout for pilferers too inclined to use their casual familiarity to help themselves in passing.[3]

What is highlighted here is the sense of drama and performance. It is all about exaggeration, talking up, overselling, doing it quite deliberately and being seen and known to be doing it; it is also about general talk and gossip among customers—the audience for the selling acts—and between them and the sellers. At the same time there is the suggestion that everyone is playing a role, playing up. The market is the moment to be more than your usual persona; and again, that goes for everyone, not just those standing behind the stalls.

In twenty-first century Britain, alongside the farmers' markets, there have also been efforts to bring back the daily liveliness of the Victorian covered markets. One that has been strikingly successful is in Shrewsbury, where an existing market, housed in a large 1960s building, and run by the local council, is open five days a week. There is a floor of food stalls, with perimeter shops and cafés, and an upstairs gallery with outlets ranging from second-hand books, to wools, to tools for cake icing. Through its management of the market and its purchase of run-down covered malls off the town's main shopping street, this council has been widely praised for showing what can be done to bring central amenities back to shopping life.

Notes

1. Dorothy Davis, *A History of Shopping* (London: Routledge & Kegan Paul Ltd., 1966), 19–20.
2. James Schmiechen and Kenneth Carls, *The British Market Hall: A Social and Architectural History* (New Haven: Yale University Press, 1999), 135, 282.
3. Stuart Hall, with Bill Schwarz, *Familiar Stranger: A Life between Two Islands* (2017; London: Penguin, 2018), 9.

7

Self-Service and Supermarkets

Figure 4. Shoppers at Sainsbury's new store in Bury St Edmunds, Suffolk, 1960
Image courtesy of Sainsbury Archive

Neat rows and stacks of canned goods are a regular feature in the stylish redesigning of grocery shop interiors between the wars. Typically, tins would be carefully placed on the shelves behind the counter, reachable to the clerk and visible to the customer as she went through her list of items. With hindsight, these orderly arrange-ments of identical packaged products look like small-scale forerun-ners of the supermarket aisles of a few decades later. They were modestly attractive displays, blending aesthetically and tidily into the well-planned space of the counter-service food store. Elsewhere, in the new American self-service stores that were appearing in the 1930s, the combination of simplification with large scale was already becoming an article of cut-price retailing faith. This was the new world of 'Pile it high and sell it cheap', to give the phrase its full imperative punch, and the tone was entirely different to that of the small grocery and provisions store, with or without the orderly displays of tins. Self-service and the supermarket did not arrive in western Europe, with the UK somewhat lagging or resisting, until after the war; even Tesco, the downmarket discount king of the first phase of bigger British self-service stores, only began to seriously stack it up in the late 1950s. Self-service plus size—the double prerequisite of the supermarket—was consciously exported from the United States, as part of an organized marketing drive, via special short courses for international food store managers taught by a charismatic Colombian entrepreneur at a venue in Dayton, Ohio. Trujillo's taglines continued to be cited by generations of appreciative French and German managers who had attended one of his famous five-day workshops.[1]

Self-service was the retailing revolution of the twentieth century, in the wake of which over-the-counter service—which still survived and survives—would come to look like history. Beginning with the con-version of existing stores, it gradually came to replace the counter for much day-to-day shopping for groceries. The Co-op was quicker than other chains of the time to switch over large numbers of branches (whereas later, when it came to building large supermarkets on new sites away from town centres, the Co-op was the one that failed to follow the trend). Black and white photographs from this post-war period show housewives being shown how to walk round the store with a basket over their arm, taking a jar or two off the shelves by themselves (see Figure 13). They look now like exhibits from some world of long ago: poor old things, it must have been confusing.

In this first phase the new way of shopping was being promoted, and sometimes criticized. The phrase 'one-stop shopping', meaning that everything you want can be found in a single outlet, was circulating already in the 1950s; it is used by the managing director of Laws Stores on Tyneside in his own writing on retail.[2] Non-specialization was a crucial innovation, alongside the supermarkets' primary deployment of self-service, not counter sales, as the mode of customer access. It made them natural successors and complements to the department stores which, a century before, had presented themselves as offering every kind of (non-food) merchandise for sale in single building, separated into different departments bur not into separate shops. Both aimed at low prices, achieved by small profit margins and high volume. Both made their appeal across all social classes. But the department store offered an elevated atmosphere, a luxury of both environment and merchandise that was now accessible to everyone. Supermarkets, while often proud of their range of goods or their fixtures, displayed a quite different kind of democratization: the absence of the grocer's rituals of deference, and the housewife's freedom to shop as the mood might take her. The counter, relegated to the past, could now be seen as a superseded obstacle on both sides.

With the food-selling chains of the past, companies had often combined into larger economic units through amalgamations and takeovers, but they retained their identities, keeping the name and the specialization. Now, the (much larger) physical shops themselves became, almost by definition, all-containing, all-supplying stores. But the companies were not the same ones as before. Tesco was relatively insignificant until it began to open supermarket-sized stores in the 1950s; while Lipton's, Home and Colonial, and the rest of the previous giants among the multiples faded away in the face of the new competition. With Sainsbury's, already a small, smart chain, and with the Co-op, the original chain and the first to engage systematically in self-service conversions after the war, there is some resilience between the two eras, before and after the supermarkets. But the Co-op, for all its continuing evolution and its many, many outlets (there were more than *twenty thousand* individual shops just after the war), has never, by any measure, been at the top of the supermarket tree.[3]

Sainsbury's first self-service store was opened in London Road, Croydon, in June, 1950, by converting both ground floor and basement on the extended site of a store that had been there since 1882. In its time this had been the flagship 'first luxury food store', with tiling on floor and walls, and a marble counter.[4] Seventy years later, the company prided itself on being the first to take advantage of the potential for self-service stores to be large; there were no fewer than five of the 'exit lanes known as "check-outs".'[5] Writing for the in-house journal, Mr Salisbury wants staff to understand the historical significance of the conversion to self-service—'Suddenly, I think it can be said, we have switched from evolution to revolution.' Let's hope Croydon was ready for it.[6]

On the long anticipated first day, 'At 8.30. a.m. the shutters went up, and in walked the queue of one.'[7] Mr Salisbury does also refer to widespread criticisms of the new phenomenon, chief of which is that it is a way for stores to cut their costs, with fewer assistants needed. In light of later environmental concerns, the counterargument is striking:

> In general much, and perhaps too much, emphasis has been laid on self-service as a cheapened form of distribution. This aspect is very open to question, particularly having regard to the additional packaging costs which are involved, but the necessity of prepackaging everything before sale does make for cleanliness.[8]

Objections to self-service continue to figure in the background of other contemporary reports of supermarket openings. Two laudatory features in local papers about the Laws chain bring out diverse aspects of the perception of the new style of store in the early years. In the first, in 1958 (see Figure 5), the principle of bulk purchasing is carefully explained. Above all, supermarkets are to be seen as money-saving for

Figure 5. *Newcastle Journal* feature on the opening of a new branch of Laws Stores in Gateshead, June 1958

customers. They are also presented as progressive and ambitious in both design and product range. The local reporter notes the lighting, the refrigeration units, and the ceiling, which is 'the most attractive thing in interior decoration I've seen in years'; 'The place is—need I say it?—architect-designed.' There are 'display gondolas laden with yet more goods', and there is also a 'connoisseurs' corner' with offerings that include spaghetti, macaroni, and 'even a tinned Scottish haggis'. Away from these exotic hints of the supermarket as an affordable luxury store, there is also a general philosophy of all-encompassing practicality: 'As for the supermarket idea, well, the advantages of being able to buy nearly all your requirements, householdwise, that is, under one roof, are surely too obvious to mention.'

Setting aside an already standard objection to self-service on the grounds of its impersonality (no conversation across the counter), the friendliness of the place is also stressed. With customers wandering round freely and staff no longer 'chained to counters', the new store is instead to be regarded as a positive liberation for all concerned. 'We can move about, chatting to customers, offering advice—giving them far more individual attention than by the old, behind-the-counter methods, in fact.' This is the opinion of the manager, Mr John Wilkin, 'a curly-headed young man' who is also described as 'Spotlessly white-clad', and 'smiling'. Happily, the opening of the new store is to be on Mr Wilkins' birthday, but that is 'pure coincidence'.[9]

In 1961, three years later, in Newcastle's other daily paper, another feature celebrates another Laws store opening in another part of Gateshead, this one with 'the first Continental corner in any super-market on Tyneside'; the delicacies of this Continent include 'octopus and reindeer steak'. There will also be 'taped background music', which is 'to make the customer's look round the store even more pleasant'.[10] As much as the muzak, notable here is that what the customer does in a food store can be casually called a 'look round'. What this means—though it is not said directly—is that she does not need be either focused or swift, and this is the vital difference of self-service from counter shopping, for which you must wait your turn and go through a list. Here, hesitation will not hold up others waiting behind you. The suggestion is that in the supermarket, far from being hurried or having a specific task to do, the shopper can have a pleasant time just looking around, with music to accompany her as she strolls.

Like the earlier article, this one is surrounded by related display advertisements. Some are for the store itself and its opening offers: not the reindeer steak, but such items as sugar, flour, Tinned Pears, Carnation Milk, Fruit Salad, Garden Peas, Fray Bentos (corned beef), and 'Defiance Orange Squash'. Many of the other advertisements are placed by firms and brands offering their congratulations to Laws on its new store; Domestos, a firm that is both local and national, is among them. The other brands include Lakeland eggs, Harris (Wiltshire) bacon, and Be-Ro self-raising flour. A second category is advertisements placed by the various companies who were privileged to do the fitting and installations for the store, from electrics to glazing to display shelving and 'dump display units' (for special offers). Some have photos of the articles they make, and every one of them is a local company.

Nearly six decades later, when supermarkets in Britain are almost all national or non-British chains, it is the local emphasis of these features, with their accompanying publicity, that stands out. The firm of Laws Stores, with its forward-looking new branches, is a regional achievement. In this context, Mr Wilkins' birthday, that pure coincidence, makes a likeable contrast to a story some decades later about the opening of a Tesco branch in Llanelli, on 4 April 1989. The day before, just in time, a daughter had been born to the wife of the man responsible at that time for the organization of Tesco store openings. The birth was a planned caesarean, to avoid any possible clash with the store event.[11]

In the late 1980s, a government-sponsored report on the future of the high street could still manage to avoid the word *supermarket* altogether, instead referring to 'modern, large foodstores' or 'large grocers', along with various other unusual expressions—as if to ignore the by then entire familiarity of these beasts.[12] Supermarket circumlocutions deserve a historical study in their own right. My favourite is James Jeffery's 'self-service combination stores'; but unlike the anonymous authors of the later report, he was writing (in the early 1950s) before any such thing had been seen in Britain, with or without a generic name. He goes on to define them, simply enough, as 'retail units selling meat and groceries and provisions'.[13] In the 1980s, though, whatever you called these places, there was no pretending they weren't there. At the turn of the twenty-first century the biggest supermarket chains in both name and statistical fact were Sainsbury's and Tesco, the king and king, accompanied by an occasionally varying mini-group of competitor-courtiers floating beneath them.

The 'biggest' supermarket might imply any one of a number of different definitions, depending on the context: numbers of branches; total or average sales area; total or average area of selling plus storage space combined; weekly or annual turnover or profits. But it is clear that at the end of the twentieth century, average store selling areas were changing in only one direction, beating a roadway by then much less resisted to the edge of town and beyond; ever more stores covering ever greater areas were put up in previously no-shops lands, at a distance from built-up residential areas. And with even more land for the cars. Precise formulae from American feasibility studies were pondered, to calculate the notionally correct ratio between the sales area and parking area—but were found, for all their mathematical exactitude, to be just not up to the planning job in a different country with, for instance, smaller cars and tighter expectations of how close the next car could be. For decades—for more than half of the twentieth century—North Americans had been motoring to the market (that is, the supermarket), near or far, and increasingly leaving the towns and cities to live in the newly built suburbs and drive to the newly built malls. In Britain (and on the Continent—with many variations) using the car to buy food was a relatively recent development—as was storing it in a refrigerator at home.

The future of the high street never stops being a subject of speculation and concern and invention. At the start, online shopping in Britain was relatively slow to progress (though that, in the context of its subsequent settled expansion, has been largely forgotten). But at the start of the 2020s news comes regularly of dwindled profits, or redundancies, or outright closure, for yet another long-term name of a chain or department store 'on the high street'—now extended to include the out-of-town shopping centre as well. As far as supermarkets are concerned, not only are they successful as online retailers themselves, but there has been a second development of equal note. This is a return to smaller-scale local shop units of the size that had been left behind, in every sense, when they first began to shift operations out to the wild ring-road west (or east, north, or south) of an average, thereby abandoned high street. This has been the surprise of the early twenty-first century food-buying and high street landscape—almost a townscape, once again. It is bound up with all sorts of other slow changes, from smaller household size (and picking up food on the way home from work) to—paradoxically—online food shopping itself (the convenience store for items forgotten on the order, the delivery not yet due). Having stretched out and away from the towns where they started; having expanded, adding larger and larger links to their long, long chains, the big supermarkets have come back to occupy small units in the centre—just as they did at first.

Notes

1. On the development of self-service and supermarkets in America and the UK, see Rachel Bowlby, *Carried Away: The Invention of Modern Shopping* (London: Faber and Faber, 2000); Lawrence Black and Thomas Spain, 'How Self-Service Happened: The Vision and Reality of Changing Market Practices in Britain', in David Thackeray, Andrew Thompson, and Richard Toye (eds), *Imagining Britain's Economic Future, c1800–1975: Trade, Consumerism and Global Markets* (London: Palgrave Macmillan, 2018), 159–80; Kim Humphery, *Shelf Life: Supermarkets and the Changing Culture of Consumption* (Cambridge: Cambridge University Press, 1998).

2. See for instance W.G. McClelland, *Studies in Retailing* (Oxford: Basil Blackwell, 1963), 54.

3. To be exact: there were 20,657 Co-op shops in Britain in 1946, including nearly ten thousand grocery and provisions stores (9,490) and almost five thousand butchers (4,536); figures in C.W.S. [Co-operative Wholesale Society], *A Consumers' Democracy* (Stockport, 1951?), 123.

4. Mr F.W. Salisbury, 'Sainsbury's Sample Self-Service', *J.S Journal* 3:4 (September 1950), 4.
5. Salisbury, 'Sainsbury's Sample Self-Service', 8.
6. Salisbury, 'Sainsbury's Sample Self-Service', 10.
7. Salisbury, 'Sainsbury's Sample Self-Service', 8.
8. Salisbury, 'Sainsbury's Sample Self-Service', 8.
9. Elizabeth Holland, 'Mr Wilkins Has a Birthday to Remember', *Newcastle Journal*, Wednesday 11 June 1958, 6.
10. 'The most modern shopping centre in North-East', *Evening Chronicle*, Monday 20 March 1961, 8–9.
11. The story is in Sarah Ryle, *The Making of Tesco: A Story of British Shopping* (London: Bantam, 2013), 212.
12. Distributive Trades EDC [Economic Development Corporation], *The Future of the High Street* (London: Her Majesty's Stationery Office, 1988), 5, 22.
13. James B. Jefferys, *Retail Trading in Britain 1850–1950* (Cambridge: Cambridge University Press, 1954), 207.

8

Shopping Centres

After the Second World War, the motor bus taking the customers into town and the delivery van taking the goods to their door disappeared from most of the talk about shops; instead of representing a mobile and forward-looking modernity, these vehicles instead came to stand for an image of bygone shopping simplicity. Closer to home, the newly built *parades* of local shops on the interwar estates were already losing their gleam—just as the older parades on the front in seaside towns would soon be showing signs of decay, with their summer visitors all flown away on package holidays abroad. The 'hit parade' of the 1950s and early 1960s, meanwhile, would be superseded by the businesslike sound of 'the charts'. By the 1960s it was possible almost to scoff at the pre-war building of 'rows of little boxes, one each for the grocer, the butcher, the greengrocer, the baker, and so on', like a sort of toy town. But it was also recognized that if the planners of shopping parades were misguided, it was unavoidably so, since 'they could not then foresee that the need in the nineteen-sixties would be for supermarkets.'[1]

In the 1950s and 1960s, the future-orientated debate was all about something by then called the 'shopping centre', soon to be purpose-built or purpose-rebuilt. For the first time, during this period, shops in the aggregate became the object of targeted planning in their own right. How many should there be? Where should they be, in relation to one another and to the dwellings of their customers? Were there, either in the country as a whole or in particular towns or neighbourhoods, too many of them for the needs of the buying population? This last phenomenon, already identified by economists in the 1930s, was known by the wonderful name of *overshopping*. Britain—and even more, England—was thought to be suffering acutely from this ailment; the always well-worn line about 'a nation of shopkeepers', supposed to have been spoken by Napoleon, was probably repeated more during this period than at any time before or since. But how was this too much or too little to be measured, especially when shops themselves were infinitely variable in size, and when even the nature of that size—whether to calculate it by selling area or turnover, for instance—was itself a matter of argument? And how, in any case, could those needs be evaluated in any reliable way when shopping was such a diffuse and variable practice, depending on the occasion, the region, or the social class (ethnicity was not yet a consideration); and when buying patterns were changing all the time, so that future projections based on present data were necessarily flawed? From a common-sense point of view, it seemed confusing that the corner shop opened up in a converted front room had the same economic status as the big branch of Marks & Spencer in the city centre. Each of them, officially and statistically, was simply 'a shop'.

Most of these questions had been mooted before, but there was a new urgency and enthusiasm for thinking about them proactively at this mid-century time. New shops needed to be built in areas that had been bombed during the war, and also in the places that were being planned in the wake of the New Towns Act of 1946. By now the many suburban estates put up in the interwar decades had generally acquired those little 'parades', of five or six shop units, dotted around, with a group of them every few streets. But with the new towns, for the first time, shops were a matter of large-scale planning for a substantial population. They were treated as an element of necessary public provision, even though it was also assumed that once operational they would be leased to private tenants, as normally happened. Basic food shops, in the same way as primary schools, should be regarded as local amenities, to be sited within walking distance of every home. At this time, it is worth recalling, very few households had refrigerators or cars; and many shops that sold perishable food did not have refrigerators either. Daily purchasing of what it was possible for one person to carry (often with the supporting help of a pram) was the norm.

For town centre shopping, the need or desirability of parking provision is a looming question, adjacent to the newly arising possibility of fully pedestrianized streets or squares (the *precinct*, taking over from the *parade*, is the new shop word at this time). In the many books that consider the subject in the post-war decades, the same few examples of newly planned centres are brought out and discussed. Coventry and Stevenage are prominent, the first as a town centre rebuilt after bombing and the second as a new town. Both, controversially, experimented early on with areas of pedestrianization, and developments in both were endlessly debated in the literature as well as on the ground, in the towns themselves and the offices that were designing them. Frank Schaffer, in a book about new towns published in 1970, is fulsome in his praise of the pioneer of true pedestrianization of the centre: 'To Stevenage goes the proud distinction of forcing the change.'[2] Brave little Stevenage!

Other new towns commonly mentioned in connection with their shops are Cumbernauld, Hemel Hempstead, and Crawley. Plymouth is sometimes cited as another redeveloped bombed city, but the brutalist shopping centre across the water in Rotterdam is a much more frequent illustration. The key topics for discussion have to do with basic planning issues, such as: the number of parking spaces (and who should provide them, and how far away from the shops); the optimum number of levels in a shopping centre (a few were built with two, sometimes resulting in unforeseen wind tunnels); the need for various facilities, from public toilets to flower beds to litter bins to sculpture to somewhere for people to sit down; the layout most likely to bring it about that most shoppers will find their way past the highest proportion of the shop frontages (this issue is sometimes referred to by the formidable term of 'pedestrian engineering'); and whether to have or not have a pram ramp.[3]

It was not only new towns or rebuilt centres that were the objects of concentrated expert attention in relation to their future shops. The detailed study headed by the sociologist Ruth Glass of the future needs of Middlesbrough considers shop provision in some detail, for outlying parts as well as the town centre. Precisely because shops had not in the past been a formal object of planning policy, Glass found, their distribution within the town had gradually ceased to be aligned with changing residential patterns as they had evolved since the last part of the nineteenth century. The existing distribution was anachronistic, with too many shops remaining at one end of the town from which people had moved away, while a newly populated district at the other end was undershopped. Drawing on the models used with other recent town surveys, the book uses a descriptive division involving multiple scales of shopping 'centre', both in relation to the present dysfunctional arrangements and as a framework for proposals for future developments. Thus a 'local centre' is the small group of shops that people use most days; between that and the shops in the centre of the town are 'district' centres, with some question also about whether even a fourth intermediate category is useful—in planning or in reality—between the district and local centres. Shopping 'centres' in this model are in no way necessarily large, or even central in relation to the town as a whole; they are more like clusters or strings to be seen in a series of varying relationships to neighbourhoods which are themselves at varying distances from the town centre proper.

Glass's book often adopts a straightforwardly economic logic (where there are redundant shops, not all can make a living), but the redistribution she advocates is also motivated by social arguments that lie at the understated heart of the book.

> One fact, in particular, which was brought to light in Middlesbrough, will not be forgotten. It was found that the chances of children of reaching higher education were multiplied fifteen times when they moved from the blighted areas to the new housing estates, and thus from the obsolete to the up-to-date school.[4]

When it comes to the much larger scale of the post-war new towns and rebuilt town centres, social issues are taken for granted as an aspect for consideration for planning in the long term and also in relation to small details of the layout of shopping streets or pedestrian 'precincts'. A common question is the desirable width of a street, with or without non-human traffic; this has repercussions for the cohesion or not of a shopping area as a whole:

> There should be enough room for people to move freely from one shop window to another. Too wide a street can effectively divide the shops that line it, while too narrow and crowded a street may lose its appeal. Ideally, a shopping centre should display its shops with as much care as each shop displays its goods.[5]

A different order of proposal, in the 1960s, for an out-of-town centre that was never actually built received more discussion subsequently than any that ever was. Haydock, somewhere in the depths of Lancashire, was to have been a private development; it was refused planning permission on the grounds of the effect it was likely to have on shops in the three nearest big towns (St Helens, Warrington, and Wigan). But much of the debate that surrounded this hypothetical implantation concentrated on the impossibility, in any case, of predicting who might ultimately go there, by what means of transport, from where, how often, and what for. A subfield of *this* argument was about how much weight to give to American mall viability studies, virtually a micro-industry by this time. The Haydock proposal made use of a 'law of retail gravitation', according to which 'two cities attract retail trade in style and fashion goods from an intermediate town approximately in direct proportion to the population of the two cities and in inverse proportion to the square of the distance from the intermediate town to the two cities.'[6] The word 'approximately' is doing some heavy lifting here.

As time went on, a further issue that emerged in the British debates was whether shopping centres should be roofed over in their entirety, not just shop by shop—thereby avoiding the creation of wind tunnels not conducive to customer calmness (and avoiding any effect at all from the ordinary variability of weather). The fully covered centre is more expensive to maintain and involves different protocols both for shopfront presentation (less individuality; no need for a door) and for service payments on the part of shop leaseholders. The place is now in effect one great big building that has to be maintained as such. It needs air conditioning and, since it is shut up at night, it needs a different order of security.

It was not just a question of how useful these studies, known as 'retail location models', might be on their own terms, for their own purposes, but of how far both shopping and shop-constructing conditions in the UK were so radically different from those in the US as to make them almost irrelevant. In policy terms, American malls were all private developments—as was the ill-fated Haydock. In practical terms, they depended on private car ownership and on space for vast car parks (with land being generally much cheaper and more readily available than in European countries). Typically, malls were situated well out of town, adjacent to the newly built centreless suburbs for which there was no direct urban equivalent in Britain. They needed massive amounts of land area far beyond the shop space per se, since they had to cater for all the cars that would carry the customers there. But British shoppers were likely not to have cars in the first place (to commentators at the time, this is the most obvious and most often stated difference); even though car ownership was growing fast, only around a third of households had one at the start of the 1960s. By the end of the 1980s, however, a government report about 'the future of the high street' is using a striking phrase for a complex subspecies of road users now to be taken into planning consideration, that of 'car-borne working wives'.[7]

It is worth pausing for a minute to wonder about the husband of this wife—or the children, for that matter. The speaker of Allen Ginsberg's poem 'A Supermarket in California' (from the 1950s, when supermarkets were well established as the primary food shopping mode in America) is mock-amazed by the unnatural sight of 'whole families shopping at night!' and 'aisles full of husbands!'[8] Husbands are unexpectedly and comically seen as a collective species, but as such they are out with their wives; whereas the car-borne wives do not have husbands or any other human associates in tow: they have jobs, which is why they now have to do the family shopping at funny times. Men in supermarkets are rarely if ever to be seen in any planning literature (to what extent they may have been there in fact, in the stores themselves, is another matter). But shopping men— including some buying household supplies—do surface here and there in the limited evidence for the history of who bought what. One very early example is none other than Samuel Pepys, whose diary has many examples of his purchasing role, both in relation to his personal needs—his clothes and, at one point, his hair—and for food and other domestic items. Here he is on a quick trip to the seventeenth-century version of an indoor shopping centre. His wife is making marmalade:

> I left her at it, and by coach I to the New Exchange and several places to buy and bring home things.[9]

For this coach-borne working husband, to 'buy and bring home things' is a normal part of his everyday life.

The absence of men as if by definition, not reality, is marked in a small British survey of the 1960s. In addition to the large feasibility studies for out-of-town projects, there were also evidence-based reports that were modest in scope, seeking to sound out a fairly small section of a fairly small population, in order to see what useful information could be gleaned for the planning of town centre shops and parking over the coming decade. Leighton Buzzard in Bedfordshire, with a population of about 15,000 at the time, commissioned its own little survey of shoppers, conducted one Friday and Saturday in April 1965. In the context of a proposal put forward the previous year for considerable expansion of shop provision in the town, the aim was to find out how this centre was currently used. People who happened to be there on those days were stopped and asked about what they were doing: where they had come from, how they had travelled in, and what other errands they had in the town in addition to shopping. The interviewees were also asked what kinds of things they generally bought in Leighton Buzzard town centre, as opposed to elsewhere— in other parts of the town, or in other towns (or villages). In all, the prepared set of questions was put to 301 people, all but one of whom turned out to be from the town itself or its surrounding districts. But only women were interviewed!—a fact that is stated but given no explanation. Is it meant to be obvious that only women shop? Or that to include any men who were out and about on those mornings might in some way have skewed the statistics? If there were none to be seen (and excluded), there would have been no need to say that only women were spoken to. More than fifty years later, though, the decision is itself of historical interest. As for the one (female) exception who did not live locally (and whose presence also prevented what would otherwise have been the statistically simple round number of 300 interviewees), she came from Wallsend on Tyneside and was 'visiting friends'. Her responses have to be explicitly excluded from the table about 'Normal Shopping Habits' (with data about other places where various goods are bought). We will never know who she was! But she has her tiny place in shopping history.

In addition to its use of respondents' answers and the contingency of who was around on these particular days, the survey drew on detailed figures from the 1961 Census of Distribution. When it came to predictions and plans, one major assumption was that the broad categories of goods purchased were not going to change in the coming years. The general conclusion was not to promote or carry out any drastic changes to the (small) town centre. A notable finding is this:

> It would appear that there are more than enough grocers in the town centre to meet growth in demand for this category of convenience goods. Should a new supermarket be located in the central area, it will have to

share trade which would naturally have been absorbed by existing shops. Competition of the severest kind would therefore be the lot of the grocery trade.[10]

In spite of the potential disruption indicated in the last sentence, the existing shops do include at least two chain store grocers, since the two of the interviewers were stationed outside Key Markets and International Stores. The report is not against chains; on the contrary, it positively looks forward to the prospect of their arrival in the areas considered appropriate for development: 'The main expansion in trade should be in the fashion trades, men's wear and household goods, and it is within these lines that trade should improve, due to expanding population, to a level which would be attractive to new traders, and multiple traders in particular.'[11] From the point of view of contemporary retail woes, it is also interesting that the survey specifically stipulates for the infilling of broken shop frontage—in other words, the occupation of presently empty units—before any new development takes place.[12] The depressing effect of such gaps is a point also made in the earlier study of Middlesbrough.

As these examples show, the extensive post-war literature of future shop provision came from many different fields; as well as from academic writing by sociologists, economists, and (increasingly) geographers, it also includes lavishly produced architectural studies and publicly sponsored reports and inquiries, both local and national. As the years moved on beyond rationing (which finally came to an end in 1954) and into the bright or garish world of the new, and newly named, 'consumer society', the thinking about shopping futures frequently took on a tone of social critique or censure. Whereas 'overshopping' was previously a word that simply meant too many shops for the needs—which were known and stable—of a given community, now it would suggest a quite different meaning: that people were shopping too much. In the process, shopping as a matter of daily sociability also went out of the window: no more local shops to do it in, or housewives at home to do it. The big stores outside towns drew people away, leaving behind and less used the small shops and the new parades, and eventually the town centres too. Whatever the plan had once been.

Notes

1. W.G. McClelland, *Studies in Retailing* (Oxford: Basil Blackwell, 1963), 179.
2. Frank Schaffer, *The New Town Story* (1970; London: Paladin, 1972), 141.
3. See Clive Darlow, *Enclosed Shopping Centres* (London: Architectural Press, 1972); David Gosling and Barry Maitland, *Design and Planning of Retail Systems* (London: Architectural Press, 1976).
4. Ruth Glass (ed.), *The Social Background of a Plan: A Study of Middlesbrough* (London: Routledge & Kegan Paul Limited, 1948), 191.
5. Glass, *Social Background of a Plan*, 183.
6. Peter Scott, *Geography and Retailing* (London: Hutchinson University Library, 1970), 169; on Haydock see also Colin S. Jones, *Regional Shopping Centres: Their Location, Planning and Design* (London: Business Books, 1969), 26–46.
7. Distributive Trades EDC [Economic Development Committee], *The Future of the High Street* (London: Her Majesty's Stationery Office, 1988), 102.
8. Allen Ginsberg, 'A Supermarket in California' (1955), in *Howl* (San Francisco: City Lights, 1955), lines 5–6.
9. Samuel Pepys, *The Diary of Samuel Pepys: A Selection*, ed. Robert Latham (London: Penguin, 2003), 318.
10. *Leighton-Linslade Central Area Shopping Survey* (Bedfordshire County Council Planning Department, 1965), 25.
11. *Leighton-Linslade Central Area Shopping Survey*, 25.
12. *Leighton-Linslade Central Area Shopping Survey*, 25, 27.

9

Shop Windows

Glass windows of any kind were late to appear at all on the street-facing fronts of shops. Before the eighteenth century, when glazing began to be used, and goods to be actively put on display behind it, the usual arrangement was the shutter that doubled as a daytime counter, with an overhead canopy. Precisely described by the nineteenth-century French architect Eugène Viollet-le-Duc, this was 'closed with lower and upper shutters, the former attached to the counter and opening downwards and outwards to form an extension of the counter, and the latter attached to the wooden lintel and opening upwards and outwards to form some protection for the goods displayed below'.[1]

In the middle of the nineteenth century, big new windows began to be seen on the front of some shops, which then stood out from more modest neighbours. With their spacious transparency, not broken up into little panes, plate-glass windows were the symbol of a new kind of city store: open to all comers, with a visibly modern outlook. In the beginning of the plate glass period, we find Charles Dickens, in his own first (journalistic) phase, having fun in his fulminations against an absurd new species of London shop. Like dogs and other animals, Dickens suggests in 1835, 'different trades run stark, staring, raving mad periodically', and that 'the contagion is general, and the quickness with which it diffuses itself, almost incredible.'[2] One instance of this trade madness looked like this:

Six or eight years ago, the epidemic began to display itself among the linen drapers and haberdashers. The primary symptoms were an inordinate love of plate glass, and a passion for gaslights and gilding. The disease gradually progressed, and at last attained a fearful height. Quiet dusty old shops in different parts of town, were pulled down; spacious premises with stuccoed fronts and gold letters, were erected instead; floors were covered with Turkey carpets; roofs supported by massive pillars; doors knocked into windows, a dozen squares of glass into one; one shopman into a dozen.[3]

The stress here is not on a contrast of size as between the small, dark windows of old back-street shops and the big new ones. Instead, Dickens describes a kind of wanton destructiveness, as the 'Quiet dusty old shops', doing no harm to anyone, are ripped out to make way for the flashy new constructions. Even the dust is neutral; whereas a century later it would be a regular sign of the carelessness in a local grocer's or butcher's that could obviously benefit from the clean sweep of modernization along newly hygienic lines.[4] Dickens objects, pure and simple, to the *décor* per se: to the attempt to make mere shops into spectacular sites of display.

George Eliot's *The Mill on the Floss* was published in 1860 but set, like most of her novels, in a provincial town some years in the past. The time distance is utilized to make a comment about recent changes to the appearance of buildings on the high street. At this earlier time:

there was no incongruous new-fashioned smartness, no plate glass in shop windows, no fresh stucco-facing or other fallacious attempt to make fine old red St Ogg's wear the air of a town that sprang up yesterday. The shop windows were small and unpretending, for the farmers' wives and daughters who came to do their shopping on market-day were not to be withdrawn from their regular, well-known shops.[5]

Here the plate-glass windows are the very image of a general aspiration to 'new-fashioned smartness'; it is the newness of having no apparent history, of a place looking like it has just been built. The reference to the farm women coming into town to make the same purchases at the same shops every week has the effect of making the pre-plate-glass shops into social institutions as old as the market and as natural as the culture of the land. It is crucial, too, that the older, unchanging town only looks that way from the later, changed perspective of the present time.

In the long term, plate glass changed the appearance of the shopping street, as window display became a minor art form, taught as such and developing talents that could be exercised through panes of modest scope as well. Plate glass had also been bound up with a whole philosophy of shop presentation, together with an array of new possibilities for the interior. From now on, the view that is shown to the world that passes by was to be regarded as essential to a shop's success. Carefully chosen fixtures and fittings such as mahogany counters and glass display cases were to complement the smart exterior. Artificial lighting—first gas and later electric—became an increasingly significant feature, both inside and outside. In the initial phase, such changes took place for the most part in shops that sold clothing and fabrics or household goods. In the later part of the nineteenth century, the first department stores brought all these things together into one vast emporium—with vast plate-glass windows an essential feature of their imposing metropolitan presence.

In the shorter term (but into the twentieth century), plate-glass windows were regularly condemned as lacking a sense of architectural proportion, as upper storeys appeared to be balanced on nothing underneath. In the 1930s, two architects write with a sense of change at last after too long a period of plate glass malpractice:

> The use of large plates of glass demanded an entirely different treatment and throughout the nineteenth century this treatment was so inadequate and crude, especially in conjunction with an elaborate top-hamper of heavy masonry, that until the last few years it seemed as if shop-design was to be for ever synonymous with bad taste.[6]

This pre-war period was a golden age of artistic window display, concentrated on an aesthetics of modernist simplicity, its clean lines contrasted with the dust and 'clutter' of the window hitherto used as if as a storage space.

Shop windows and their displays can also be seen to have the effect of artificially altering the spectator's view of themselves, by acting as mirrors or magnifiers (or reducers) of their current self-perception, if not the of way that they actually look. The mannequin in the plate-glass window invites the spectator outside to stop and see themselves in this image of another self, and then to step into the shop and try it on for themselves.[7] Thus the window offers an idealizing view which may then have the effect of downgrading in their own eyes the person who now sees their present appearance as inferior (to be rectified or improved by the acquisition of what is seen); alternatively, it may lead to an inflation of self-esteem, in connection with the prestigious objects they are looking at.

In Virginia Woolf's novel of the mid-1920s, *Mrs Dalloway*, where shopping possibilities are to be found at the turn of every page, the middle-aged Peter Walsh comes across an impressive picture of himself in the large window of a London car showroom: a new kind of commercial venue in the early 1920s. Here the window has become not just a form of display for the shop and its wares, but also a way of perceiving the self, in a newly flattering light. The image that Peter sees is gratifyingly unique: 'Only one person could be as he was, in love. And there he was, this fortunate man, himself, reflected in the plate-glass window of a motor-car manufacturer in Victoria Street.'[8] An enlarged sense of his own importance as a colonial administrator in India of 'a district twice as big as Ireland' then easily promotes further thoughts of the performance of the products on sale. He is 'looking at the great motor cars capable of doing—how many miles on how many gallons? For he had a turn for mechanics; had invented a plough in his district.'[9] In this specifically masculine version of the scene of consumer desire in front of the shop window, both the man and the motor car are magnified by the big glass, at once mirror and window.

So it is that Peter Walsh, invited to a society party, is gratified by the sight of a superior masculine self, 'this effigy of a man in a tail-coat with a carnation in his button-hole coming towards him.'[10] Exactly the opposite glass effect is produced in the case of a man without means, confronted with his material descent in the world. In George Gissing's *New Grub Street* (1891), the once promising novelist Edwin Reardon is almost proud to wander the (back) streets wearing clothes that might have been cast-offs:

> In his present state of mind he cared nothing how he looked to passers-by. These seedy habiliments were the token of his degradation, and at times he regarded them (happening to see himself in a shop-mirror) with pleasurable contempt.[11]

The clothes reflected back to him are like a proudly negative self-advertisement for his fallen condition, as he shows himself to his own mocking view, and to the public sight of other passers-by. There is also an occasion when a shop window takes Reardon away altogether from his sense of public decorum: 'when walking in one of the back streets of Islington'—a poor area—'he stopped idly to gaze into the window of some small shop'. He starts reciting out loud some lines from Shakespeare about a ruler fallen on hard times; and he is brought back to reality by 'the loud mocking laugh of two men standing close by, who evidently looked upon him as a strayed lunatic'.[12] In harmony with Reardon's reduced circumstances and self-esteem, the modest window of 'some small shop' has none of the pretensions of the grand spectacle of the plate-glass image. Thus the windows talk back to the passers-by, an image of their dreams or their descent.

More warehouse than showroom, supermarkets did away with the display of the window altogether. No more views of the style of the shop, whether ultra-modern (the motor car) or discreetly elegant (on her morning walk, Mrs Dalloway passes the exclusive tailor's long patronized by her father, showing its single, sufficient roll of quality tweed).[13] Just a functional, light-admitting sheet of glass, facing out to the concrete of a car park. No street from which to draw the customers in, to make them want to stop and admire the display. By making the journey and parking the car they have already taken the decision to come here; an alluring window would be redundant.

Notes

1. Cited in Raymond McGrath and A.C. Frost, *Glass in Architecture and Decoration* (London: Architectural Press, 1937), 136.
2. Charles Dickens, 'Gin Shops' (1835), *Dickens' Journalism: Sketches by Boz and Other Early Papers 1833–39*, ed. Michael Slater (1994; London: Phoenix, 1996), 180.
3. Dickens, 'Gin Shops', 180.
4. See Rachel Bowlby, 'The Passer-by and the Shop Window', in *Carried Away: The Invention of Modern Shopping* (London: Faber, 2000), 49–78.
5. George Eliot, *The Mill on the Floss* (1860; Harmondsworth: Penguin, 1979), 117.
6. McGrath and Frost, *Glass in Architecture and Decoration*, 137.
7. See Bowlby, *Just Looking: Consumer Culture in Dreiser, Gissing and Zola*(1985; London: Routledge, 2009), 30–2.
8. Virginia Woolf, *Mrs Dalloway* (1925), ed. David Bradshaw (Oxford: Oxford University Press, 2000), 41.
9. Woolf, *Mrs Dalloway*, 41.
10. Woolf, *Mrs Dalloway*, 41.
11. George Gissing, *New Grub Street* (1891; Harmondsworth: Penguin, 1980), 377.
12. Gissing, *New Grub Street*, 376.
13. Woolf, *Mrs Dalloway*, 9.

10

Sources

In October 1826, the campaigning writer William Cobbett was travelling up from Southampton, back to London. On the way he found matter for argument at Netley Abbey, where he fulminated about the disappearance of the 'ancient *fish-ponds*' of the place—'"reclaimed," as they call it.' What had gone was a valuable and simple source of food:

> What a *loss*, what a national loss, there has been in this way, and in the article of *water fowl*! I am quite satisfied, that, in these two articles and in that of *rabbits*, the nation has lost, has had annihilated (within the last 250 years) food sufficient for *two days in the week*, on an average, taking the year throughout. These are things, too, which cost so little labour![1]

The perspective is one of planning on a national scale, with the deployment of averages, time periods, and cost-effectiveness to elaborate the case. Starting from this particular place, the view pans out to encompass innumerably more: all the ponds that Cobbett has seen on his travels, a justification for the generalization that he has already made: 'You can see the marks of old fish-ponds in thousands and thousands of places. I have noticed, I dare say, *five hundred*, since I left home.'[2]

What is to be done? The solution would be straightforward, just like the yield that could then be obtained again from these sources—but it is a solution which, Cobbett declares, is thwarted from the start, and that is because of a new social practice which has effectively made the ponds redundant:

A trifling expense would, in most cases, restore them; but now-a-days, all
is looked for at *shops*: all is to be had by *trafficking*: scarcely any one thinks
of providing for his own wants *out of his own land* and ... his own domestic
means.[3]

Cobbett casually identifies a momentous change: from the default
position of growing your own and using the local resources, to
seeking what is needed elsewhere—and above all with *shops*, the
word speared with those savage italics. Cobbett identifies the difficulty
primarily as a matter of mindset: today 'scarcely any one thinks of'
being self-sufficient.

Then Cobbett says more on shops and what is wrong with them:
'To buy the thing, *ready made*, is the taste of the day: thousands, who are
housekeepers, buy their dinners ready cooked.'[4] Apart from some now
unlikely characters and turns of phrase—the housekeepers, 'the taste
of the day'—this could be the beginning of a well-meaning post about
'cooking from scratch', as currently used to mean preparing food at
home, as opposed to buying a ready meal from the shop (or having it
delivered). As it stands, Cobbett's harangue could well be the earliest
example of this argument. To be sure, this is not yet the world of
Deliveroo, or even the not so long ago world of Vesta curries, those
packets from half a century ago that are sometimes spoken of now
with a sort of nostalgic horror. In their twentieth-century time, such
things—loved and loathed—seemed like a new idea. In his monu-
mental history of the past century of British retailing, published in the
mid-1950s, James Jefferys ventured the thought that future developments in food sales might include 'even the sale of ready-cooked meat
and meals'.[5]

Hence, it is striking that two hundred years ago, Cobbett articulates
his environmental and lifestyle concerns about the food we eat in
terms that are not very different from those of today. He deplores the
way that new modes of consumption have taken people away from
local making—growing, rearing, and food preparation—and taken
them out to the *shops* to get what they need (he is not, in this passage,

condemning the desire for new commodities as such: that comes elsewhere). That *ready* meal epitomizes a different relationship to what is eaten because it does away with the sense of a long and slow process in which nature and then people take the time to make the food. Ready is instant, is now; it has no particular connection with the place of consumption or preparation. But for some reason, it is what people seem to want, and Cobbett's aim is to change their minds.

On another journey, the previous year, this time going through Surrey, Cobbett set off on a related train of polemic, this time prompted by a farmhouse rather than a fishpond. Again, an exemplary sighting: 'Here I had a view of what has long been going on all over the country.' What he spots this time is a sale taking place because the long-standing leasehold farmer is moving out. Cobbett's interest and upset is directed at the change in custom which has led to a fine old table no longer being used or cared for, or even now kept at all. This table being put out for sale is the symbol of a whole way of life that has been abandoned:

> Every thing about this farm-house was formerly the scene of *plain manners* and *plentiful living*. Oak clothes-chests, oak bedsteads, oak chests of drawers, and oak tables to eat on, long, strong, and well supplied with joint stools. Some of the things are many hundreds of years old. But all appeared to be in a state of decay and nearly of *disuse*. There appeared to have been hardly any *family* in that house, where formerly there were, in all probability, from ten to fifteen men, boys, and maids: and, which was the worst of all, there was a *parlour*! Aye, and a *carpet* and *bell-pull* too![6]

Cobbett even imagines the future upcycled fate of the long table as part of an ornamental bridge for the residence of a stockbroker ('stock-jobber')—and decides to rescue it by buying it himself. He also goes into details about the end of the communal household that he supposes to have been there—the 'family' including the live-in workers and servants. All of them would have been eating together, with not much privileged difference in the master's entitlement, Cobbett thinks. But now the extra people have been cast out to live in separate small households, much more expensive to run, and not earning enough to do so; meanwhile, in the big house, the remaining immediate family of the farmer is playing out an imitation of an already degraded contemporary mode of life, epitomized by that ghastly new kind of room, the *parlour*. Like the *shops*, it is shown up in italics and also, this time, for good measure, with scare quotes. Inside it is an array of the things that go with the different way of living:

> One end of the front of this once plain and substantial house had been moulded into a *'parlour;'* and there was the mahogany table, and the fine chairs, and the fine glass, and all as bare-faced upstart as any stock-jobber in the kingdom can boast of. And, there were the decanters, the glasses, the 'dinner-set' of crockery ware, and all just in the true stock-jobber style. And I dare say it has been '*Squire* Charington and the *Miss* Charingtons; and not plain Master Charington, and his son Hodge, and his daughter Betty Charington, all of whom this accursed system has, in all likelihood, transmuted into a species of mock gentlefolks.[7]

This transformation involves everything from the building work to create the *parlour* to the buying in of the upmarket china and glass that were beginning to be grandly promoted as aspirational commodities.[8] All of a piece, you can't put the old things in with the new, and 'That long table could not share in the work of the decanters.'

The italics added to the *parlour* and the inverted commas to the 'dinner set' convey the condemnation in another way, now as a matter of a special language; the things are like self-citations, or brand names of themselves. The fancy font twists the straight letter, and 'plain' Master Charington and his children have to be addressed with fussy titles. The 'plain' house and 'plain' name have been falsely changed into fake versions of a superior class, 'mock' gentlefolks; but this needless, almost absurd performance does harm as well, by its detrimental effects on the farm workers.

Cobbett goes on—and on—about the Charington farmhouse (owned, as it happens—and as he tells his readers—by the public school Christ's Hospital). To ears and eyes familiar, as ours may be, with property advertising and lifestyle features across many media, Cobbett seems to be instituting a sort of angry reversal of the genre before it has even begun. He moves away from the specifics of the place he visited to make a general critique of current new-build farmhouses. Once again, this involves a detailed imagining of exactly what the interior will be like:

> Those that are now erected are mere painted shells, with a Mistress within, who is stuck up in a place she calls a *parlour*, with, if she have children, the 'young ladies and gentlemen' about her: some showy chairs and a sofa (a *sofa* by all means): half a dozen prints in gilt frames hanging up: some swinging book-shelves with novels and tracts upon them: a dinner brought in by a girl that is perhaps better 'educated' than she: two or three nick-nacks to eat instead of a piece of bacon and a pudding: the house too neat for a dirty-shoed carter to be allowed to come into; and every thing proclaiming to every sensible beholder that there is a constant anxiety to make a *show* not warranted by the reality.[9]

All the features, decorative and rhetorical, of the earlier section are resumed in this one: the superficiality of the houses that are just 'painted shells', the calling ordinary things and people by fancy names; the mockery of 'showy' furniture—including, here, a sofa (no, a *sofa*), one of the must-haves of these softly sitting times. And there is more, with the tacky display of cultural objects: gilt frames and prints, not real paintings; novels and tracts, the latest ephemera of the too light or too serious—rather than decent old books. Instead of proper food, a solid two courses of meat then pudding, the people are just grazing on snacks—on 'two or three nick-nacks'. Not even 'ready' meals, which are bad enough. Then there are the artificial separations of space and employment, allied to mistaken ideas of rank. These people cut themselves off from the ordinary dirt of the outside; and they want nothing to do with actual work. Instead of farming, the sons are meant to get jobs in an office—jobs that are as inauthentic as the food their parents consume. 'Good God! What, "young gentlemen" go to plough! They become *clerks*, or some skimmy-dish thing or other.'[10]

Lamenting the fate of the fishpond and the farmhouse, Cobbett's two reports both work in the same way. They home in on one place where a change has occurred, by human intervention, from age-old consuming practices to new ones. The evidence of the change he has seen with his own eyes and now describes. The new practice lacks all the virtue and good sense of the old. It involves purchases, whether of fixtures and furnishings or food—where previously no money was involved, because the table had been there for ever and the meal was sourced and prepared at home. It involves, in the farmhouse case, the loss of a harmonious mixed community and the substitution of an unequal division in which the master class cuts itself off from real work and requires a fabricated language to go with its fabricated roles and possessions.

Cobbett's characteristic style moves from a here (in this very place) to all over, as he starts with a show and tell—look what I saw!—and then makes it a microcosm of broad and regrettable ongoing changes. From the sight of this one particular place—and all the more because this one particular place is self-evidently real, is here and now—we are assured that the story that surrounds it is true. And that sense of righteous rightness is presented as all the stronger because Cobbett is already talking, directly, about contrasts between the true and the false, the real and the fake, which are inseparable, he suggests, from the language in which they are lived and spoken. The *Miss* Charingtons, as opposed to plain Betty Charington, belong with the *sofa* on which, inevitably, they are seated.

The changes that Cobbett describes are all interrelated. If 'now-a-days, all is looked for at *shops*', it is also the case that more and more elements of everyday life—more and more goods and services, new and old—are now being bought with money rather than made or maintained or performed by those who use them. An old table becomes something to be sold off and replaced, rather than something whose age, as it always has done, confirms its continuing value and usefulness. The home, having previously been a place of communal habitation for an extended working group, is now isolated as the residence of a nuclear family whose adults seek to mark their social superiority; new paid-for projects of improvement and new pur-chased objects of interior décor are to extend and demonstrate that status. The home is 'showy' rather than for living in.

The generalization of the cases means that Cobbett goes out of his way to point out that these new consumers, consumers of the new, are not individually at fault. The choice is not their own:

> the blame belongs to the infernal stock-jobbing system. There was no reason to expect, that farmers would not endeavour to keep pace, in point of show and luxury, with fund-holders, and with all the tribes that *war* and *taxes* created. Farmers were not the authors of the mischief; and *now* they are compelled to shut the labourers out of their houses, and to pinch them in their wages, in order to be able to pay their own taxes.

This twofold explanation—social emulation on the one hand and a tax burden on the other—departs from the emphasis elsewhere, which gives no explanation for what the farmers have been doing. The two reasons now brought forward are different in kind—and also in forcefulness. The first, fairly plausible, is economic. The farm workers are thrown out of the house because saving on their wages is the only way for employers to pay their taxes. The second, much less tangible and much more complex, is vaguely psychological and social. It is hedged about with the uncertain double negatives of there being 'no reason' to expect that farmers 'would not' do what they are doing. And what they are doing is copying. In a phrase that is almost exactly equivalent to 'keeping up with the Joneses' (which enters the language much later), Cobbett says that this happens because the farmers want to 'keep pace, in point of show and luxury, with fund-holders' and all the rest of them. The old table is swapped for a new one because that's how the new moneyed classes behave—and impli-citly, therefore, it is the stockjobbers and their ilk that the farmers want to be seen to keep up with. But why?

Keeping pace is equally curious as it introduces, all of a sudden, and again without further explanation, the idea of speed and contest. Why would rural farmers be measuring themselves at all in relation to such a different class, that of the moneyed *nouveaux riches* of the city—let alone comparing a rate of advance? Moving away from a formerly stable situation would seem to be part of the image of false progress that Cobbett condemns the farmers for buying into. He doesn't approve the attitude, but he presents it as if it were somehow bound to be: 'no reason to expect, that farmers would not...'. But why would anyone ever have abandoned the food-rich fishpond and sent out to the shops instead? It's not even that they have taken to selling the pond's easy produce for profit. It seems that the pond and its contents lack the appeal of the shops, have just been let go: 'scarcely any one thinks of providing for his own wants *out of his own land* and other domestic means.'

This slightly slippery moment in Cobbett's arguments suggests that there must be more to say: hidden depths, perhaps. It may indicate that there is something in the social situations he is trying to give an account of that does not fit easily into the categories he wants to maintain. The farmers endeavouring to keep pace are a particularly strong illustration of this hesitation, since the idea of social emulation as a reason for going out to buy new stuff—especially stuff for the home—is today one of the dominant ways of explaining why and how people might do such a thing. It is the phenomenon brilliantly labelled *conspicuous consumption* in Thorstein Veblen's work of semi-satirical anthropology, *The Theory of the Leisure Class*. From the tasteful parlour to its appropriately accompanying lady and the display of cultured accessories, many of the elements that Veblen singled out to describe affluent Americans in 1900 are present in Cobbett's description of buying for show. Veblen's phrase *conspicuous consumption* is now used without any sense of the where and when of its origins; and the emulation and aspiration it describes are taken so patently to be how people really are motivated that they are not seen as needing any further explanation.[11]

In Cobbett's time, that general expectation is not yet the case, which is why the affirmation—he says it, but says no more—is so interesting. The logical jump occurs just when he is articulating the sense of a break that is taking place between the enduring and the emerging; between the permanent source (the old oak table, the ever plentiful fish) and the quick new thing (the bought-in décor and dinners). But as an argument, this contrast is also what gives his writing its power. Something has happened—is happening—right in front of us, if only we have eyes to see it. Think about it! Do something!

Two centuries after Cobbett's time, what he says shouts out once again with the urgency of anger and activism about the environmental damage that humans have done and are doing to their immediate and larger worlds. Why did we turn our backs on local sources of sustenance? How can we step back now from the false appeals of the fast? Fast fashion, fast food—and yes, fast furniture. Once again, there is a wish to consider the long-term effects of short-term satisfactions—and to challenge the dominance of buying and selling, and throwing away, in almost every aspect of ordinary living. The scope of the challenge extends to the whole global economy, from the destruction of natural balances and resources to the perpetuation of glaring human inequalities: in Cobbett's picture, from the fishpond to the downgraded farm workers.

In the passages from Cobbett quoted above, history is an indefinite period of unbroken usage, and the present a sudden and stupid shock of the needless new. At other times, on other occasions, he offers instead layered and detailed accounts of the idiosyncrasies of one region or another as they have interacted with human history over time. There is both a use and a risk in the defining polemical illustration. A use because it shows what it shows so clearly, as if beyond the need for further evidence. A risk, by the same token, because it stands alone, without more ado: as if history, up to the present time of observing and writing, had been gently passing or flowing by, without disturbance; whereas now, dramatically, all is changed. But equally, there is both risk and use in staying only with the gentler graduations of change: as if nothing was ever contested, and everything happened along slow and settled pathways towards the destination of the present.

Cobbett's rage at the commodification of just about everything, and at the happy accommodation to that, continues to reverberate today, but in a different way precisely because the purchasability of almost anything has extended so much further since his time. Take the passage about the neglected fish, which doesn't end with the purchase of pre-cooked food:

> To buy the thing, *ready made*, is the taste of the day: thousands, who are *housekeepers*, buy their dinners ready cooked: nothing is so common as to *rent breasts* for children to suck: a man *actually advertised*, in the London papers, about two months ago, to *supply childless husbands with heirs!* In this case the articles were of course, to be *ready made*; for, to make them *'to order'* would be the devil of a business; though, in desperate cases, even this is, I believe, sometimes resorted to.[12]

Then, as now, the buying of babies can be presented as the ultimate scandal: if even a baby can be pre-ordered and paid for, then surely nothing is out of the reach of marketization.[13] Cobbett also highlights the promotion of the practice: they don't just do this, they *actually advertise* that they do it. Thus, the fact that baby-buying might not be scandalous is itself a scandal. But at the same time as this final example is continuous with present-day sensibilities, the specific practices are not the same. In the nineteenth century, wet-nursing, the rented breast, is commonplace; although Cobbett clearly doesn't like it, he takes it for granted and treats it as the everyday habit that offsets the truly appalling—but unspecified—practices that may happen in 'desperate cases'. What is being referred to? The advertisement, here, is left to speak uninterpreted, in its euphemistically riddling way (the childless wife who must belong with the childless husband is not even mentioned). The ready-made baby probably means a clandestine adoption, while a baby made to order may involve some form of surrogacy or supposition (a newborn passed off as the offspring of another woman who is not in reality its birth mother). Just possibly the reference might be to artificial insemination. The difficulty now is not only to identify what Cobbett intended to suggest—if indeed it was any specific practice—but also to know whether he expected his readers to get it at the time.

Cobbett's pre-ordered baby does two things in his argument. On the one hand it is there to show the arrival at an extreme limit of commodification: even babies can be bought. On the other hand, it is meant to seem almost silly—the very idea of an advertisement to *supply childless husbands with heirs!*—and so to discredit or mock the more ordinary examples of buying just anything too. Seen in this company, the idea of the food to go could begin to look as ridiculous as the idea of the baby to go. Of course we should make them ourselves!

But the logic is also one of retreat to the small-scale rural unit. Which is all very well if you have a fishpond (or a fertile spouse) of your own, but sometimes it may be necessary to trade or at least to exchange with others to get what you modestly want or need. Not everything is already given for everyone by bountiful nature. But if it is, look no further.

Notes

1. William Cobbett, *Rural Rides*, (1830), ed. George Woodcock (Harmondsworth: Penguin, 1975), 475.
2. Cobbett, *Rural Rides*, 475.
3. Cobbett, *Rural Rides*, 475.
4. Cobbett, *Rural Rides*, 475.
5. James B. Jefferys, *Retail Trading in Britain 1850–1950* (Cambridge: Cambridge University Press, 1954), 207.
6. Cobbett, *Rural Rides*, 226–7.
7. Cobbett, *Rural Rides*, 227.
8. On the innovative marketing practices of Josiah Wedgwood's company in the second half of the eighteenth century see Neil McKendrick, 'Josiah Wedgwood and the Commercialization of the Potteries', in McKendrick, John Brewer, and J.H. Plumb, *The Birth of a Consumer Society: The Commercialization of Eighteenth-Century England* (Bloomington: Indiana University Press, 1982), 100–45.
9. Cobbett, *Rural Rides*, 229.
10. Cobbett, *Rural Rides*, 229.
11. See Thorstein Veblen, *The Theory of the Leisure Class* (1900), ed. Martha Banta (Oxford: Oxford University Press, 2007).

12. Cobbett, *Rural Rides*, 475.
13. On the repudiation of baby-buying, both today and as far back as Sophocles' *Oedipus the King*, see Rachel Bowlby, *A Child of One's Own: Parental Stories* (Oxford: Oxford University Press, 2013).

PART II

ROLES

11

Collections

There were numerous manuals and textbooks for novice shop-workers or shopkeepers in the first decades of the twentieth century. Some specialized in the skills and knowledge required to run one particular type of shop, with more broadly applicable instruction about every facet of retailing, from window display to account keeping. For trade in general, and most of all for the one in focus, there is usually a tone of lovingly detailed promotion of the cause. The young person is invited to share in the privilege of rare knowledge, to be valued both for its own sake and as something that can be shared with customers as a demonstration of expertise, as the need or wish arises. A beautiful example of this can be found in *The Retail Grocery Trade*, a book published by Methuen in 1938. It is further described in the subtitle as '*A Book of General Guidance for Apprentices and Assistants— particularly for those studying for the Examinations of the Institute of Certificated Grocers.*' And it is. Its three hundred and more pages contain a great deal of information relevant to those exams—whose syllabuses included not just trade-specific material, such as bookkeeping and the history of grocery commodities, but also essay-based tests on British history from the Middle Ages to the present.

There is also considerable attention given to the decision about where—in what size of town—the prospective assistant or apprentice should seek to find their first job, one factor being the greater availability of evening classes in a larger place. The author, C.J. Elliott, does emphasize the advantages of being able to attend a live course, but he is not discouraging to those who, for whatever reasons, find it necessary to study at a distance, by correspondence. Elliott stresses throughout that grocery apprentices should know about each of the many types of product that they are likely to be selling. His book provides much of that knowledge. There is an account, for instance, of the life cycle of the tea plant and the history of the British East India Company, dominant in the trade between Asian countries and the British Isles. There is a separate chapter on canned goods, with details of what has to happen first to the fruit or vegetables or fish, as well as a marvelling description of the efficiency of today's technology: 'Modern can-making machinery is a revelation to those who view the processes for the first time; the production rate is over 250 cans per minute.'[1] Different sets of knowledge about the many commodities are provided for three separate levels of exam, which the apprentice will take in sequence.

To readers now many decades on from the advances of the 1930s, what stands out in Elliott's often enchanting book is a different kind of detail. He instructs his young would-be grocer to send away for the study materials he will be missing if he cannot attend an actual class:

> The student in the smaller town will...be compelled to rely much upon himself and the help he can get from books. But opportunities are open to him, as follows:
>
> If he writes to the Secretary of the Institute he will find that he can buy samples of the various raw products that he will be expected to recognize in his examinations.
>
> For the FIRST Examination he will receive, for the sum of 10s., samples as follows:
>
> TEAS (9); SUGARS (3); DRIED FRUITS (9); CEREALS (18). Total 39.[2]

For the INTERMEDIATE and then the FINAL examination there are progressively higher costs for the associated package, with more samples and more types of product. Expenditure goes up from the ten shillings of the first stage to thirteen and then thirty shillings. This is a considerable outlay for a young person, almost equivalent to a family's average weekly expenditure on groceries, which the book itself gives as being, on average, thirty-two to thirty-five shillings.[3] The number of samples rises to forty-five and then to over a hundred (precisely given, of course, in Elliott's listings, as '108'). More specific varieties of the products already included will be sent in the second and final packages, with the addition as well of new categories: EVAPORATED FRUITS (in both), and SPICES (only in the last).

After providing these details of the three phased deliveries, Elliott goes on to say what should happen next. It is unexpected: 'As soon as these are received—39 for the First Examination, and the additional ones for the higher examinations later—the student can start his own museum.' This museum is not open to any public, however close by; it is purely for the student's own use and pleasure: 'he should closely examine the samples referred to' and doing so amounts to a 'practical application of book knowledge'. That in turn is the only way to acquire the 'essential confidence which he will require in the examination room'.[4] Everything is concentrated on the learning; no shop, not even a private display, is yet in view.

There are no instructions as to how or where to put or keep the personal mail-order museum; and there is no illustration of one, even though the book has many glossy photographs of shopfronts and shop interiors and various natural species of commodity. Any of these pictures today, at a distance approaching a century, might themselves pass for exhibits from a museum. Or as a 'living museum', in the case of the handsome images of the latest 1930s counters and cabinets, only awaiting the addition of a couple of millennials dressed up in starched white aprons, or else self-consciously balancing baskets on their arms. The most gorgeous of the interiors to my twenty-first-century eyes shows an angled view inside a store called Fasham's, in Margate. There is a glass-fronted 'provisions counter' with ham and cheese, backed by three neatly stacked shelves of branded bottles, and the shop's own logo in elegant lettering above the shelves. In front of the counter are black and white tiles with a single chair at the end for the customer while she orders. As with the images of rooms in the present-day marketing of furniture or flats and houses, these photos of store interiors avoid the distraction of showing any actual people, as if human particularity might detract from their aesthetic perfection.

In its own images, the book itself is a thing to be looked at, like a special collection of contemporary grocerly curiosities. In connection with the information on different types of tea plant, there is a half-page image showing four different views of tea plant leaves of the high-quality kind that the young apprentice will be receiving in the sample pack ('For the finest teas, the youngest leaves and the "tip" are plucked', the caption reads). Below this is a photograph of beautifully piled cubic chests of 'Indian and Ceylon tea', with a barrow carrying small white bales alongside; this tranquil scene, once again without human presence, is 'the Commercial Road Warehouses, London, E.'[5]

Also featured are various machines for manual operation in the preparatory work of the shop. There is a photograph, for instance, of a 'Hand-operated Bacon Slicing Machine—the "Asco"'. Grocers' manuals of this period stress the advantages, both practical and presentational, of acquiring the latest equipment for preparing and storing your goods, with hire purchase facilities available for obtaining it. For shops selling provisions (cheese and ham) as well as dry goods, a further state-of-the-art machine is a refrigerator. Another picture in Elliott's book (see Figure 6) shows (in the words of the super-informative caption) 'An Electric Coffee Grinding Mill ("Uno") with flashing signs for advertising purposes. Its output is 1lb. of ground coffee per minute.' This particular exhibit is a sign of the developing importance of branded electrical products at this time, and also of the conscious new sophistication of shops' fittings and equipment. With a kind of covert product placement, the example is both advertising these machines to prospective shop workers, and also showing how they will be advertising themselves by name once they are *in situ* in the store. The flash of the 'Uno' takes place in a special oval bulb on which are imprinted (top down, upper case) the words 'Freshly Roasted COFFEE Freshly Ground'. Much as with miles-per-gallon specs that were beginning to be cited in car advertisements at this time, the

*An Electric Coffee Grinding Mill ("Uno") with
flashing sign for advertising purposes.
Its output is 1 lb. of ground coffee per minute*

Figure 6. 'Uno' coffee grinder, late 1930s

statement here of a precise productivity rate—an *output* of a pound's
weight per minute—presents the coffee grinder as primarily an industrial machine at the same time as it is also being shown as part of the
attractive furnishings of a superior modern store. The visibility as well
as the actual use of this object is part of the shop's own image; and
today, it is suggested, a shop—even a regular grocer's shop—should

appear as an advertisement for itself as a destination, a place to come and see.

The novice assistant's private museum is connected, it turns out, to all sorts of forward developments in the provincial food store for which he is being trained. But the link between shops and museums has other kinds of association too. Above all, on a grand Victorian scale, there is the nineteenth-century congruity, as places for ordinary people to go and look at extraordinary things, between the big new city department stores, and those other contemporary exhibition venues, art galleries and museums. There was also the succession of 'world's fairs', starting with the Great Exhibition in London of 1851, which took place in some of the major cities of the world: London, Paris, Chicago. Continuing well into the twentieth century, these international fairs were staged as short-term spectacular events which drew in tourists of every social class; in Britain, cheap long-distance travel was newly enabled by the rapid development of the railway network from the 1830s. All sorts of people came from all over to look at the marvels of modern invention on display.

As if acknowledging or recommending their kinship with the less commercial institutions, Paris department stores used the same word *exposition*, exhibition, to promote their special themed events—the January sale of household linens ('whites'), or the December toys, pre-Christmas (some shopping things don't change). The only formal difference from the museum (or the Great Exhibition) was that the things on view in a department store could be bought—were shown to be bought. But they could also simply be looked at, and the great innovation of these new huge stores with their diversity of merchandise was that they not only allowed but encouraged their customers to do just that; and, if they chose, only that (no pressure to make a purchase). Just looking became the mode of modern shopping—as it was also, in another register, the mode of contemplative looking for the person walking around a picture gallery or a museum. In London, the various Kensington museums—of science, geology, natural history, or applied and decorative arts (the Victoria and Albert

Museum)—were all built and opened during the 1850s, the same decade as the Great Exhibition. So the practice of going into town to look at things—and only to look—was a familiar one by the time that the major department stores began to emerge a few years later.

From the other side of the counter, though, the point of putting on a department store show—and the point of shop display more broadly—was that it should be temporary, for goods that were only passing through. Stores' displays were not, like those of museums, permanent collections, though the word was used in their advertising to announce the arrival of new seasonal fashions: the autumn or spring collection. The display was only for now, with the purpose of creating an event to draw customers in. And even though customers were entitled and enabled to look, and just to look, it was equally true that all the goods, at some point, were meant to go!—thereby reaching a place where, in twenty-first-century fashion parlance, they would be part of a further 'collection', now a personal wardrobe to be carefully *edited* and *curated*.

There is one instance of a nineteenth-century village grocer whose own historical researches, beyond his shopkeeping duties, gained national attention, and ultimately some permanent notice. Benjamin Harrison, born in 1837, lived all his life in the village of Ightham, not far from Sevenoaks. He managed the grocer's shop (see Figure 7) that had been in his family for a century and a half, and he was also, in the limited free time he had, an archaeologist who worked with flints collected in the area. In 1889, Harrison was awarded a grant to conduct 'excavations at Oldbury Hill, near where he lived. The significance of his work is brought out in a local newspaper's write-up at the time of the award:

For it is no small credit to a village grocer to have divined the existence of an ancient flint period around his own home; to have 'made a collection' is also something; but these ends have always been subsidiary in Mr Harrison's mind to truly understanding the scope of the facts which came before him. And this scientific study he has pursued under great

Figure 7. Benjamin Harrison's shop in the village of Ightham, Kent, c.1900
Image courtesy of Ightham History Project

> difficulties: stolen hours before sunrise, rare Bank Holidays, and occasional half Sundays, have, we imagine, been all the time that Mr Harrison has been able to spare from the hours of business.[6]

Harrison discovered the first specimens of what were subsequently named eoliths, and his work was promoted in papers written by the distinguished geologist Joseph Prestwich. His death in 1921 merited a substantial *Times* obituary, which was unambiguous in its praise: 'Many are the archaeologists and geologists whose publications draw for much of their material on the observations and collections made by this village grocer.'[7] The obituary mentions the powerful influence on Harrison as a boy of Hooker's Curiosity Shop in Sevenoaks. In the Tunbridge Wells Museum today is a glass case, itself deserving to be a museum piece now, which holds a display about him and his work.

Notes

1. C.J. Elliott, *The Retail Grocery Trade: A Book of General Guidance for Apprentices and Assistants—particularly for those studying for the Examinations of the Institute of Certificated Grocers* (London: Methuen & Co. Ltd., 1938), 125.

2. Elliott, *Retail Grocery Trade*, 65.
3. Elliott, *Retail Grocery Trade*, 4.
4. Elliott, *Retail Grocery Trade*, 65.
5. Elliott, *Retail Grocery Trade*, plates facing p. 92.
6. *Sussex Agricultural Express*, Saturday 28 September 1889, 7.
7. 'Geologist and Grocer. Death of Mr Benjamin Harrison. Discoverer of Eoliths', *The Times*, Monday 3 October 1921, 12.

12

Counters

Prior to self-service, and still in many small outlets, a counter is the defining piece of shop furniture. It is where goods are asked for or proposed, then fetched, supplied, and sometimes wrapped; it is also, usually, where they are paid for (some shops had a separate desk for that). As the universal point of purchase, the counter involves four primary elements: the merchandise, the money, the shopper, and the salesperson. Initially, the goods and the seller are on one side, the customer and the money on the other. In the process of the purchase, the non-human articles cross the counter while the others stay where they are. It is the most ordinary of sequences, repeated a hundred times in the same spot every day.

A common counter set-up in earlier shops (until recently, for some butchers and fishmongers) was a hinged flat surface outside the shop, which doubled as a shutter overnight. It was drawn down in the morning to make, in both senses, the 'open' shop. The counter would then be put back up at closing time; in this respect it resembled the stall in an outdoor market, also set up and dismantled at the start and end of each trading day. This external table, again like a market stall, was typically used as a place to lay out some or all of the available merchandise and make a display of it.

The interior counter differs from the market stall because it is not normally a surface for general display, though goods are placed on it when the customer is being shown some item. Just on the cusp of it being decisively superseded by self-service, the counter's use as a surface of work as well as service is well described by the economist Patrick McAnally, in a book of 1971:

> In earlier days the fundamental object was the counter. Goods were taken by assistants out of drawers or cupboards—where they had been invisible—and placed on the counter for inspection. If yards of material or pounds of bacon had to be cut, this was done on the counter. The sales document was written on the counter, the goods were packed on the counter, and after the customer had visited a cash desk to pay and had obtained a receipted bill, she returned to the counter to pick up her parcel.[1]

The separate cash desk applies only to a shop of some magnitude; but the length and complexity of the process indicate the practical benefits of the ongoing change to self-service, which can now be presented as if it had been the solution to a perennial problem:

> time was wasted by the customers and assistants, and space was wasted by counters which could not be fully used and by the customers going to and fro from the cash desks, and as a result of these causes as is well known the 'self-service' revolution has taken place.[2]

The logic is to do with waste, but there are two different applications of that term: to a waste of physical floor space in the shop, and to a waste of time for the human participants. In the human category, time is itself of two sorts: the employee's (which is paid at a certain rate and could be put to some other use), and the customer's (a limited personal resource of subjective, not monetary value). These conflations are worth highlighting today when forceful critique is made of the 'waste' of shopping, now meaning something else again: an overuse of natural resources.

In addition, as the word most simply says, a counter is for counting out the money. The cash register, precursor of later computerized tills, came into use in the early twentieth century; it was heavily promoted by the American National Cash Register Company that had patented it, and it represented a considerable financial commitment for a small shop—as well as taking up precious space. Before there were cash registers sitting on top, coins and notes would normally be kept in a drawer behind the counter—that is, underneath it: unlike the drop-down external device or the market stall, the in-store counter was more like a chest than a table. Other things might live on the surface of the counter, too. Chemists or sweet shops would typically have one or two items in small display units, 'counter stands', provided as point-of-sale advertising by manufacturers of branded goods.

Where the customer stood or sat was a vertical surface dropping down from the counter proper; in front of the shopkeeper, on the other side, were numerous small spaces of drawers and cavities, including anything that might be offered or asked for from the nebulous domain that was *under the counter*. Under-the-counter goods might be clandestine or simply sold in a different way: if a show is made of suggesting that something is *not* on show, then the sale acquires a different kind of value for the purchaser who has been given the special treatment. Before the separate licensing of book-makers in 1961, local shopkeepers sometimes acted as betting agents; in the 1930s one Brighton newsagent 'took bets in under the counter where the police wouldn't get them. The bookies' runners, as they called them—if you come for your newspapers you'd slip your bets in.'[3] More mundanely—without the dynamics of secrecy or singling out—there were sensitive items sold by pharmacies for which open visibility, on the shelves behind the shopkeeper, might be embarrassing.

Aside from the merchandise, seen and unseen, the counter's face-to-face exchange is also a conversation at close quarters between two people. As such, there is always the potential for romance, with one or both of them suddenly removed from their routine retailing roles and transported into some other scene. The one-sided version of this is dramatized in Henry James's story *In the Cage*, about a London post office clerk who becomes infatuated with a gentleman whose personal telegrams she receives from him across the counter. Eventually, after some moderate stalking in the world outside the shop, she gives up and goes back to what James calls the 'reality' of her solid fiancé, a future grocer.[4]

Elsewhere the anonymity of the big city store is the setting, all of a sudden, for an *encounter*. In Patricia Highsmith's novel *Carol* (first published, in 1952, under a pseudonym and with a different title, *The Price of Salt*), the scene is the toy department of a Manhattan department store, where Therese has a temporary job during the Christmas rush in the dolls section. Then Carol appears:

> Their eyes met at the same instant, Therese glancing up from a box she was opening, and the woman just turning her head so she looked directly at Therese....Therese could not look away. She heard the customer in front of her repeat a question, and Therese stood there, mute....Then Therese saw her walk slowly towards the counter, heard her heart stumble to catch up with the moment it had let pass, and felt her face grow hot as the woman came nearer and nearer.[5]

'Their eyes met at the same instant': the classic moment of love at first sight locks the two women together, and away from the people surrounding them. Therese has eyes only for the stranger, and is deaf and fails to respond to the customer she is meant to be serving. There is a sense of something imminent and inevitable.

'The woman' wants a particular 'valise', the one in the show window—and Therese breaks the rules by taking it out of the display for her. The scene goes on to show in painstaking detail the outward business of a customer making a purchase, with documented arrangements for payment and delivery—all the more to bring out the contrast of these procedures with the unspoken exchange that is taking place at the same time. For Therese, these practical facts are exalted: 'The name, the address, the town appeared beneath the pencil point like a secret Therese would never forget, like something stamping itself in her memory for ever.'[6]

At a later stage of the novel, when Therese and Carol have embarked on a road trip across the continent, another kind of counter scene takes place, now to do with gaping social differences of access to what can be bought and enjoyed. The two women stop off at a delicatessen in Pennsylvania. This is linked to a café with a model of a Dutch village in its window, constructed by the elderly owner. The meat for the sausages sold by the deli is from pigs raised on the premises. Therese is taken back to the thought of an older fellow worker who made friends with her in the department store, and whose home she visited one evening. On that occasion too they had stopped off in a deli to buy food. This Mrs Robichek had previously had her own dress shop ('I managed four girls'), and had wanted to give Therese one that she had made herself, in what had been her shop's distinctive style.[7] With the many connections now coming into her mind—the two delis, two shop owners, their skills of making—Therese sees a way to make some return:

> A sign on the till said they shipped anywhere, and she thought of sending Mrs Robichek one of the big cloth-wrapped sausages, imagined the delight on Mrs Robichek's face when she opened the package with her trembling hands and found a sausage.[8]

But behind Therese now stands the poised Carol, wondering 'if she thought they should buy a whole ham'.[9] They are buying quite a lot: 'The young man slid all the bundles across the counter, and took Carol's twenty-dollar bill. And Therese thought of Mrs Robichek tremulously pushing her single dollar bill and a quarter across the counter that evening.'[10] Here, the counter's simple function as a surface for the physical exchange of merchandise and money is freighted with all the difference between the two amounts, as between the two women—arrogant and diminished, rich and poor.

Mrs Robichek had been reduced to taking a position in a big store after having a shop of her own; as a customer herself, buying food, she has little cash to spare. To be an employee in a big shop, put behind the counter, is socially and personally demeaning for her. When Therese begins work there, early in the novel, she learns that she is to be identified by number, not by name. This extreme impersonality of the American department store is parodied in a short story of the 1940s by Shirley Jackson, in which, while the new recruit is known by her number, slightly more senior staff are all called 'Miss Cooper'.[11] In Highsmith's novel, Mrs Robichek is the only fellow employee to make a gesture of friendship towards Therese. This one human touch, from a woman whose hopelessness also fills her with dread, is a kind of negative rehearsal for the other significant meeting, with Carol—this second time with different contrasts of class and wealth, and directly across the counter.

In the normal order of things, communication over the counter of a department store was kept at its given distance. Emile Zola's novel about a nineteenth-century department store has a brief scene that brilliantly dissects these expectations from the points of view of a wealthy customer and the male assistant who is helping her try on pairs of gloves. He is disappointed in her lack of reaction to an experience he finds erotic, in part because of the animal odour of the gloves' material. But 'in front of this ordinary counter, she did not smell the gloves, they did not set up any sensual heat between her and this random salesman doing his job.'[12] Between them is not just the difference of class and sex, but also their separate experiences of that. For the assistant, she is a woman—or is to be reduced to that. After she has moved away from the counter, he boasts to a colleague— 'crudely', says Zola—saying something like, she'd be well glovable, that one.[13] For the woman's part, and this is explicit:

With her elbow next to the velvet and her hand raised, she gave him her fingers in the calm way she put out her foot to her chambermaid for her to button her boots. He was not a man, she was using him for intimate habits with her usual disdain for people in her service.[14]

For her, 'He was not a man' because he is a servant; and for him, she is not superior because she is a female.

In English at this period the class difference across the two sides of the counter was marked by a special word, *counter-jumper*, meaning someone with the transgressive temerity to try to cross over. W.M. Thackeray's brief essay 'Waiting at the Station' is a strong indictment of the society that pushes poor women to emigrate from England—although, he trusts, they will meet with a less constricted world in Australia, their children growing up 'in the midst of plenty, freedom, and manly brotherhood'.[15] Thackeray berates the unthinking and ignorant behaviour of his own class:

> We never speak to the servant who waits on us for twenty years; we condescend to employ a tradesman, keeping him at a proper distance, mind, of course, at a proper distance—we laugh at his young men, if they dance, jig, and amuse themselves like their betters, and call them counter-jumpers.[16]

Notes

1. Patrick McAnally, *The Economics of the Distributive Trades* (London: George Allen & Unwin, 1971), 112.
2. McAnally, *Economics of the Distributive Trades*, 112.
3. Quoted in Neil Griffiths, *Shops Book: Shopkeepers and Street Traders in East Brighton 1900–1930* (Brighton: QueenSpark Books, 1978), 63.
4. Henry James, *In the Cage* (1898), in *In the Cage and Other Stories* (1972; Harmondsworth: Penguin, 1987), 96.
5. Patricia Highsmith, *Carol* (1952; London: Bloomsbury, 2010), 35–6; ellipses added.
6. Highsmith, *Carol*, 37.
7. Highsmith, *Carol*, 15.
8. Highsmith, *Carol*, 187.
9. Highsmith, *Carol*, 188.
10. Highsmith, *Carol*, 188.
11. See Shirley Jackson, 'My Life with R.H. Macy' (1941), in *The Lottery and Other Stories* (London: Penguin, 2009), 57–62.
12. Emile Zola, *Au Bonheur des Dames* (1883; Paris: Garnier-Flammarion, 1971), 133. The novel is translated by Brian Nelson as *The Ladies' Paradise* (Oxford: Oxford World's Classics, 1993).

13. Zola, *Au Bonheur des Dames*, 133.
14. Zola, *Au Bonheur des Dames*, 133.
15. W.M. Thackeray, *Sketches and Travels in London* (1853; Gloucester: Alan Sutton, 1989), 165.
16. Thackeray, *Sketches and Travels*, 166.

13

Credit and Credibility

A*ccess Takes the Waiting out of Wanting*. In 1972, with a swirling sense of 'the sixties', the slogan that launched the new credit card suggested the heady charge of new desires. You can have what you want, and have it now. But what customers might actually go on to buy, as shown in pictorial ads at the same time, was surprisingly homely: a cooker; baby equipment or winter clothes in good time; a nice meal out with old friends.

Before credit cards, hire purchase had provided a common means of extended credit for the acquisition of major household items. Goods regularly sold in this way had included (with different emphases in different periods) pianos, vacuum cleaners, refrigerators. More broadly, a much older history of credit and debit sits on the other side of such aspirational projects, instead exposing the barest need to keep going or just to keep up with minimal daily buying. Here, want is not desire, but need and lack: the want of hunger or home-lessness, and no money to pay. Local food stores generally offered credit or put up with providing it for regular customers, even—or especially—when times were hard and shopkeepers, part of the same community, were suffering too. In the normal course of things they were put in the position of having to act as informal arbiters of their neighbours' creditworthiness. But customers could also decide to go elsewhere. As Neil Griffiths summarizes it, in relation to small Brighton food shops in the early twentieth century: 'There was a fine line between being too free with credit and taking on too many bad debts, and not being free enough and losing custom as a result.'[1] Here the new plastic cards clearly had a use for shopkeepers as well, since they permitted credit but passed on the responsibility for debt collection to the bank. The shop would get its money without having to worry about who to trust or how or when to pursue them. But the cost of using the facility put it beyond viability for smaller businesses and small purchases.

Credit was not necessarily prompted by absence of means to pay. Keeping a customer account was simpler and remained the norm for many forms of trading, local and otherwise, with or without a need to defer: whether for newspaper deliveries or purchases from the local department store, a monthly or quarterly bill was often the expected and most practical arrangement. The history of informal credit for everyday purchasing has a further dimension, too, apart from simplification or want of means. In pre-industrial times, ready money was itself in short supply, and if there was no change to give—with naturally no local bank for float—the use of coins for every small purchase might be needlessly complicated, if it was even possible. Today, once again, the use of ready money in small transactions is diminishing, as that function is superseded by the use of contactless debit and credit cards, or smartphones.

This present shift away from the use of cash may be compared to something like an equivalent development half a century ago. Before the 1960s, and later than that for many, weekly wages usually came in a pay packet that actually was one: an envelope containing coins and notes. The method of payment that replaced it, via transfer to bank accounts, meant that employees had to have them. As soon as they did, one prerequisite on the customer's side for the as yet uninvented credit card was in place.

The subject of spending beyond your means, whatever the social level, is one that lends itself to story, with standard character types that range from the carelessly irresponsible young lady to the impoverished worker's wife. A novel called *Helen* by Maria Edgeworth, published in 1834, opens with events leading up to the death of a gentleman who cannot manage his money and leaves insurmountable debts. In the case of this dissolute if well-meaning senior clergyman, a habit of specialized foreign spending means that his adored dependent niece will have no money to live on: 'All was desolation and dismay at the deanery'![2] Edgeworth spells out the economic circumstances with some directness. The problem is not to do with not paying, but with paying too much and too often: 'in money matters he was inconceivably imprudent and extravagant—extravagant from charity, from taste, from habit.'[3] He has no boundaries: 'Cursed with too fine a taste, and with too soft a heart—a heart too well knowing how to yield—never could he deny himself, much less any other human being, any gratification which money could command.'[4]

Long before credit cards, the man has more than maxed out—but nothing stops him. Already, in the first half of the nineteenth century, Edgeworth is using the proto-psychoanalytical language of a boundless 'gratification' from any and every kind of purchasable object or experience. With the help of money, these pleasures can be childishly shared and enjoyed. But it is the body as well as the mind that suffers when 'pecuniary difficulties' develop.[5] He goes to Florence to recover:

> There his health and spirits seemed at first, by the change of climate, to be renovated; but in Italy he found fresh temptations to extravagance, his learning and his fancy combined to lead him on from day to day to new expense, and he satisfied his conscience by saying to himself that all the purchases which he now made were only so much capital, which would, when sold in England, bring more than their original price, and would, he flattered himself, increase the fortune he intended for his niece.[6]

By this time the gratification, such as it still is, is at a remove: 'he satisfied his conscience', that being an intermediate factor which previously played no part. Edgeworth shows how spending, for Dean Stanley, is a type of addiction, fuelled not stalled by the expertise of his unusual 'learning' that combines with his 'fancy' to 'lead him on from day to day to new expense'.[7] The change of scene cannot cure him because he is surrounded by 'fresh temptations'. With conscience now also of the party, the unintended succumbings have to be rationalized in a new way as saleable investments. But the imagining of monetary profits is never a primary aim for this amiable character.

It is striking that Edgeworth should open with a portrait of someone who is an overspending purchaser of small *objets* as well as a generous dispenser of *largesse*—two consumerly roles that are frequently held apart and attributed to women or men, differentially. It is another type of division that Dean Stanley, this consummate omnigratifier, has never imposed on his all-consuming nature. Later in the novel there is a gorgeous vignette of an extreme version of the former category, the practitioner of retail therapy or buyer of extra special things. The star of this show is a minor female character who has married above the class she comes from. After dinner, when the ladies are sat together, Lady Bearcroft charms or shocks with her unguarded tale of lawless luxury pursuits:

> She opened to both friends cordially, *a propos* to some love of a lace trimming. Of lace she was a famous judge, and she went into details of her own good bargains, with histories of her expeditions into the extremity of the City in search of cheap goods and unheard-of wonders at prime cost, in regions unknown. She told how it was her clever way to leave her carriage and her *people*, and go herself down narrow streets and alleys, where only wheel-barrows and herself could go; she boasted of her fears in diving into dark dens in search of run goods, charming things—French warranted—that could be had for next to nothing, and, in exemplification, showed the fineness of her embroidered cambric handkerchiefs, and told their price to a farthing![8]

Like the Dean with his Florentine art finds, Lady Bearcroft is clearly a connoisseur in her small field, someone for whom part of the pleasure of this 'love of a lace trimming' comes from the process of the purchase itself, then the telling of that as a story. From the very beginning, the bargain aspect is just as important as the extraordinary beauty of the goods themselves: the 'unheard-of wonders' are all the more gorgeous for having been got 'at prime cost', and a cost that is now specified as part of the narrative, 'told...to a farthing!' To the double triumph of getting the treasure and getting it for 'next to nothing' is also then added the pleasure of the tale to tell: a story of difficulties overcome in the quest for these coveted objects. There is the 'dark' and 'narrow' of the streets and alleyways and the shops themselves, the 'dens' and the 'regions unknown' that are the opposite of the elegant establishments on the genteel new West End shopping streets elsewhere in the city; and there is the slumming separation as the lady goes incognito, away from her carriage and 'down' into depths that are beyond the accessible pale even for servants, one's *people*. At the end, the production of the pretty things themselves for all to see and touch seems to work as a seal of authenticity—'French warranted'!—for the story as well as the handkerchieves.

Lady Bearcroft's recounting of her shopping adventures is interesting in several other ways. First of all, it is clear that the cost price deal and the inside knowledge—she is sure she has got the real thing—are just as important to her enjoyment as the having and handling of the lace itself. For Dean Stanley, on the other hand, the practical considerations—the price to be fetched by a precious thing in different countries and at different times, or the difference between what he paid and what he can sell for—is a secondary consideration. The love of the objects is almost all, and the possibility of selling them on at a profit comes in as a later rationalization to justify or make up for having paid for them in the first place, with money he didn't still have.

A further point of interest in Lady Bearcroft's story is the way that it offers a sort of consumerly reversal of sales talk. It is not the buyer, but the person with something to sell who is meant to be the one with the patter, the story, the brilliant or ludicrous account of where this came from and why you should get it now. Lady Bearcroft's story is also about provenance—guaranteed French provenance, combined with the romantic expedition to the dark hidden place where no lady has gone before. But the point is not to persuade her audience to buy what she shows them, but rather to promote an image of herself as shopper-gatherer *extraordinaire*. Shopping provides her with daredevil heroic stories as well as with beautiful feminine fabrics.

Lady Bearcroft's bragging does not stop with the laces. 'From her amazing bargains', and after a pause for audience appreciation, the lady 'went on to smuggling':

> the last trip I made to Paris—coming back, I set at defiance all the searchers and *stabbers* and custom-house officers of both nations. I had hundreds of pounds worth of Valenciennes and Brussels lace hid—you would never guess where. I never told a servant—not a mortal maid even; that's the only way; had only a confidant of a coachmaker. But when it came to packing-up time, my own maid smelt out the lace was missing; and gave notice, I am confident, to the custom-house people to search me. So much the more glory to me. I got off clear; and when they had stabbed the cushions, and torn the inside of my carriage all to pieces, I very coolly made them repair the mischief at their own cost. Oh, I do love to do these things bravely! and away I drove triumphant with the lace, well stuffed, packed, and covered within the pole leather of the carriage they had been searching all the time.[9]

In the first story, the excitement is about knowing your stuff and where to get hold of 'run goods' that have crossed the border illegally, for 'next to nothing'. In this one there is a thrill in turning a purchase into a haul, in outwitting officials even when they have been tipped off by the servant. The maid's accurate guess might be a match for the mistress's cunning, but Lady Bearcroft gets away with it, even claiming, in the aftermath of the men having 'torn the inside of my carriage all to pieces', that it is she who has been ripped off: 'Oh, I do love to do these things bravely!'

Perhaps Edgeworth doesn't know where to go next with her loud lady teller of outlandish tales, since she now cuts her off through the unanswerable device of having 'the gentlemen' rejoin the ladies after the post-dinner separation of the sexes. This has the effect of ratifying the shopping-heist tales as being for women only, a sort of fantasy experience not for re-communication beyond this private feminine world. The smuggling story already enacts a symbolic version of this set-up, with the woman secreting the contraband goods in the most unfindable places of the interior of her private coach and the men seeing nothing of what's really been going on. More broadly, though, the story takes its place within a novel that is itself occupied with problems arising from the unwarranted circulation and threatened publication of a potentially compromising private image of one of the leading lady characters. As much as its other effects and aims, Lady Bearcroft's bravado in telling her stories, and doing the deeds she claims she did, is a double performance, like that of some compulsive blogger constantly offering supposedly insider tips about where and how she picked up this amazing deal or steal. The storytelling is a show in its own right, but so is the scene being re-enacted, complete with its moment of coolly playing the woman who claims her privacy has been shockingly violated.

A quite different kind of female purchasing triumph is recounted, admiringly, by a shop assistant who wrongly thinks that theft or damage, at least, might be in the offing. In the mid-1950s the portable typewriter was being marketed as a highly desirable piece of personal equipment—as with the personal computer when it arrived in the 1980s. The WHSmith in-house journal, *Talking Shop*, abounds in little articles about how best to display and sell this especially expensive item, if you venture to stock it. A wonderful anecdote was sent in by E.R. Luke, of the Stockton-on-Tees branch of the store:

> During last month I saw two schoolgirls, aged about 15, testing a type-writer. This is a worry on so valuable an article. I said to one, 'I imagine you would like to have that.' She said, 'Yes, I am going to have it,' and handed me £20.[10]

It is the minimal information which makes this so perfectly tantalizing as a story.

In its own extraordinary way, Lady Bearcroft's narrative has to be taken, if taken it is, on trust: look how I conned them! Believed or not, it makes for an excellent narrative entertainment for its genteel audience, a report from another shopping world. But there are also more reputable ways in which shopping has appeared as a hidden and privileged spectacle that can only be imagined. For most people, the world of the fashionable is seen at a definite distance—sometimes literally so. In an essay of 1830 by William Hazlitt, it is the waiting presence of the footmen with the carriage on the street that conveys the aura of an absent lady, invisibly shopping within:

> What would become of the coronet-coach filled with elegant and languid forms, if it were not for the triple row of powdered, laced, and liveried footmen, clustering, fluttering, and lounging behind it? What an idea do we not conceive of the fashionable *belle* who is making the most her time and tumbling over silks and satins within at Sewell and Cross's, or at the Bazaar in Soho-square, from the tall laquey in blue and silver with gold-headed cane, cocked-hat, white thread stocking and large calves to his legs, who stands as her representative without! The sleek shopman appears at the door, at an understood signal the livery-servant starts from his position, the coach-door flies open, the steps are let down, the young lady enters the carriage as young ladies are taught to step into carriages, the footman closes the door, mounts behind, and the glossy vehicle rolls off, bearing its lovely burden and her gaudy attendant from the gaze of the gaping crowd![11]

Hazlitt's recounted moment encapsulates a fascination with the marks of difference. There is no mistaking the lackey for a man of the upper class, in spite of his labourless livery. But the visible lavishness of the footman's appearance stands for that of the unseen personage within: 'You do not indeed penetrate to the interior of the mansion where sits the stately possessor, luxurious and refined; but you draw your inference from the lazy, pampered, motley crew poured forth from his portals.'[12] Glimpsed at the moment of her departure, the 'fashionable *belle*' attended by her footman has no name—unlike the well-known store whose 'sleek shopman' is ready to give the nod to her attendant. She can be imagined, though, 'tumbling over silks and satins' in a sort of voluptuous rummage, and 'making the most of her time', which even for such a leisured young lady is apparently to be thought of as a limited resource. Hazlitt not only specifies which shop she is in, he also mentions one like it, as though to provide an exclusive list of the places patronized by the rich if not famous.

This Soho Bazaar was not, in fact, exclusive in quite the way that Hazlitt's satirical outside view suggests. Started by John Trotter in 1816 with some support from a clergyman called James Nightingale, its purpose, in part, was to provide work for women who needed it. Inside there were 160 separate fixed selling booths, each with its own counter. These could be rented out for different lengths of time, as short as a week, at twopence or threepence a day. The interior was a dramatically appealing large space, on two floors: a prototype of department store design. There were rules to define the respectability of the place (not that that stopped jokes about just what kind of female goods might be on offer); these included a strict limitation, compared to other shops, of opening hours.[13]

Thus the kind of social exclusiveness that Hazlitt alludes to was in the process of changing: there was growing access, for more people, to more of the shopping spaces patronized by the well-to-do. By the end of the nineteenth century, with the availability of cheaper, ready-made clothes and the building of big city department stores whose clientele was more mixed, that *belle* inside the shop might be almost any woman, dressed at the height of fashion. In this new shopping scene, the blurring of social differences would proceed apace, leaving behind the old world in which the signs of status (or lack of it) could be read at a glance, and for those without it, nothing would take the waiting out of want and wanting, in all their forms. In the department store, selling it all and open to all, the upper-class lady is in the same elegant place as the ordinary housewife, both of them treated with deference.

Elizabeth Gaskell's novels dramatize the sheer injustice of the social divisions of shopping in a way that makes Hazlitt's satirical critique of them seem beside the point. Difference often comes down to who does or does not have the means to buy food. In *Mary Barton* (1848), during a recession, with men laid off, 'the shops for expensive luxuries still find daily customers, while the workman loiters away his unemployed time in watching these things, and thinking of the pale, uncomplaining wife at home, and the wailing children asking in vain for enough food.'[14] John Barton 'tried credit; but it was worn out at the little provision shops, which were now suffering in their turn.'[15] With a sick child he is desperate:

> Hungry himself, almost to an animal pitch of ravenousness, but with the bodily pain swallowed up in anxiety for his little sinking lad, he stood at one of the shop windows where all edible luxuries are displayed; haunches of venison, Stilton cheeses, moulds of jelly—all appetising sights to the common passer by. And out of this shop came Mrs Hunter! She crossed to her carriage, followed by the shopman loaded with purchases for a party.[16]

The lavish display and the casual entitlement of the lady, even the enjoyment of a 'common passer by', all become grotesque when presented as what is visible to John Barton, but inaccessible. There is waiting, and there is want. To complete the melodrama of the contrast with Mrs Hunter and her party, he goes home 'to see his only boy a corpse!'[17]

In George Orwell's novel *A Clergyman's Daughter*, the shop itself does not appear, but the opening situation is that of the daily distress of owing a local shop money that there is no way to pay:

> She had remembered, with the ugly shock with which one remembers something disagreeable for the first time in the morning, the bill at Cargill's, the butcher's, which had been owing for seven months. That dreadful bill—it might be nineteen pounds or even twenty, and there was hardly the remotest hope of paying it—was one of the chief torments of her life. At all hours of the night or day it was waiting just round the corner of her consciousness, ready to spring upon her and agonize her; and with it came the memory of a score of lesser bills, mounting up to a

figure of which she dare not even think. Almost involuntarily she began to pray, 'Please God, let not Cargill send in his bill today!'[18]

In this misery of debt upon debt, the initial numbers, 'seven months' and 'nineteen or even twenty pounds', which are frightening enough ('that dreadful bill'), then trigger thoughts of further amounts, now too many even to count ('a score of lesser bills'), and their totals mount up to 'a figure of which she dare not even think'. Orwell takes this waking 'shock' of a remembered worry to be a common type of everyday horror, the magnification of its details not just to do with the particular material—the number of bills and the sum of the debts—but also with the force of the fear that takes over. In this inescapable occupation, it is the mind itself that has been taken over; the threat is always there, out of the region of mental control, and 'ready' to pounce from 'the corner of her consciousness'. As the too dutiful housekeeping daughter of an incompetent father—the village rector of the title— Dorothy represents a common enough character in social reality as well as in English fiction of the nineteenth and earlier twentieth centuries. Her scared and subservient situation (until she breaks away, which she does) is sharply elaborated in Orwell's dissection of its moment-by-moment psychological reality.

Orwell's rector has an unreflecting indifference to the means of procuring, preparing, and paying for the meals that will fit his expectations and habits (there is no difference between the two). With a house that came with the job and an income for life (no requirement to retire at any age), a rural clergyman was one of those fortunate employees whose livelihood would never be threatened, not even during the 1930s. He was assured of a roof over his head and the means of purchasing his daily bread. The butcher's bills (and the rest of them) in Rev. Hare's household are unpaid, we learn, not because there was never enough money to pay them, nor even because the food ordered was beyond his means, but because much of the regular income, instead of being used for immediate requirements, has been lost in bad investments. This mode of spending casts away daily housekeeping money in the hope of an eventual 'return' when it will come back accompanied by additions. The speculations are neither savvy nor successful, and Orwell makes it clear that the money problems that ensue are caused not so much by the legendary low budgets of clergy households—'poor as church mice'—but by the weak attempts of the man to play an un-Christian capitalist game for which he has neither the talent nor the knowledge. Far from proposing to change his behaviour, or seeing the problem at all, the rector regards it as a sort of inherited patriarchal tradition, a class privilege of ignoring the importunate demands of an inferior: 'Doesn't everyone owe money to his tradesmen? ... I distinctly remember that when I was up at Oxford, my father had still not paid some of his own Oxford bills of thirty years earlier'.[19] In this case the situation does not continue for thirty years, and Orwell offers a satisfyingly retributive ending. After the departure of the long-suffering daughter, the rector's creditors round on him as a group, so that 'He has been obliged to pay off all his debts.'[20] The deadlock from which Dorothy suffered had only continued because the shopkeepers liked her: 'You, evidently, were the only person who could keep the tradesmen permanently at bay.'[21]

At the other extreme from Orwell's decent Dorothy is the non-paying customer who normally 'keeps the tradesmen ... at bay' by sheer charm. Hazlitt recites a whole string of tales about the eighteenth-century dramatist Richard Sheridan, who was legendary for his manoeuvres. His servants had to join in the act, not always successfully:

> so sharp-set were they, that to cut short a debate with a butcher's apprentice about leaving a leg of mutton without the money, the cook clapped it into the pot: the butcher's boy, probably used to such encounters, with equal coolness took it out again, and marched off with it in his tray in triumph.[22]

It is a performance almost worthy of Lady Bearcroft.

Notes

1. Neil Griffiths, *Shops Book: Shopkeepers and Street Traders in Brighton 1900–1930* (Brighton: QueenSpark Books, 1978), 53.
2. Maria Edgeworth, *Helen* (1834; London: Pandora, 1987), 3.
3. Edgeworth, *Helen*, 2.
4. Edgeworth, *Helen*, 2.
5. Edgeworth, *Helen*, 2.
6. Edgeworth, *Helen*, 2.
7. Edgeworth, *Helen*, 2.
8. Edgeworth, *Helen*, 232.
9. Edgeworth, *Helen*, 232–3.
10. From a letter forming part of 'The Outlook for 1954', *Talking Shop*, January 1954, 6–7.
11. William Hazlitt, 'On Footmen' (1830), *Metropolitan Writings*, ed. Gregory Dart (London: Fyfield Books, 2005), 147.
12. Hazlitt, 'On Footmen', 149.
13. On the Soho Bazaar see Ian Mitchell, 'Innovation in non-food retailing in the early nineteenth century: The curious case of the bazaar', *Business History* 52:6 (2010), 875–91; Alison Adburgham, *Shops and Shopping 1800–1914* (1964; 2nd edn London: George Allen and Unwin, 1981), 23; Jon Stobart, *Spend Spend Spend! A History of Shopping* (Stroud: The History Press, 2008), 109–10.
14. Elizabeth Gaskell, *Mary Barton: A Tale of Manchester Life* (1848), ed. Stephen Gill (Harmondsworth: Penguin, 1970), 59–60.
15. Gaskell, *Mary Barton*, 60.
16. Gaskell, *Mary Barton*, 61.
17. Gaskell, *Mary Barton*, 61.
18. George Orwell, *A Clergyman's Daughter* (1935; London: Penguin, 1988), 8.
19. Orwell, *A Clergyman's Daughter*, 29.
20. Orwell, *A Clergyman's Daughter*, 223–4.
21. Orwell, *A Clergyman's Daughter*, 224.
22. Hazlitt, 'On the Want of Money' (1827), *Metropolitan Writings*, 107.

14

Customer Loyalty

In Jane Austen's *Emma* (1816), one character suggests that a shop called Ford's is the object of local 'patriotism'.[1] It is just an affectionate joke: everyone loves Ford's. But the commercial fortunes of such a feeling are considered more seriously in another classic novel a century later, when those two kinds of attachment, love of country and love of shopping, come close together. Virginia Woolf's *Mrs Dalloway* (1925) shows a flurry of speculation one morning about the possibly royal passenger of an imposing motor car which is making its way through the streets in the centre of London. Could this be 'The Queen going to some hospital; the Queen opening some bazaar'? Or could it even—extraordinary thought!—be 'the Queen going shopping?'[2] Whichever, the royal sighting takes precedence over all ongoing ordinary retail pursuits on the part of anyone else, and the novel's own narrative is paused as Mrs Dalloway, in the middle of buying her flowers, goes to the window of the shop to look out. Crowds gather near Buckingham Palace to wait for the car's return. Patriotic attachment is primary and compelling, so far.

But while this is going on, a sound is heard and everyone looks upwards, to stare at that rare phenomenon in the 1920s, an aeroplane. Here is a new enigma, as the plane is seen to be streaming out letters to make up a word, which all now attempt to decipher. It is a brand of toffee. So instead of a glimpse of the queen, what the spectators have witnessed is a show of the new art of *skywriting*. It is the highest of high-tech advertising, used to promote newly ubiquitous type of packaged commodity. The marketing of confectionery was taking off at that time, urging customers to ask for a brand by name in the sweet shop. Change is in the air! In this initial era of brash brand promotion, it might be that even Woolf, not a normally symbolic writer, is suggesting a broad shift of public attachment from patriotic to commercial allegiances. In the century that followed this novel, the royal family itself would become one of the biggest brands, a major international marketing draw in the British tourist industry of the early twenty-first century. Perhaps this is already adumbrated in the celebrity mystique surrounding the unidentified person within the motor car. And from the viewpoint of the twenty-first century, one other thing to be seen in the sequence is real shopping—buying some flowers in a particular shop—being superseded by mass marketing.

The loyalty of brand believers has not always taken the passive form that it does for Woolf's London crowd, as if compelled to raise their eyes to the mystery name magically unfurling far above them. When the members of Co-operative societies began—from the mid-nineteenth century—to sell and then also to manufacture commodities collectively, on their own behalf, they had invented a new kind of retail institution, with no formal distinction between customers and owners. These were one and the same, and the benefits were shared. Customers were loyal to the institution because it belonged to them. The dividend, or 'divi', was a system of regular returns in proportion to customers' retail purchases whereby the surplus—what was not retained for running costs and reinvestment—was distributed among the members of a given local Co-op. Individual amounts were calculated from stamps supplied at the time of the purchase and pasted into a book; in good years, this could be 5 per cent of the total spent, sometimes more. Saving and redemption: the culture of Co-op stamps was attuned to cardinal values of work and reward. It was also, as economists put it admiringly in the 1930s, 'a most valuable method of accumulating small savings almost unconsciously.'[3] But this was more than a reflex, with members having deliberately 'allowed a good deal of their dividend to accumulate', as they 'used the Retail Societies as Savings Banks'. In a protective capacity, 'The retail societies have willingly undertaken this task of looking after their members' savings.'[4]

In the early twentieth century, branded goods with minimum prices set by manufacturers became common; this became known as resale price maintenance or RPM, and lasted until into the 1960s. The brand itself was meant to appear in its own right, a known name specifically asked for over the counter. RPM was supported by small independent shops as a protection from the chains' undercutting of their prices. In this context, there was considerable resentment, by independents and manufacturers alike, of the Co-op's ability to reduce prices indirectly, since the dividend was paid on all purchases, brands included. Other companies introduced their own stamp schemes; the north-eastern chain of Broughs did this in the 1930s, for instance.[5] Beginning in 1958, when self-service and supermarkets were starting to develop rapidly, Tesco launched their Green Shield Stamps as a competitive alternative to the supremacy of the Co-op's dividend. These stamps were exchanged for stuff, not money: for 'gifts' from a catalogue.

For Tesco, it was a major decision to discontinue these stamps in 1977, and a further gamble two decades later, in 1995, to bring on the Tesco Clubcard, with its matchless tracking capacities in the dawning age of data. The Co-op kept up its dividend in various incarnations, with its level of return still today much higher than that of Tesco or other chains using loyalty cards. But as an emblem of allegiance to an ethos, the divi had dwindled, along with the perceived ideological importance of the Co-op itself. In its peak time, extending into much of the twentieth century, the Co-op's moral as well as financial significance gave it national prominence in grocery sales and in many other key products and services too, from milk and bread deliveries to furniture or funerals or travel. In 1950, Co-operative societies accounted for 15 per cent of food and household retail sales, virtually equal to the market share of all other chains at the time put together. Co-ops also accounted for almost the same proportion of clothing and footwear sales—though with chain stores in that category much exceeding them, at almost 30 per cent.[6] But in the last part of the twentieth century the organization declined, as other companies jostled for now much-mediatized positions in various rankings of profits and popularity. Above all, Tesco and Sainsbury's took turns at the top of the supermarket league tables from the 1980s through to the 2010s.

During the time when Tesco had its Green Shield Stamps and the Co-op with its dividend remained significant, Sainsbury's had stood aloof from the frivolity of such bonuses. 'Good Food Costs Less at Sainsbury's' was the message, printed in orange on plain white carrier bags. But in the newly digital cut and thrust of the early twenty-first century, Sainsbury's lined up alongside the Tesco card with its own equivalent, Nectar. And when, from the 1990s, the German companies Aldi and Lidl entered the field with a smaller but low-priced choice of lines, they appealed across the complex British social range, to hit both Tesco and Sainsbury's, as well as the cheaper Asda, in equal measure. Like Sainsbury's, back in the clear twentieth-century day, the new discounters have no stamps, and no loyalty cards, and no online delivery, either. What you carry is what you get.

The Co-op's trading stamps offered customer benefits as direct profit-sharing, an offshoot of the movement's community ethos. Other stores' stamp or (later) plastic card loyalty schemes have had no participatory component, operating instead more like a kind of feudal largesse or 'reward', a patronizing handout: Every Little Helps! (The Tesco slogan, shamelessly appropriating an old saying, may also have succeeded by the gratifying suggestion that a spending customer was somehow by nature hardworking and underappreciated.) But today, beyond Tesco's long ago Green Shield trading stamps, a new green has come into view. This time it is green for the (global) community, not for the individual customer. In retrospect, the (anti-)tipping point into this new green naturalization may have been the abolition of free plastic bags in England in 2015—a move which, before it happened, was widely thought likely to fail. It has subsequently been compared to such earlier reforms as the introduction of compulsory seat belts in cars, or of alcohol limits for driving, both quickly absorbed, despite other expectations, into cultural common sense. But the timing is not always right in this way. Excessive packaging had long been criticized by groups such as Friends of the Earth, going back to the 1970s, without ever generating a wider movement against it. In the late 1980s there was a period of environmental awareness that had some effect on the marketing of cleaning products—with *eco* the key word to mean the same thing, more or less, as *green* does today. But widespread interest was short-lived, and change could be merely cosmetic, with products in practice unmodified behind the brightly new label to mark that they did not contain certain ingredients.

In the late 2010s, stores had to adapt to the new anti-packaging environment, and it was complicated to do so for both practical and commercial reasons. Plastic carrier bags had long played a sideline promotional role, with buyers swinging the name of a store as they walked down the street. If the shop was prestigious and the customer suited the image, the benefits were mutual, as with the celebrity papped with a Prada bag. In an earlier period, standardized packaging was a novelty in itself and could be promoted to customers, over the counter, as if it represented a special bonus that the store was offering. One 1930s textbook proposed phrases for memorization that the assistant might like to use: '"This is a new way they have of packing—." "This is rather a novelty—the package is so easily opened—no tearing—no scissors or knife required—look!"'[7] The author, C.J. Elliott, is keen to stress that drawing attention to something new in this way is nothing but helpful, since 'All new goods—or new and novel packings—give the sales assistant a chance to render a service to the customer.'[8] It sounds like a worthwhile ambition, and it is explained in meticulous detail, including some more suggested sentences to use and a description of the back-up work done by point-of-sale publicity materials:

> The sales assistant brings a line to the notice of a customer in this way:
> 'This is quite a new way of packing table-jellies; this booklet tells you all

about them.' This is all he or she says—but the display on the counter says more. There is a showcard which says still more.[9]

Elliott initially recommends leaving it at that and letting the showcard and booklet do the talking. That way, 'When she gets home, she may regret her purchase, but she will blame herself—*not* the shop, or the over-anxious assistant.'[10] The post-sale addition to the story inadvertently acknowledges that the overpersuasive assistant may not have rendered a real service after all: quite the reverse. But never mind: the customer has only herself to blame; it is '*not* the shop' or the poor man behind the counter doing his best. Painfully, this is one kind of customer loyalty.

The invented story about the jelly disappointment also reflects another aspect of the tension that developed throughout the twentieth century between independent retailers and the manufacturers of pre-packaged brands. The expertise of the shopkeeper now counted for nothing; instead there were the goods that were supposedly 'pre-sold' (via advertising), meaning that there was no longer any persuasive or suggestive work for the shop assistant to do. But as the already packaged brands appropriated the grocer's own preparation of goods or packs (the laborious weighing out and packing up of tea or biscuits or spices in different quantities), the effect was to shift the sense of loyalty away from individual shops to the trademark names of the products. As a point of recognition and reliability, the well-known brand—obtainable in every high street, if not in the sky above—was taking over from the small and local shop.

Notes

1. Jane Austen, *Emma* (1816), ed. James Kinsley (Oxford: Oxford University Press, 1995), 179.
2. Virginia Woolf, *Mrs Dalloway* (1925), ed. David Bradshaw (Oxford: Oxford University Press, World's Classics, 2000), 13.
3. Dorothea Braithwaite and S.P. Dobbs, *The Distribution of Consumable Goods: An Economic Study* (London: George Routledge & Sons Ltd., 1932), 255.

4. C.W.S. [Co-operative Wholesale Society], *A Consumers' Democracy* (Stockport: C.W.S., 1951), 42.
5. See Peter Mathias, *Retailing Revolution: A History of Multiple Retailing in the Food Trades* (London: Longmans 1967), 90.
6. For these sales figures see James B. Jefferys, *Retail Trading in Britain 1850–1950* (Cambridge: Cambridge University Press, 1954), 75, 77.
7. C.J. Elliott, *The Retail Grocery Trade* (London: Methuen, 1938), 232.
8. Elliott, *Retail Grocery Trade*, 231.
9. Elliott, *Retail Grocery Trade*, 231.
10. Elliott, *Retail Grocery Trade*, 231.

15

Motor Vans and Motor Buses

In the 1930s, the motor bus and the motor van were the talk of the town and the country. *Motor* being, in both cases, the operative word; it would fall away from the front when these splendid new vehicles became familiar enough to be seen as just buses and vans. The same thing occurred with the *motor car*, soon downsized to the car. But the *motor bicycle*, proudly individual, has kept to its formal beginning and remains, in a single word, the *motorbike*—probably to distinguish it from the (simple, unmotorized) *bike* which, unlike the horse-drawn carriage or coach that the car and bus replaced, continues to have a life.

Like the train and the tram, the fast new motor bus brought the country visitor into the town to shop, and the town or suburban visitor into the city. (It also took city dwellers out to the country, but that is a different story.) The fast new delivery van, transporting meat or bread, or a whole supply of general groceries—the 'mobile shop'— saved customers from having to lug these things back themselves (see Figure 8). This was not yet the time of the car—or not for many. But the motor bus could go faster and further than the person walking from the home to the shop, or the journey in a horse-drawn convey-ance; faster too than the delivery boy on his legs or his bike. In the country his 'motor bicycle' often replaced it. In the words of Hermann Levy, an economist writing just after the war, 'The motor-van and the highly specialized commercial vehicle have had a revolutionary effect, enabling shoppers to buy goods in person at distant stores without regard to their bulk.'[1]

Figure 8. Berkhamsted and Hemel Hempstead Co-operative Society mobile shop in Hemel Hempstead, 1950s, marked GROCERY SELF-SERVICE
Image courtesy of Hertfordshire Archives and Local Studies

Motor vans were among the extra facilities that smaller as well as central shops were urged to equip themselves with during this period (at the same time as they were also meant to think about investing in better fixtures and fittings for the shop interior, from counters to flooring). These vans were typically small, but differences were noticeable, such as whether and how the name of the shop was painted on. Some companies were ready with generic designs for different trades; a manual for fruiterers and florists, meanwhile, points out that 'a lorry which is travelling about the district acts as a very good advertisement, provided it is clean and smartly turned out, with the name of the retailer prominently displayed.'[2] On the other hand, Levy sounds a cautionary note about going too far:

> When the small retailer aspires to deliver in a luxurious van, to indulge in costly advertisement, to renovate his shop at high expense, to imitate the modern chain store in expensive outfit, to exaggerate his ranges of goods in order to follow the line of the big department store, he very soon finds himself in difficulties as to his costs.[3]

One day you buy a nice new motor van for the shop, and before you know it you think you are Swan & Edgar.

The delivery van's gentler cousin was the diesel milk float, which has survived (just) into the following century. Its rounds are vastly diminished from the near universality of daily deliveries up to the 1980s; but in response to present-day environmental concerns about containers it has been making a small comeback, with returnable glass bottles still on board. In the middle decades of the twentieth century everyone had their milk delivered every day, sometimes in half pint as well as pint bottles, and sometimes twice a day, with home refrigerators unusual before the 1960s. Schools received a daily supply in special per-pupil bottles of a third of a pint, in time for the morning break. (Government funding for this free school milk was ended in 1972 by the then Minister of Education, Margaret Thatcher, dubbed the Milk Snatcher as a result.)

The motor bus was a visible sign of changing consumer behaviour between the wars. All going shopping! For one observer, it could be seen that 'Improved transport has brought with it the possibilities of far more fluid purchasing, in place of relatively fixed habits of shopping': the mind was moving forward along with the vehicle that was taking you into town.[4] From a marketing perspective (the writer was managing director of Daniel Neal's, a prominent children's outfitters) the 'change in emphasis' could be summarily stated as being 'from the old outlook which said "This need is not being met," to one which today says rather: "This latent desire should be stimulated and catered for"'. The psychological vocabulary is striking, with its new desires to be seen as already present in each consumer and simply awaiting the trigger to bring them out. Neal adds a crucial further point: 'Naturally also the difference shows itself not merely in the types of merchandise sold, but in the trappings and attractions with which the sale has to be invested.'[5] That is, shops themselves are now meant to offer a pleasurable experience to match the qualities of their goods. The manifestation of this movement of shopping psychology from the satisfaction of needs to the response to newly emerging and mobile desires depends, it is insisted, on the design of the shops themselves, not only on what they sell.

It is not uncommon for commentators about their own times and past times to talk about a shift from fixed needs to mobile desires, and a shopping experience to go with it. But this same story of a change in shopping minds has been identified for many different periods, not just the twentieth century. Most notably, it was deployed (both then and in later retellings) in relation to the nineteenth-century rise of the grand city centre department stores, inciting new desires for purchasable luxuries in their female clientele, and making shopping—*going shopping*—into a pleasure of its own. In the mid-twentieth-century motor bus iteration of the story, the emphasis is smaller in scale. It is about ordinary trips into a maybe not so big town, and manageable modifications in the presentation of not so big shops, with every kind of retailer being urged to make their shop a more attractive space to come into. For the customer who might have travelled to get there, it had to be worth the trip.

But the motor bus was not only for country ladies doing a morning's shopping in town, nor were the newly motorized deliveries only for those who were paying a premium for special services. In the words of a children's encyclopaedia from the early 1950s, 'The women need not go to town to do the week's shopping, for the merchants drive up to the door.'[6] (The reference to the *week*'s shopping is notable here.) Thus, a further type of vehicle that took to the roads in the middle of the motorized century was the mobile shop—often itself a former (motor) bus now converted inside for this second life. The shop would park up in the same spot at the same regular times, and either the driver-shopkeeper served from out of a hatch at the side, or customers went in and picked out what they wanted from shelves along the sides (this was one of the early experiments in self-service). A large part of this trade took goods to the new housing estates that were being built on the outskirts of towns during these years, and to the post-war new towns. By the 1950s, the travelling shops were an established feature of local retailing.

With the mobile shop, as with the pedlar, the shop came all the way to the customer, and then departed. Unlike with mail order or online shopping, the customer was both choosing and receiving the goods at the same time, in the same place—without leaving home, or not more than a step or two. In the words of Henry Smith, an economist writing in the late 1930s:

> it may be convenient for goods to be delivered to their door from a shop some distance away, or for the shop to come close to them, as in the familiar street-corner shop of the older industrial districts, or for the 'shop' itself to come right on to the doorstep, as with the pedlar or the modern motor-van housing a butcher's or draper's shop.[7]

As ever, that word 'convenience' is the criterion. By the late 1950s, mobile greengrocers were singled out as being particularly successful: 'a force to be reckoned with'.[8] The town planner Wilfred Burns considers that they will eventually even see off the fixed greengrocer, because 'the housewife does not have to carry heavy greengroceries further than the length of the garden path.'[9] This is also, although 'clearly arduous and most uncomfortable in inclement weather', one of the few trades that can be started with almost no capital.[10] The mobile greengrocer also 'has the freedom of a self-employed person who is not tied to the ordinary shopping hours (an advantage for the working woman)'.[11] That small addition, acknowledging that in practice not all women are at home all day, unknowingly opens out to a future in which almost none of them would be. But by then the greengrocer's van would have disappeared.

The food delivery trade was not only of the high-class variety deemed to be out of reasonable reach for Hermann Levy's small retailer. There were also deliveries to isolated industrial communities. Broughs, for instance, was a small chain based in Newcastle. Initially, in the 1890s, miners' wives came in to buy from the villages weekly or fortnightly (fortnightly when that was the frequency of the pay packet, not weekly). Broughs sold at low prices for large quantities, but 'bulk orders could not be conveniently carried back in shopping baskets', and so an extensive delivery service developed to meet a need: 'The trade had to be carried to the customers.'[12] In the branches, Wednesdays and Thursdays were mainly spent 'putting up' the orders, with Fridays and Saturdays set aside for deliveries, and the collection of cash (Broughs did not take credit).

Improved transport from one town to another might have different effects on existing shops. In Arnold Bennett's novel *The Old Wives' Tale*, published in 1908, a once prosperous square of shops in a provincial town called Bursley is now fallen on hard times. A neighbouring place has taken away the best of the trade, by offering incentives for customers to shop there:

> People would not go to Hanbridge for their bread or for their groceries, but they would go for their cakes. These electric trams had simply carried to Hanbridge the cream, and much of the milk, of Bursley's retail trade. There were unprincipled tradesmen in Hanbridge ready to pay the car-fares of any customer who spent a crown in their establishment.[13]

This phenomenon of new public transport taking trade from local shops was widespread, such that 'it was not uncommon for customers travelling by train or tram from one town to have their fare paid by grateful shopkeepers in another town.'[14] The means of travel may be public and carbon-neutral, but this is the equivalent, more than a century ago, of the supermarket that refunds a Pay and Display car park ticket in return for a minimum spend.

Notes

1. Hermann Levy, *The Shops of Britain: A Study of Retail Distribution* (London: Kegan Paul, Trench, Trubner & Co., Ltd., 1947), 3–4.
2. W.B. Shearn (ed.), *The Practical Fruiterer and Florist*, Vol. II (London: George Newnes, 1930s [n.d.]), 192.
3. Levy, *Shops of Britain*, 109.
4. Lawrence E. Neal, *Retailing and the Public* (London: George Allen & Unwin, 1932), 178.

5. Neal, *Retailing and the Public*, 178.
6. 'Market-Towns', *Oxford Junior Encyclopaedia*, vol. VI (London: Geoffrey Cumberlege, Oxford University Press, 1952), 285.
7. Henry Smith, *Retail Distribution: A Critical Analysis* (London: Oxford University Press, 1937), 5.
8. Wilfred Burns, *British Shopping Centres: New Trends in Layout and Distribution* (London: Leonard Hill, 1959), 39.
9. Burns, *British Shopping Centres*, 16.
10. Burns, *British Shopping Centres*, 40.
11. Burns, *British Shopping Centres*, 16.
12. Peter Mathias, *Retailing Revolution: A History of Multiple Retailing in the Food Trades* (London: Longmans, 1967), 83.
13. Arnold Bennett, *The Old Wives' Tale* (1908; Harmondsworth: Penguin, 1985), 598.
14. James Schmiechen and Kenneth Carls, *The British Market Hall: A Social and Architectural History* (New Haven: Yale University Press, 1999), 158.

16

Nineteenth-Century Bazaars

In another world from the Indian trading stations, going back hundreds of years, whose name they took, charity bazaars were a standard feature of provincial life in nineteenth- and early twentieth-century England. Along with the village *fête*, which names almost the same event, *bazaar* is one of not many words in the middle England social repertoire to be noticeably foreign, with an appeal that comes over as both exotic and familiar. In modern times the word *fair* also sometimes names the same kind of show and sale, and its fancy spelling as *fayre* in the twentieth century may look like invented olde-world authenticity. But (perhaps accidentally) it is genuine: *fayre*, like *fair*, was a medieval word.

Nineteenth-century charity bazaars were shops of a very particular sort. Their purpose was the sale of goods for a profit—but the profits were all for a good cause. This might be a political cause: perhaps the most spectacular such event of the century was the Anti-Corn Law League Bazaar held at Covent Garden in 1845, in aid of the free trade movement. Special trains were laid on to bring both goods and visitors down to London for the event, with samples of the latest or proudest local manufactures being contributed for display and sale by almost fifty towns around the country.[1] It was like a dress rehearsal for the international Great Exhibition that would take place in 1851—but with the vital distinction that at the later event, what was shown was not for sale.

Closer to home, bazaars featured as part of the annual round of ladies' community activity, often attached to the church. They were middle-class or moderately aristocratic, perhaps with a titled person doing the honours of the opening ceremony. In this common, small-scale type of charity bazaar, the merchandise was handmade—mainly by ladies, who did this work for nothing in their own homes; this at a time when, by contrast, many ordinary commodities were made or finished through low-paid, home-based piecework, with minimal returns to the producer. The same ladies generally also managed every aspect of planning and accounting, so that the short-term shop was a semi-simulacrum of the regular type. It had manufacturers, salespeople, and managers—with the same participants often fulfilling all three roles, as with tailors or dressmakers or any other workshop enterprise. There would also be donations of both new and not new goods, for sale on the day.

In one aspect, bazaars gave unoccupied ladies something worth-while to do. The enterprise made use of all the domestic crafts of women's making. Even so, the actual work of the production (the making of the goods, and the delivery of the event) was easily trivialized: 'the ideas associated with a Bazaar are those of the luxurious products of laborious idleness—fancy work, screens, cush-ions, workbags, purses, and similar nicknackeries', pronounced one critic, suggesting that the big Anti-Corn Law event had been wrongly named.[2] A bazaar just suggested pointless accessories, so why call it that?

As with any good cause, the customers at a regular parish bazaar often bought not because they had any wish or need for an object as such, but to be useful in making a purchase. All the more so if they were men, not accustomed to shopping, and if the vendors were young ladies of their social acquaintance whose worthy efforts clearly deserved reward. Bazaars were an opportunity for flirtation, with young ladies playing the part of shopgirls as an added bonus. At a bazaar, unlike almost any other shop setting of this time, male cus-tomers are at the forefront of customer visibility, if only because all the women are occupied with the work of selling. In George Eliot's novel *The Mill on the Floss* (1860), the local bazaar brings out the interest in Maggie Tulliver as well as in her wares. It happens too that what Maggie is selling is well suited to potential customers:

> the gentlemen's dressing gowns, which were among her commodities, were objects of such general attention and inquiry and excited so troublesome a curiosity as to their lining and comparative merits, together with a determination to test them by trying on, as to make her post a very conspicuous one.[3]

The bazaar scene comes over as a parody of the normal shopping division, with the men here busy purchasing and parading in their gowns. But this attraction to Maggie's stall gives rise to a counter-feeling of some force, stated with Eliot's trademark irony: 'The ladies who had commodities of their own to sell and did not want dressing-gowns saw at once the frivolity and bad taste of this masculine preference for goods which any tailor could furnish'—as if the men after all might be buying for practical reasons.

In Virginia Woolf's novel *Mrs Dalloway* (1925), the fortitude or repression of an aristocratic character in the face of personal tragedy is marked by the case of one Lady Bexborough 'who opened a bazaar, they said, with the telegram in her hand'—the telegram, that is, from which she has just learned of the death of her son in action.[4] That small 'they said' gives the status of the story as a kind of public myth whereby the bazaar, as a planned community endeavour, must be seen to be carrying on, come what may. Winifred Holtby's novel *The Crowded Street*, published the year before *Mrs Dalloway*, has a more comic take on the bazaar taking precedence over everything else. On the night when war breaks out, a Mrs Hammond sends her daughter out to buy an evening paper, and when she gets there, 'Little knots of people stood round the open doorways of shops that should have been shut long ago.' All the same, war or no war, Mrs Hammond wants 'to talk to Mrs. Cartwright. There's that bazaar on the 4th.'[5]

A twentieth-century cousin of the bazaar was the jumble sale, still sometimes to be seen where it has not been superseded completely by boot fairs and charity shops. Both of these last are sales of cast-off goods, not new ones, let alone handmade ones; the car boot sale for the profit of the Sunday sellers themselves who bring their car to the field, and the charity shop, in true bazaar tradition, a store whose staff are mostly unpaid and whose stock is mostly donated. A jumble sale is generally held to be less grand or pretentious than a bazaar, in relation to both what it sold and who is expected to buy the stuff.[6] Unlike the bazaar, everything is second-hand and cheap. When the doors open, there may be a rush for the bargains, which is not bazaar behaviour. The jumble sale was a regular form of recycling and reuse long before those ideas were being widely promoted; it was also, if you were lucky—if you got there early or waited till the final reductions—an occasion for real bargains. And as with the bazaar, it was also a way to raise money for a chosen local charity.

The perceived difference of quality between the bazaar and the jumble sale may have been a late separation. A 1916 announcement in a Northamptonshire newspaper proclaims that the Town and Country Jumble Sale 'tomorrow' will be opened by the Right Hon. the Earl Spencer, K.C. (Princess Diana's great-grandfather), and continues:

THE SALE WILL INCLUDE—
SHIRE MARE AND FOAL,
17 FAT BEAST,
150 FAT SHEEP AND LAMBS,
16 FAT STORE PIGS
SHEEP DIPPING APPARATUS, with Drainer
complete, given by Mr. F.H. Thornton, J.P.,
besides Donkeys, Goats, 11 Dogs, Harness,
Two Spring Carts, Traps, Trucks, Flour,
Hams, Meat, Wine, Cigars, Implements,
Corn, Cake, Flour, Fruit, Vegetables. Also
    THREE MOTOR CARS,
200 HEAD OF POULTRY, Etc. Etc.[7]

(Yes, the flour is listed twice.) What this noble assortment of items suggests is that the jumble of the jumble sale began as a reference to the mixture of types—only later developing the connotation of any old things, what a household has no more use for. On the same page of the paper is a second and larger advertisement for 'NORTHAMP-TON'S GREAT PATRIOTIC GIFT SALE AND WAR BAZAAR'.

In its local, temporary settings the justification for the bazaar, or fête, or fayre, is its charitable objective: 'come buy', with a noble purpose. Profits—or rather, the 'proceeds'—are given 'in aid of' a charity or local project, on whose behalf the appeal is made. But long-term for-profit shops also took possession of the non-European name. The Soho Bazaar was a famous London emporium of the first half of the nineteenth century, which had copied its selling model from a Manchester store called simply The Bazaar. It consisted of units rented out to tenants who were required to conform to extensive regulations, from opening hours to dress code; in return, the building was cleaned and security provided. In the terms of later time, it was a covered shopping centre; it had precedents in the seventeenth-century New Exchange, and the Royal Exchange, which goes back to the late 1500s and was opened by Elizabeth I herself. A detailed document, published in the *Manchester Guardian* when The Bazaar opened in new premises in 1821, laid out terms and conditions for those seeking to rent 'counters' within it, which could be flexibly done for short or longer periods, as little as a day at a time. Arrangements for the separation of the sexes were specified, with one floor to be let to 'males' and the other, above it, to 'females'; it is notable too that a primary objective of the new establishment was 'to give employment to industrious females'. Another striking stipulation, ahead of its time, was the banning of customer discounts, together with the requirement that: 'the Prices shall be marked on all the Goods'.[8]

These pre-Victorian commercial bazaars, in addition to having some features of twentieth-century purpose-built shopping centres, also anticipated the later nineteenth-century retailing invention of the department store; the Manchester Bazaar itself evolved into the business that became the department store Kendal Milne. That is, they sold all sorts of things, all in one building; customers could walk round a large indoor space of displays without any obligation to buy; prices were marked and fixed (no bargaining allowed), and the interior as a whole was a spectacle. As with the arcades developed in many cities at the same time, their design was innovative, often with skylights and a galleried upper floor with shops round the sides.[9]

In their architectural ambition the bazaars were also related to the many new municipal market halls for food constructed in the first half of the nineteenth century; those built in later decades often incorporated space for shops or stalls selling haberdashery, hosiery, trinkets, ribbons, and other such staples of the bazaars.[10] One small-scale outlet in such a place was the Penny Bazaar that opened in Leeds' Kirkgate covered market in 1884. It was run by a man called Michael Marks, who later joined up with a Mr Spencer; for most of the twentieth century, Marks and Spencer stores and own-brand goods ('St Michael', no less, until 2000) were emblematic of a dependable quality in clothing, and later in food and furnishings as well.

The charity bazaar's definingly brief duration, a few days at most, links it to a related shopping phenomenon, one equally old but which has recently been given the bright new name of the *pop-up*. The *pop-up* came to stay in the first decade of the twenty-first century, as a term for short-term shop rentals, which were then becoming frequent in shopping centres with empty retail units. From the point of view of a landlord, better six weeks than no tenant at all. From the point of view of a seller, no long-term risk and a lower rent.

The specific type of enterprise represented by the pop-up—sharp new shop, short term—goes back at least to the eighteenth century. The diary of the Sussex village shopkeeper Thomas Turner includes a disruptive moment when a salesman passes through the village and sets up temporary shop in the pub, called Jones's:

> At home all day and thank God pretty busy. This day came to Jones's a man with a cartload of millinery, mercery, linen drapery, silver etc. to

keep a sale for two days. This must undoubtedly be some hurt to trade, for the novelty of the thing (and novelty is surely the predominant passion of the English nation, and of Sussex in particular) will catch the ignorant multitude and perhaps not them only, but people of sense who are not judges of goods and trade, as indeed very few people are, but however as it is it must pass.[11]

This is the one-off flash sale, confined to a specific brief period at a specific address—not the repeated or weekly competition of the pedlar or market. But as with both of these, the short-term seller is able to undercut the prices of fixed shops. Overheads are negligible, and often there is the claim to have access to unusual merchandise or some alleged exceptional source like the cargo of a shipwreck. Understandably, Turner is not pleased. But he is not distraught either ('it must pass'), perhaps because he has just had a good trading day in the shop, 'pretty busy'. The unwelcome and unusual event also prompts some rare reflections on the motivations of consumers and their national, regional, and class variations, as everyone, wherever their place geographically or socially, turns out to be liable to misjudgement. That error is (negatively) down to ignorance, but it is initially stated as the active attraction—a 'passion', no less—to 'novelty': and not only a passion but 'the predominant passion' across the county. Novelty, in the century after Turner, would come to be widely understood as a universal stimulating force in a world driven ever more by consumption. However woodenly delivered, these are far-reaching speculations—both ahead of their time and moving way beyond a small village shop—even one placed in those unique conditions of 'Sussex in particular'.

Typically, a pop-up shop sells products that have a natural sell-now season, such as themed wall calendars in November and December. Short-term Christmas shops of this sort go back to the end of the nineteenth century. In the fictional *Diary of a Nobody*, Mr Pooter pays a visit to 'Smirksons', the draper's, in the Strand, who this year have turned out everything in the shop and devoted the whole place to the sale of Christmas cards':[12]

Shop crowded with people, who seemed to take up the cards rather roughly, and after a hurried glance at them, throw them down again. I remarked to one of the young persons serving that carelessness appeared to be a disease with some purchasers.[13]

True to the slapstick style of the book, the pompous observation of course precedes Pooter tipping over a pile of cards himself, after which he has a new source of annoyance in feeling duty-bound to buy more than he wants to.

Part of the essence of the pop-up is its responsiveness to the here and now of a trading opportunity: the unlicensed street seller who is always ready to pack up the goods and be gone. But for all the appearance, this is not true of the market stallholder, whose setting up and dismantling of makeshift premises is regular and regulated. The time limit, whether a real one or set for the purpose, is an age-old promotional strategy: Must End Today! For an online retailer, who can never shut up the shop at the end of the day, it is the only way of creating a sense of pressure. In current polemics, it is real-space shops that are represented as immutably solid, the bricks and mortar as opposed to the light mobility of the internet. But in reality it is the online outlets that are rigidly there all the time and the built shops that come and go, like daytime pop-ups.

Notes

1. See Peter Gurney, '"The Sublime of the Bazaar": A Moment in the Making of a Consumer Culture in Mid-Nineteenth Century England', *Journal of Social History* 40: 2 (Winter 2006), 385–405.
2. Quoted in Gurney, '"The Sublime of the Bazaar"', 388.
3. Eliot, *The Mill on the Floss*, 441.
4. Virginia Woolf, *Mrs Dalloway* (1925), ed. David Bradshaw (Oxford: Oxford University Press, 2000), 4.
5. Winifred Holtby, *The Crowded Street* (1924; London: Persephone, 2008), 121.
6. A point made also by F.K. Prochaska, 'Charity Bazaars in Nineteenth-Century England', *Journal of British History* 16:2 (1977), 62.
7. *Northampton Daily Echo*, Wednesday 11 October 1916, 5.

8. The document is reproduced in Alison Adburgham, *Shops and Shopping 1800–1914* (1964; 2nd edn London: George Allen and Unwin, 1981), 19–21.

9. See Kathryn A. Morrison, *English Shops and Shopping* (New Haven: Yale University Press), 92–108.

10. See Ian Mitchell, 'Innovation in Non-Food Retailing in the Early Nineteenth Century: The Curious Case of the Bazaar', *Business History* 52:6 (October 2010), 886.

11. *The Diary of Thomas Turner 1754–1765*, ed. David Vaisey (Oxford: Oxford University Press, 1984), 302–3, entry for Thursday 6 September 1764.

12. George and Weedon Grossmith, *The Diary of a Nobody* (1892), ed. Kate Flint (Oxford: Oxford University Press, 1995), 76; this section was first published (in *Punch*) in 1889.

13. Grossmith, *Diary of a Nobody*, 76–7.

17

Pedlars

A moving shop, in the times when there were no shops, the pedlar is an ancient figure of folk tale—as old as the hills. He was the source of the few far-fetched things that reached people, beyond what was traded with neighbours or bought at the market: cloths and yarns, spices or rings or ribbons. In later centuries the pedlar would also be carrying the printed word, in the form of pamphlets and almanacs.

As with other everyday practices in pre-modern centuries, there are few formal records of pedlars' movements or of just what they carried. But in stories and poems their presence continues long past the time when they were the first shop of surprises, both their visits and their goods unusual and unexpected. The pedlar had none of the market's regularity of times and products, but his seasonal journeyings were a vital element of rural culture. Pedlars also continued to play a part in the centuries when shops had almost completely taken over their earlier function of supplying the rarer goods of regular purchase—most of all in remoter areas, where dwellings were scattered and local shops not within easy walking distance. For William Wordsworth, writing at the turn of the nineteenth century, the pedlar represents a romantic figure of solitary independence, going his own way at a distance from the demands of modern urban life.

In the absence of more prosaic documentation for the long ages when pedlars were always moving through the landscape, Autolycus in *The Winter's Tale* arrives like a special gift from out of the pack. A Shakespearean pedlar: priceless! And all the more as the play provides, at intervals, detailed suggestion of a pedlar's likely merchandise and technique of selling. To begin with, his supplies are sought out by one character for a special occasion:

> Let me see; what am I to buy for our sheep-shearing feast? Three pound of sugar, five pound of currants, rice—what will this sister of mine do with rice?...I must have saffron to colour the warden pies; mace; dates—none, that's out of my note; nutmegs, seven; a race or two of ginger, but that I may beg; four pound of prunes, and as many of raisins o'th'sun.[1]

With its specification of weights and quantities this is as detailed as a recipe. Its uncommon dry goods include many that only a pedlar would supply, likely to have been carried over hundreds and thousands of miles from their places of origin and intermediate trading.

Exotic foodstuffs would not be all that was in the pack. Later, Autolycus provides something like an inventory of his standard stock. Worthless as the contents may be, the pack needs filling up:

> I have sold all my trumpery: not a counterfeit stone, not a ribbon, glass, pomander, brooch, table-book, ballad, knife, tape, glove, shoe tie, bracelet, horn-ring, to keep my pack from fasting. They throng who should buy first, as if my trinkets had been hallowed and brought a benediction to the buyer.[2]

With his 'throng' and his 'buy first', Autolycus could be summarizing future centuries of marketing psychology in a few choice words. Through objects claimed as unique, he creates a collective desire for personal satisfaction.

This is not the only advertisement for Autolycus' wares. While he may be a supplier of general merchandise, it seems he is superior to any specialist in apparel and its accessories: 'He hath songs for man or woman, of all sizes: no milliner can so fit his customers with gloves.'[3] And there is more advertising of the advertising: 'He hath ribbons of all the colours i' th' rainbow...inkles, caddisses, cambrics, lawns. Why, he sings 'em o'er as they were gods or goddesses, you would think a smock were a she-angel, he so chants to the sleevehand and the work about the square on't.'[4]

Then comes Autolycus' lyrical-promotional take on his offers, including the gloves:

> Lawn as white as driven snow;
> Cypress black as e'r was crow;
> Gloves as sweet as damask roses;
> Masks for faces, and for noses;
> Bugle-bracelet, necklace-amber;
> Perfume for a lady's chamber;
> Golden coifs and stomachers
> For my lads to give their dears;
> Pins and poking-sticks of steel;
> What maids lack from head to heel
> Come buy of me, come, come come buy, come buy;
> Buy, lads, or else your lasses cry: Come buy.[5]

Autolycus presents himself as something like a complete outfitter, creating demand for his goods as 'What maids lack from head to heel'. There is the suggestion of a higher life—'a lady's chamber'—to which you might imagine yourself introduced if you will only buy, come buy. There is some particularity about the actual things, but also an indication of their use as lovers' gifts: buy from me, give to her. The pins and poking-sticks, as well as being alliterative, are more practical. The Clown, to whom all these offers are being rehearsed, knows that he is being had but is persuaded because of his own romantic situation: 'If I were not in love with Mopsa, thou shouldst take no money of me; but being enthralled as I am, it will also be the bondage of certain ribbons and gloves.'[6]

Autolycus also advertises the ballads he has in stock, including his current hit ('There's scarce a maid westward but she sings it; 'tis in request, I can tell you'),[7] and departs with another jingle:

> Will you buy any tape,
> Or lace for your cape,

My dainty duck, my dear-a?
Any silk, any thread,
Any toys for your head,
Of the new'st and fin'st, 'fin'st wear'a?
Come to the pedlar:
Money's a meddler
That doth utter all men's ware-a.[8]

The claim is not just about quality—'fin'st'—or, implicitly, the scarcity and specialness of these pretty materials; but also that they are 'the new'st'. New is the selling point that underpins the very idea of fashion, at this stage rare and slow, and especially for the ordinary people being addressed here. The word also implies, quite simply, that the toys and threads and the rest are fresh: not used before.

Wordsworth's poem 'The Pedlar', which ultimately became part of the long work called *The Excursion*, depicts a character who is quite different from Autolycus. This is a pedlar who, far from being a trickster or cheeky salesman, is one of Wordsworth's authentic solitary characters, born and bred into an original wonder and love of the natural world, and with an abundance of human sympathy. With his 'freight of winter raiment' he is also like those who really travelled at the time in rural areas of the north-west, distributing textiles and garments.[9] This (nameless) man tells the long sad story of those who used to live in a now empty cottage where he is resting, and where the poet encounters him. The pedlar's own story is, in turn, recounted, going back to how he came to choose what is later described, as if for a priest or poet, his 'calling'—despite it being, Wordsworth says, a job that is now both denigrated and on the wane:

An irksome drudgery seems it to plod on,
Through hot and dusty ways, or pelting storm,
A vagrant Merchant under a heavy load
Bent as he moves, and needing frequent rest;
Yet do such travellers find their own delight;
And their hard service, deemed debasing now,

> Gained merited respect in simpler times;
> When squire, and priest, and they who round them dwelt
> In rustic sequestration—all dependent
> Upon the PEDLAR's toil—supplied their wants,
> Or pleased their fancies, with the wares he brought.[10]

A pedlar is the all-round provider, for the whole village, covering both what people need and their 'fancies'. The job is one that can definitely appeal:

> Not ignorant was the Youth that still no few
> Of his adventurous countrymen were led
> By perseverance in this track of life
> To competence and ease:—to him it offered
> Attractions manifold;—and this he chose.[11]

The poem's lines are themselves like a quiet advertisement for the pedlar's walk of life, as it 'offered / Attractions manifold'. Aged now, he has given up his work after saving enough for retirement:

> This active course
> He followed till provision for his wants
> Had been obtained; — the Wanderer then resolved
> To pass the remnant of his days, untasked
> With needless services, from hardship free.
> His calling laid aside, he lived at ease.[12]

So while the 'simpler' world is no more, in which the common life of a 'vagrant Merchant' was not 'debased', still things have worked out just as planned for this one. Especially in the setting of the ruined cottage and its story of slow diminishment and loss, the story is positive almost in spite of itself. The pedlar has lived the life of his choice.

George Eliot's mid-nineteenth-century novel *The Mill on the Floss* (1860) features an amiable 'packman' called Bob Jakin whose sales talk, and talk about his sales talk, she shows off in her own pastiche.

On one occasion, Bob persuades a lady to buy from him through an extended play of deference: of course she won't be wanting his damaged but quality fabrics, because then she would be depriving 'them poor women up i' the villages there, as niver stir a hundred yards from home ... it 'ud be a pity for anybody to buy up their bargains'.[13] The to and fro of this sit-com scene is carried on for several pages. But the opening pitch, apart from being based on flattery of the addressee, makes a different kind of appeal:

> It's a thousand pities such a lady as you shouldn't deal with a packman, i'stead of goin' into these new-fangled shops, where there's half a dozen fine gents wi' their chins propped up wi' a stiff stock, a-looking like bottles wi' ornamental stoppers, an' all got to get their dinner out o' a bit o' calico; it stan's to reason you must pay three times the price you pay a packman, as is the nat'ral way o' getting' goods—an' pays no rent, an' isn't forced to throttle himself till the lies are squeezed out on' him, whether he will or not. But lors, mum, you know what it is better nor I do; you can see through them shopmen, I'll be bound.[14]

Economics textbooks of the mid-twentieth century would say just the same about the 'waste' of excessive shops, fancy and otherwise, and the same argument played out endlessly over the virtues of the bottom-end, no-frills presentation of the discount store as opposed to (in later language) the shopping 'experience' of the one that is lavishly provided with 'fine gents' or any other accessory. But as Bob's speech demonstrates to good effect (his target of course succumbs in the end), either version can be effective as a mode of advertising. First version: you are getting a bargain (without any additional cost due to needless expenditure on extras). Second version: you have the pleasure and privilege of enjoying special services and décor.

The lonely wife up in the villages was not a rhetorical invention. In a study of Middlesbrough people in 1907, the limitations of non-work life for both men and women are described. There is a form of confinement that can be psychological as well as physical:

One woman, Mrs Z., whose husband had one of the most arduous 'jobs' at the works, was a typical and extreme case of want of interest in her surroundings, and, indeed, in her existence. She was born in the next street to the mews she now lives in, and this was almost all she had seen of the town. From year's end to year's end she hardly ever went out of the house, excepting to shop as near her home as convenient. It did not occur to her to go out for air and exercise; she had never been down to the river, or across the ferry to see where her husband worked.[15]

It is only the need to get food from a shop that draws the woman out of the house at all; yet even in this extreme situation, the practical word 'convenient' is at the ready: it is the one connection to normality. The vignette is all the more striking because the isolation and depression of staying at home all day is almost always associated with the lives of more wealthy women: women with nothing to do—or nothing to do but shop for pleasure, rather than, as here; for a household's daily needs.

Eliot's Bob is a modern packman whose pitch is adapted to the shops of his times, but he also plays to the traditional view of the pedlar as trickster—not only embodying it (he distorts cloth measurements by bending a thumb) but also by using the prejudice as a way to flatter the present customer as clearly being no fool. *The Mill on the Floss* refers as well to more gruesome pedlar traditions. Mrs Glegg makes out that she thinks Bob may be violent—'it isn't many 'sizes ago since a packman murdered a young woman in a lone place, and stole her thimble, and threw her body into a ditch.'[16]

As shops developed, and more especially after they were required to pay national or local taxes and rates, shopkeepers' objections to pedlars were commonplace. What could be the justification for them plying their unsolicited trade, when shops had been 'open'd in *every* corner, and in the most *remote parts*' of the country?[17] Licensing requirements for pedlars came in during the seventeenth century, and towards the end of the eighteenth century there was a proposal to make the practice outright illegal—in supposed fairness to shopkeepers, always potentially undermined by their cheaper prices, and now having to pay a newly introduced Shop Tax. But there was a strong defence to be made for pedlars' essential role in the distribution to outlying areas of manufactured fabrics—linen, cotton, and wool—from the mills of Glasgow and northern England. This was a large part of the business of those who belonged to organized networks: Manchester men, Shrewsbury men, and Scotch drapers, among others. A petition from Whitehaven in Cumbria put this case:

> The Mode of Sale which is wholly confined to small Villages and Places remote from general Markets tends very greatly to diffuse the Manufactures of the Kingdom in general and is a source of great convenience to those Inhabitants who live at a Distance from the principal Towns, great Quantities of goods of almost every Description being vended in detail, which the remote Inhabitants could not find leisure to seek and when Necessity might compel him to go from Home, the Expence of his Journey would frequently be as great as the Object of his Purchase.[18]

It is a concise argument for the usefulness of the pedlar, bringing the goods that the buyer does not have the time or money to travel for. The pedlar provides the original 'convenience' store: here is the word already.

In the past few decades it has been possible to reconstruct some complex trade networks for parts of Europe during the later centuries of this primary form of rural trading. Long established merchant families based in the Alps or southern Spain sent out their representatives, among them trainee family members, to distant parts of France and elsewhere. The summer months were for travelling, the same routes every year, and in the winter the pedlars were back at home. Stock would come from many sources, including the oriental spices and fabrics picked up at the markets and trading stations of Italy and the Middle East.[19]

As a one-on-one vendor who comes to the home of his prospects and woos them with words, as well as with goods, the pedlar has had some unlikely later incarnations. One is the travelling salesman of the first half of the twentieth century, with a particular commodity to

promote on behalf of a company. Vacuum cleaners and encyclopae-
dias were two primary products, with hire purchase an essential part
of the pitch for these expensive items. The encyclopaedia was the
distant descendant of the seventeenth-century almanac, bringing a
special form of printed knowledge into the home. To some extent,
the butchers' and bakers' delivery boys of the nineteenth and twentieth
centuries are also latter-day pedlars—but there are two crucial differences: that they have only come from the local shop, and that they
bring what has already been ordered by the customer. They are not, in
other words, from far away, with goods to be sold with the pedlar's art
of talk and timing.

One other characteristic that marks out the pedlar from every later
mode of selling is that he is slow. He moves about on his own two feet
or at most with the aid of a horse; he is in no hurry, and takes his time
with each call. As such, at the other end of history, he can appear now
as an embodiment of the antithesis of the pace of contemporary
consumer culture, in which fashion is not just new but always a new
new; and in which customers and suppliers alike are always in a hurry
to buy or to order replacements, 'just in time'. The Victorians already
described the changes they saw going on in a language of acceleration.
In *The Mill on the Floss*, the husband of Mrs Glegg (the woman who
eventually succumbs to Tom's packman patter) speaks about the old
days in terms of a different cultural speed: 'The looms went slowish, the
fashions didn't alter quite so fast.'[20] Though the context is different (he
is not concerned about the environment or the working conditions of
the weavers), this succinct statement could not be bettered now as a
call-out of fast fashion. Like the pedlar, we should slow down.

Notes

1. William Shakespeare, *The Winter's Tale*, ed. Ernest Schanzer (London: Penguin, 1986), IV. 3.35ff.
2. Shakespeare, *Winter's Tale*, IV.4.593ff.
3. Shakespeare, *Winter's Tale*, IV.4.193ff.
4. Shakespeare, *Winter's Tale*, IV.4.205ff.

5. Shakespeare, *Winter's Tale*, IV.220ff.

6. Shakespeare, *Winter's Tale*, IV.232ff.

7. Shakespeare, *Winter's Tale*, IV.288f.

8. Shakespeare, *Winter's Tale*, IV.313ff.

9. William Wordsworth, *The Excursion* (1814) in *Poems, Volume II*, ed. John O. Hayden (Harmondsworth: Penguin, 1977), 55 (line 542). The section on the pedlar was first drafted in the late 1890s.

10. Wordsworth, *Excursion*, 49 (lines 322–32).

11. Wordsworth, *Excursion*, 49–50 (lines 333–7).

12. Wordsworth, *Excursion*, 51 (lines 381–5).

13. George Eliot, *The Mill on the Floss* (1860; Harmondsworth: Penguin, 1979), 327.

14. Eliot, *Mill on the Floss*, 323.

15. Lady Bell, *At the Works* (1907; London: Virago, 1985), 234.

16. Eliot, *Mill on the Floss*, 322.

17. Quoted in David Alexander, *Retailing in England during the Industrial Revolution* (London: Athlone Press, 1969), 66; the document has no date.

18. Quoted in Dorothy Davis, *A History of Shopping* (London: Routledge & Kegan Paul Ltd., 1966), 246. See also Margaret Spufford, *The Great Reclothing of Rural England: Petty Chapmen and their Wares in the Seventeenth Century* (London: Hambledon Press, 1984).

19. See Laurence Fontaine, *Histoire du colportage en Europe XVe–XLXe siècle* (Paris: Albin Michel, 1993).

20. Eliot, *The Mill on the Floss*, 405.

18

Saturday Nights and Sundays

In the Middle Ages, going to church and going to the market were the two established weekly events of rural life. As time went on, there would commonly be a church clock to show or sound the hour. Church and market had fixed and declared hours of starting—and in the case of the market, fixed hours of ending as well.[1]

In later times, when shops rather than markets had become the primary places for buying and selling, and when working life for most people was industrial, not agricultural, the days and times of opening and closing were specified in all but the smallest establishments. Over the centuries these weekly times have off and on been the subject of argument and negotiation, often acrimoniously. In the nineteenth century, trading hours, like factory hours, became an explicit question of workers' rights, though the small size and family basis of most retail enterprises made it hard to enforce regulations, especially when—as very commonly—the shop was also the shopkeeper's home and the workers were members of the family, or apprentices who lodged there. Another issue was the dispersal of employees because of the physical separation of shop units, so that unionization was difficult to organize, as well as going against the grain of the small business ethos. Most of the many debates in different periods about the state or future of the shop-hours schedule point out that the changes proposed would benefit either the customer (by extending the hours) or the employee (by reducing them)—but it is never both: no benefit for one without harm for the other. In the succinct but weary words of one government report from the mid-twentieth century, 'the law tries over much to combine the incompatibles of compelling shops to shut and allowing people to buy.'[2]

With a larger shop the conflict of interests between customers and employees does not arise in the same way, since additional hours can be distributed across different shifts. W.G. McClelland, then managing director of the Tyneside-based Laws supermarket chain, and a thoughtful commentator on retailing in the early 1960s, made a pair of radical suggestions, intended to be beneficial to workers and customers alike. At the time most regular food shops, including supermarkets, closed at 5 or 5.30 p.m. on weekdays and Saturdays, except for the legally required early closing day, when they were shut in the afternoon; apart from newsagents and a few other exceptions, no shops at all were open on Sundays. Why not look forward, McClelland proposed, 'to the era of the seven-day trading week coupled with the four-day working week'?[3]

An adjacent problem that regularly occupied economists was the anomalous status of shops. Were they, like factories, to be seen as productive units? And if they were, how could their productivity be measured when there were so many unavoidably variable conditions? Which element of what they did was the output, in any case? You could control the flow of the physical goods coming in (the stock) but you could not control their flow in the other direction (when they left the shop after being sold). In particular, there was no way to get your customers through the door and out again at a regular rate during the hours of opening, and that meant that for much of the time the staff might be idle, whereas at other times there might not be enough of them to keep up with demand (long queues at the counter). In the Preface to a book of 1932 a novel suggestion was made in passing by F.J. Marquis, who was chair of the Lewis's group of department stores (not the same as John Lewis). Marquis emphasizes the significance of women as the chief purchasers, doing the shopping each day. The cost-effectiveness of retailing, he says, depends on their daily shopping habits, not in the sense of them being the buyers (which is assumed) but in relation to when in the day they choose to do it. And this is where change could happen:

> If those who could shop in the morning would do so: if the peaks and valleys of shopping could be levelled somewhat, the large army of shop assistants would lead much happier lives, the services the public received would be much more efficient—and the cost of it could be reduced.[4]

The specific agenda here is clear from the next sentence, when Marquis states that 'The intelligent use of spending power would be infinitely more effective than restrictive legislation in bringing down cost': persuading is better than compelling.[5] All the same, the spectre of 'restrictive legislation' is not quite off the table of future shopping prospects. It is significant that women are being co-opted into what is presented as a shared policy of cost-cutting efficiency; the shop-workers are called an 'army', but the customers too are asked to practise some self-discipline. In 1940, by this time Lord Woolton, Marquis went on to be appointed by the Prime Minister, Neville Chamberlain, as the wartime Minister of Food, tasked with overseeing the organization of rationing—which made the equal distribution of supplies a matter of state regulation.

In the later twentieth century, most arguments about shop hours were centred on the issue of Sunday trading: whether or not to permit it, and if so whether it should take place on the same terms (for the same hours and the same range of goods) as for other days of the week. For years this argument went back and forth at intervals, with various government-sponsored reports followed by failed attempts to legislate. Eventually in 1994, after heated campaigning over the previous decade, a Sunday Trading Act licensed six hours of opening for all types of shop on every Sunday of the year except Easter Day. Many had opposed change on the grounds that there was a 'traditional' Sunday in relation to which open shops would represent an incursion. Given the plausibility of this Sunday exceptionalism, it is interesting to note that in the Middle Ages the opposite had been true, with Sunday being not the day when shopping was banned, but the only one when it took place: 'In early times Sunday had been the normal market-day. Everyone was then free from his accustomed labour and at leisure to attend to his weekly shopping.'[6] Thus churchgoing was naturally, not abnormally, combined with making purchases. (There was however some challenge to this practice, with some success, from reformers in the thirteenth century and after.)

In medieval times, the bond between church and commerce was also demonstrated in both the timing and the control of many of the country's annual fairs. Fairs were huge events, lasting for days if not weeks, and almost always linked to church festivals; St Giles at Winchester and St Bartholomew in London, to name two, were world famous. Often the ownership of a fair or market was ecclesiastical, too; the proceeds from the fair of St Giles went to the Bishop of Winchester, and the income from tolls and dues was substantial. Today, the connection between church and large-scale commerce is still of great significance. The Metro Centre at Gateshead on Tyneside was the largest purpose-built shopping centre in the country when it opened in the 1980s (it is still second only to Bluewater, outside London). It was financed by the Church Commissioners (the investments arm of the Church of England). It has its own full-time Church of England chaplain on site.

Sundays were not the primary issue in the initial regulation of shop opening hours. Most employees worked what are now unimaginably long hours—for very low wages, or for none at all, usually, if they were apprentices or members of the family. The Shops Act of 1911 introduced the requirement of that 'early closing day', providing an afternoon off for employees on one day a week. Before that, the full six-day working week was normal, and those days were long. So while it is often assumed that supermarkets' eventual extension of food shopping hours into the evening was unprecedented, once again, the opposite is the case. Before the war, most shops used to stay open until mid-evening on normal days; on Saturdays, depending on the location and the type of shop, this might be as late as midnight or even beyond. Saturday night was the big shopping night at shops and indoor markets, with prices for meat and fish and other perishable goods coming down as the evening drew on (because the food would deteriorate before the next opening on Monday). The historian James Jefferys spoke in the early 1950s of 'the price-cutting and auctioneering frenzies of Saturday night' that went on, right up to the Second World War; in the precise, measured prose of this writer's usual style, *frenzies* stands out as a highly charged word.[7]

Before the direct concerns about Sunday, this Saturday night shopping was itself the subject of anxious debate about hours. In the 1850s there was a modest campaign in Sussex for food shops to close on Saturdays by 9p.m.; that would have been early at the time. The negative concern here was equally religious, with the thought that the late hours affected shopworkers' capacity to get up and go to church on the following morning.[8] On the other side, Saturday night shopping, especially in the markets, was just as much a fixture of weekly social life as the Sunday morning service. As with the interminable twentieth-century debate about Sundays, this one about Saturday nights somehow never seemed to get to the point of closing. Exeter's town council, allegedly, 'debated a proposal to shorten Saturday-night hours for thirty-six years'.[9]

Local and village shops, with owners (and family) living in, were more of a law unto themselves for opening hours—even after there were actual laws that might have regulated them. A South Shields man recalls the shop where he grew up in the 1930s:

> They were open from early morning till late at night. Even when they were shut they were open.... Really it was our store-cupboard, we didn't keep anything at home because you could just pop in there.[10]

Where the shop is a store, in this full, original sense of the word, it can be almost like an extension of the home. It has its separate but accessible space, over the road or round the corner. As in the name of the 1970s BBC sitcom about a shop in a suburb of Doncaster, it is as if *open all hours*: welcoming in a way that the coldly digital 24/7 of more recent years could surely never be.

Notes

1. On the history of public clocks and timekeeping, see Paul Glennie and Nigel Thrift, *Shaping the Day: A History of Timekeeping in England and Wales, 1300–1800* (Oxford: Oxford University Press, 2009).
2. Gowers Committee Report (1947), quoted in *The Shops Acts: Late-Night and Sunday Opening*, Report of the Committee of Inquiry into Proposals to Amend the Shops Acts (London: Her Majesty's Stationery Office, 1984), 3.
3. W.G. McClelland, *Studies in Retailing* (Oxford: Basil Blackwell, 1963), 182.
4. F.J. Marquis, Foreword to Lawrence E. Neal, *Retailing and the Public* (London: George Allen & Unwin Ltd, 1932), p. xi.
5. Marquis, Foreword, *Retailing and the Public*, p. xi.
6. A.L. Poole, *From Domesday Book to Magna Carta 1087–1216* (1951; 2nd edn Oxford: Clarendon Press, 1955), 76.
7. James B. Jefferys, *Retail Trading in Britain 1850–1950* (Cambridge: Cambridge University Press, 1954), 198.
8. See Helena Wojtczak, *Women of Victorian Sussex: Their Status, Occupations, and Dealings with the Law 1830–1870* (Hastings: The Hastings Press, 2003), 66.
9. James Schmeichen and Kenneth Carls, *The British Market Hall: A Social and Architectural History* (New Haven: Yale University Press, 1999), 168.
10. Quoted in Avram Taylor, *Working Class Credit and Community since 1918* (London: Palgrave Macmillan, 2002), 96.

19

Scenes of Shopping

Figure 9. Lingerie department, Marks and Spencer, Middlesbrough, late 1950s or early 1960s
Image courtesy of Marks and Spencers plc

Near the end of William Cowper's *The Task* (1785), embarking on a quiet passage in praise of countryside contemplation, the poem suddenly shifts away from this kind of timeless retreat. We are in the city, and in a shop—or rather, in a series of similar fashion shops. What these represent, for Cowper, is the place not to be; they are where a man would find himself if he made the mistake of passing his time not in philosophical thoughtfulness but in the company of the sort of young lady who always has to be drifting about from one such place to another. These are the lines that describe that fool

> who gives his noon
> To Miss, the Mercer's plague, from shop to shop
> Wand'ring, and litt'ring with unfolded silks
> The polished counter, and approving none,
> Or promising with smiles to call again.[1]

This person is a pain not only for her gentleman companion, tired out by having to accompany her shop-hopping, but also for the man on the other side of the counter. She is 'the Mercer's plague', no less: a special female contagion tormenting the innocent shopkeeper who cannot resist her uncharming charm: 'with smiles', she says she'll be back. She has taken up his time, asking for one roll of fabric after another to be taken down and shown to her. But she hasn't bought a thing. Both men, it is implied, would agree on the serial annoyances of this young woman, with her multiple shops and multiple silks. Time and again, she presents herself as being on the point of purchase, inside a shop and with merchandise ready to buy—but she never settles for any particular item.

We can unroll and replay this scene from many perspectives. First of all, it is a set-piece drama of gender relations. Not just one but two men are made to succumb to the whims of a flighty female who does what she wants with both of them, wasting the time of the man of leisure and the man of business alike. She benefits neither: the shop-keeper makes no money, while the gentleman seemingly has no pleasure in sharing *her* pleasure, her 'wand'ring' movement from one shop to the next and her indirect 'litt'ring' of the counter with everything she has wanted to handle and have a close look at. So the two of them are in the same position, in relation to both her and their lost time—in one case probably valuable time.

But there is no mutual acknowledgement of this. Because at the same time, the two men are also in quite different positions in relation to both the shop and the woman who has entered it. They are on either side of the counter, in two clearly separate classes, with one giving her the service of a specialist trade and the other the chivalrous, socially equal attentions of the *beau*. And just as the roles of each player are allocated according to gender and occupation (or lack of it), so they are specific to the situation inside a shop. The customer, the customer's friend, and the salesman can all, so the poem implies, be given their likely characteristics and parts, with this type of difficult woman determining the playing out of partial, repeated events.

For the young lady is confidently represented as a stock type: 'Miss, the Mercer's plague', whose defining feature it is to act in this maddening fashion, trying everything and buying nothing. As such she is a literary forerunner of a much later and longer cast of typical shopping characters, who feature for instance in textbooks for shop assistants of the twentieth century. These contain colourful synopses of the likely behaviour of this or that sort of woman (it is always a woman) who will present you with her own particular obstacles to the smooth making of a sale. On the one hand, the store assistant is elevated to the role of an expert who knows her or his psychological types, just as she knows about the goods she is selling. And on the other hand, this specialist knowledge of customer profiles is also a way of mitigating the annoyance of having to deal with such people. Converted into representative characters, embodiments of a single type, they are placed at a distance and are halfway to being controlled and kept at a distance. You know what you are dealing with (and what you are dealing with has no surprises, no individual differences). More broadly, the same is true of the shopping scenario itself. In its basic elements—customer, shopkeeper, something to sell or to buy—it is scripted in advance with a number of key roles, a *dramatis personae* with both a set and a likely plot in view (the shop itself, and the purchase, made or thwarted).[2]

Cowper's vignette with its repeat non-buyer and its purposeless but apparently deliberate feminine drift (the girl's 'Wand'ring' habit) may look like a possible hint at the unmarried Miss who refuses to make up her mind, enjoying her power to receive an offer before smiling sweetly and moving on to the next one—swiping left, in eighteenth-century style. But it is placed, in the poem, as one of a series of negative illustrations for men of how not to spend time that would be better devoted to contemplation. The other bad occupations are playing billiards or board games, and going to auctions but never making a bid—the point in common with all of them being the waste of time and the last example closely resembling the practice of the unpurchasing girl shopper.

The problem of the non-buying customer had been raised before. In a number of *The Spectator* published in 1712, a shopkeeper's complaint is voiced in a fictional letter:

> I am, dear Sir, one of the top China-Women about Town; and though I say it, keep as good Things, and receive as fine Company as any o' this End of the Town, let the other be who she will: In short, I am in a fair way to be easy, were it not for a Club of Female Rakes, who, under pretence of taking their innocent Rambles, forsooth, and diverting the Spleen, seldom fail to plague me twice or thrice a Day, to cheapen Tea, or buy a Screen; *what else should they mean?* as they often repeat it. These Rakes are your idle Ladies of Fashion, who having nothing to do, employ themselves in tumbling over my Ware. One of these No-Customers (for by the way they seldom or never buy any thing) calls for a set of Tea-Dishes, another for a Bason, a third for my best Green-Tea; and even to the Punch-Bowl there's scarce a Piece in my Shop but must be displaced, and the whole agreeable Architecture disordered.[3]

The letter is signed by 'Rebecca the Distress'd'. In this all-female shopping world, all the sexual privileges of being a man are suspended: here are Women about Town (one of the 'top' ones, even), who keep their own shops, and here are other women strolling about in a group, on their 'innocent Rambles'. The writer is bitingly sarcastic—'*what else should they mean?*'—in her criticism of her 'No-Customers' who bargain over the price of tea (then don't buy it) and mess up the shop's interior display of china, 'the whole agreeable Architecture disordered'. They behave in this way, she says, because they are 'idle', with 'nothing to do'; they only make more work (and no profit) for the shopkeeper.

For Cowper, the error in the shopping example is that of a male companion sharing in a purposeless female outing. There is no shadow here of a closely related scene, often described in nineteenth-century advice to would-be (male) strollers in the city, to avoid at all costs the company of a woman, who is bound to make you stop and shop (and spend your money at her request).[4] In contrast, Cowper's young lady ought to figure as a delightfully cheap date; but perhaps at this early stage in the evolution of city shopping the absence of a loss of money fails to be noticeable in the face of the palpable loss of time, which is presented as a useful and finite resource even for those who are under no obligation to work.

Cowper's female 'plague' on the mercer also has her modern counterpart. In the passage about the time-taking, non-buying shopper, we might as well be in the early twenty-first century, denouncing the sort of customer who taps the expertise of a specialized high street retailer before making a more or less awkward exit and buying online instead. In The Task, though, there is no suggestion that the Miss is out to save money or seek information; it is not clear that she has any plan of purchasing at all. Instead, her behaviour seems to be tailor-made for the sort of enjoyable looking and not yet quite buying that would be enabled if not invited in the city shops of the decades that followed. Already, in Cowper's own time, there were showroom-style shops for the display of attractive china or glassware.[5] Such commodities were tasteful accessories that aspiring customers came to see for themselves, in a space whose own design and location became part of the products' own prestige. Such developments can now be seen to mark the beginning of a culture of commodity display that would be more and more visible and accessible in the nineteenth century. The shops of a city centre became places to go and see, to spend time and not necessarily money just looking at what was there: admiring, perhaps desiring. *Shopping* became established as part of a lady's life: the word as well as the habit, in the sense of an open-ended activity, without a precise buying purpose.

Cowper's Miss is given short shrift, as a time-consumer for men who might have been otherwise occupied. She is clearly a nuisance, but the few lines given to her do not explore why she might have been acting the way she does. That balance is amply redressed by a work from a few years before *The Task*. Fanny Burney's novel *Evelina* presents a young lady whose initiation by other women into the social habits of modern London includes introducing her to a practice so new that it has to be garlanded with a special description as well as its own special word. Writing to her guardian back home, Evelina says: 'We have been *a shopping*, as Mrs Mirvan calls it, all this morning, to buy silks, caps, gauzes, and so forth.'[6] She expands on what is meant by this; it involves, it would seem, a male performance:

> The shops are really very entertaining, especially the mercers; there seem to be six or seven men belonging to each shop, and every one took care, by bowing and smirking, to be noticed; we were conducted from one to another, and carried from room to room, with so much ceremony, that at first I was almost afraid to follow.[7]

In Evelina's account, as in Cowper's, there is not just one article brought out in answer to the customer's request. But in this case, rather than being the result of a girl's not deciding or not wanting to make a choice at all, the showing of many possible things is all part of the flashy service:

> I thought I should never have chosen a silk, for they produced so many, I knew not which to fix upon; and they recommended them all so strongly, that I fancy they thought I only wanted persuasion to buy every thing they shewed me. And indeed, they took so much trouble, that I was almost ashamed I could not.[8]

'I fancy they thought': not only is Evelina reporting on a new experience for herself, as a woman *a shopping*; she is also putting herself in the place of the men in the shops and thus adding to their persuasive performance her own imagining of what they think she, the soon to be buyer, is thinking. Her 'almost ashamed' and not settling for the entire stock is Burney's cue for us to see Evelina's reading of these men as naively echoing their own design as salesmen: we know (so Burney allows us to think) that they are only too pleased for this first-time shopper to feel there might be something wrong in not buying enough, let alone in not buying at all. And there is also a personal element. Even though this is clearly recognized, by Evelina herself, as an elaborately orchestrated scene, complete with its stage moves as she is guided from one part of the shop to another, she also perceives the assistants as likely to suffer real disappointment if she doesn't do what she thinks they think she would do with just that little extra push of completing 'persuasion': that is why she is 'almost ashamed', with a warmth of feeling that echoes what she takes to be theirs.

For a first shopping expedition, so early in Evelina's urban experi-ence as well as in the history of modern shopping, Evelina is already up to her ears and eyes in all the interpretative intricacies of shopping psychology, as the passage goes to and fro between different under-standings of what is going on, both in the shop and in the minds of the buying and selling characters. And it is not over yet!

> At the milliners, the ladies we met were so much dressed, that I should rather have imagined they were making visits than purchases. But what most diverted me was, that we were more frequently served by men than by women; and such men! So finical, so affected! They seemed to understand every part of a woman's dress better than we do ourselves; and they recommended caps and ribbands with an air of so much importance, that I wished to ask them how long they had left off wearing them![9]

Being served by men is not different from what happened before, in the mercer's, where there were six or seven of them; for some reason it seems that the phenomenon is more to be noted as such in relation to the milliner's—selling not just finished hats, but all the accessories and variations implied by the 'caps and ribbands' which the men are said to be so familiar with. All the way to the 1970s BBC sitcom *Are You Being Served?*, about a provincial department store, this may well be the first in a long tradition, in more than one medium, of representations of the camp male shop assistant: obsequious, emphatic—'so much importance'!—and fond of female fashion. And it is via that parade on the men's part of such an intimate familiarity with femininity that Evelina is led to situate herself as part of a community of actual women, 'we...ourselves'.

With the 'so much dressed' ladies at the beginning, the paragraph also indicates something about the subtle shift that is taking place in the invention of this new thing called shopping. The practice is seen as both excessive—'so much'—and ritually social, like making a formal visit. This is the sort of occasion for which dressing up is clearly required; as opposed to buying things, even pretty feminine things, which is not—or has not been till now—regarded in the same way, Evelina implies. But despite all the fussing and frippery, there is also a point to be made—in a firm, single-sentence paragraph of its own—about a quite different feature of this kind of shop: 'The dispatch with which they work in these great shops is amazing, for they have promised me a compleat suit of linen against the evening.'[10] This is the first time there has been a direct mention of the size of the establishments, previously suggested only in the proliferation of their front-of-house personnel. But here the large scale implies not excess, but a new kind of efficiency: they can make her a whole customized outfit by the end of the day, in time for tonight's event. In its own way it is the first fast fashion.

Evelina ends the account of her remarkable morning by describing a further new experience: 'I have just had my hair dressed. You can't think how oddly my head feels...' Though this work is also, as with *shopping*, an occasion for noting a new word—'frizled they call it'—there is no mention of the man, or woman, who does it, or where the transformation happens.[11] Whereas the buying of fashionable clothing would come to lose the prestige of a personal service bestowed or inflicted on the well-to-do young lady, *hairdressing*—compacted into one word—would expand to become every woman's regular special occasion, a standard amenity on side streets as well as in city centres—and many women's adaptable lifelong job. In the late 1950s, the town planner Wilfred Burns referred to the tendency of housewives who had been hairdressers before marriage to open up a part-time business in a bedroom, with service 'provided outside normal working hours when it is most appreciated by a large number of working women'.[12] In Britain, the hairdressing salon was up there in numbers with the equally ubiquitous newsagent's and sweet shop in the mid-twentieth-century heyday of local shops and shopping. In terms of daft punning names, an English speciality, the hairdresser is almost the equal of the fish and chip shop, the original takeaway fast food outlet: A Cut Above meets The Codfather. Hairdressing salons and barbers are also among the few types of business whose presence on shopping streets has not declined in the twenty-first century. You can't get a haircut online.

By the time of Jane Austen's novels, a few decades after Burney's, ladies' shopping for new fashions is part of the fabric of middle-class life. Along with their mother, the Bennet sisters in *Pride and Prejudice* (1813) enjoy their London aunt's descriptions of the new season's latest styles, and when one of them visits her, the round of metropolitan entertainments includes not only an evening at the theatre but also some daytime 'bustle and shopping': the word has by now become a regular noun.[13] But this is only a more glamorous version of what happens at home all the time, with the fun-seeking youngest girls, Lydia and Kitty, transfixed by the latest accessories in the windows of the milliner's in the small town near where they live. For them, these are natural objects of feminine desire, just like the young men in uniform who saunter up and down the same street—and they can walk into town to gaze at them whenever they want.

In Austen's *Emma* (1816) a comparable establishment is shown as a focal point for another such provincial place. It is talked up by the visiting Frank Churchill, who wants to impress Emma Woodhouse with his local knowledge. He describes the shop, with mock exaggeration (and also as a quick change of subject from Emma's grilling), as an essential part of local life—every day and for everyone:

> At this moment they were approaching Ford's, and he hastily exclaimed, 'Ha! this must be the very shop that every body attends every day of their lives, as my father informs me. He comes to Highbury himself, he says, six days out of the seven, and has always business at Ford's.'[14]

Not only does Frank's father supposedly have something to buy at Ford's all the time, but the claim has been made by a man to a man (even if it is now being reported, with possible ulterior intent, to please a lady). And now Frank himself proposes to follow in his father's regular footsteps:

> If it be not inconvenient to you, pray let us go in, that I may prove myself to belong to the place, to be a true citizen of Highbury. I must buy something at Ford's. It will be taking out my freedom.—I dare say they sell gloves.[15]

Local initiation, at least in jest, is making a purchase, at Ford's—and the choice of a specific 'something' to get is subordinate to this larger intention. At any rate, Emma warmly responds to both sides of Frank's declarations: 'Oh! Yes, gloves and everything. I do admire your patriotism.'[16]

> They went in; and while the sleek, well-tied parcels of 'Men's Beaver' and 'York Tan' were bringing down and displaying on the counter, he said—'But I beg your pardon, Miss Woodhouse, you were speaking to me, you were saying something at the very moment of this burst of my *amor patriae*.'[17]

There is no direct mention of the person performing the actions of bringing down and displaying, even though the naming of two of the sample styles of men's gloves could not be more precise. The narrator is specific about commodity specifications, and is also attentive to good-looking, effective packaging ('sleek, well-tied parcels') as part of the service. Frank and Emma, though, continue to talk for the length of a page before the storyline momentarily returns to the setting, and then only in an introductory clause, 'When the gloves were brought and they had quitted the shop again'. The transaction is passed over without details of what kind of gloves, or the moment of choosing, as if now it is merely a background to the main stream of a conversation about something else.[18]

In keeping with Frank's father's alleged pronouncement of the shop's importance, this is not the first time that Ford's features in *Emma*. On its initial appearance, in fact, it is given a plug which sounds like a formal equivalent of what Mr Churchill said to his son: 'Ford's was the principal woollen-draper, linen-draper, and haberdasher's shop united; the shop first in size and fashion in the place.'[19] This concise tour-guide aside comes in the middle of a long paragraph in which Harriet Smith is ramblingly recounting how she got caught in the rain, and entered the shop for shelter. The narrator puts in the sudden promotion without any diminishing distance: it comes over like paid-for content surrounded by fairly banal local news. Inside the shop, though, an emotional drama ensues, as Harriet finds herself sharing space with her just-rejected suitor and his nice sister, and there is the problem for all concerned of how they should act and react. As with Frank Churchill's glove-buying moment, the shop scene's narrative interest is not about any actual or potential purchase (although the Martins appear to have made one); here Ford's becomes, in effect, just like any enclosed space, public or private, in which people negotiate an embarrassing meeting by chance. Anxious words and movements are painstakingly charted— 'I found he was coming towards me too—slowly you know, and as if he did not quite know what to do'—until, the rain having stopped, Harriet finally gets herself out of the door.[20] There is no suggestion, whether from the (again, unmentioned) proprietor or assistant, or from the narrator, or even from the guilty Harriet herself, that popping in to get out of the wet, and not buying a thing, is something that should not be done. The shop has its non-commercial uses.

Yet another scene at Ford's does involve, this time, a definite plan of purchase—'Harriet had business at Ford's'—but one that then turns out to be painfully protracted, as she fails to make up her mind.[21] Harriet's delay is open-ended, but Austen is specific about its twofold cause, from both a multiplicity of desirable possibilities and the persuasive force of any remark: 'Harriet, tempted by everything and swayed by half a word, was always very long at a purchase; and while she was still hanging over muslins and changing her mind, Emma went to the door for amusement.—'[22] After a while, along comes Frank Churchill in the company of his stepmother, Mrs Weston, this time presenting himself not as a natural patron of Ford's, but as a likely encumbrance: 'My aunt always sends me off when she is shopping.'[23] After her exchange with him, Emma has reason to hurry Harriet along, and goes over to 'the interesting counter—trying, with all the force of her own mind, to convince her that if she wanted plain muslin it was of no use to look at figured; and that a blue ribbon, be it ever so beautiful, would still never match her yellow pattern.' The deal is finally clinched—'At last it was all settled'—by the persuasive 'force' of the friend rather than by 'Mrs. Ford', who does this time appear by name in the subsequent discussion, recorded in all its dithering detail, about whether or not the purchase should be put into two parcels for two destinations. This is an issue to do with where it will be needed by Harriet, who moves between two places, and also, as pointed out by Emma, to do with the limits of customer service: 'It is not worth while, Harriet, to give Mrs. Ford the trouble of two parcels.' To which, after Harriet's agreement, deferential to both, the response from 'the obliging Mrs. Ford' is: 'No trouble in the world, ma'am.'[24]

Emma's indefinite stationing of herself at the door of the shop puts her in an unlikely position, more like an unoccupied shopkeeper than what she presently is, a regular customer waiting for someone else to make a purchase. A full picture, minute by minute, is given of the just about urban scene she can see:

Much could not be hoped from the traffic of even the busiest part of Highbury;—Mr. Perry walking hastily by, Mr. William Cox letting himself in at the office door, Mrs. Cole's carriage horses returning from exercise, or a stray letter-boy on an obstinate mule, were the liveliest objects she could presume to expect; and when her eyes fell only on the butcher with his tray, a tidy old woman travelling homewards from shop with her full basket, two curs quarreling over a dirty bone, and a string of dawdling children round the baker's little bow-window eyeing the gingerbread, she knew she had no reason to complain, and was amused enough; quite enough still to stand at the door.[25]

The 'traffic' includes a number of people, a generational cross-section of a small community, from the children to the old lady. They are mostly engaged in commercial or shopping errands of one sort or another—beginning with the dogs and the bone. 'Mr. William Cox' has an office he lets himself in to, Mr Perry is just in a walking hurry of unspecified aim, but everyone else's movement or attitude has something to do with food buying. The old lady and the butcher are both carrying out the final stage of completed purchases that need to be conveyed from shop to home, while the children, not going anywhere, are collectively captivated by the sweet things to be seen in the baker's window. For Emma, even though 'Much could not be hoped' from it, this everyday spectacle is *enough* (twice said) to keep her where she is: it amuses her. It is enough, because it is various, each separate actor or group singled out with their particular activity as buyer, seller, or would-be consumer: the children 'eyeing' the cakes that are there but not theirs, tantalizingly visible but not accessible.

With Emma, there is nothing significant—nothing that changes the story—in what she witnesses of local shop life. She just looks, and takes pleasure in the looking. Like her own creator, Emma enjoys observing the ordinary ways in which life goes on in a little place; and at this particular moment in her novel what she takes in is the simple street scene of the shops and a typical morning's activities that they elicit. Butcher, baker, and buyers, present and future: all the small-town shopping world passes before Emma's eyes as she waits in the draper's for Harriet to sort out her ribbons.

But Emma's perspective, viewed with a sense of the longer implications of what she sees, can also be critical. In its small way, Ford's of Highbury is a local beacon offering services more and less commercial of many kinds. It is where the customer, even a fairly insignificant customer like Harriet Smith, gets to stop off in a shower of rain, to have what she's bought packaged up and delivered, to her particular requirements—and to hesitate about whether or what to buy, for minutes on end. Among possible classifications of customer stalling, she stands in a different place from Cowper's young lady who leaves (again and again) with a charming smile, buying nothing. Harriet hates her own hesitation and is also chastised for it by her superior female companion.

In *Emma*, the shop itself is half personified as a focus of local affections and identifications. Ford's is a semi-public space in which the customer is given all kinds of personal attention and practical assistance, in addition to the basic buying of this or that article. It is solidly anchored on the main street; it stands for much more than the 'bricks and mortar' that have become the dismissive phrase for shops that exist in a place that is not the internet. In later times, the corporate tracking of 'customer loyalty' would take away the lightness of Frank Churchill's little joke. And so would the patronizing—not patriotic— attitude to the 'small man' (or woman) of the standard high street shop, half indicated, perhaps, in the virtual absence of Mrs Ford or any other shop personnel from the scenes in *Emma*. He—or she—plays a vital social role.

Notes

1. William Cowper, *The Task* (1785), in *Cowper: Verse and Letters*, ed. Brian Spiller (London: Rupert Hart-Davis, 1968), 522.
2. See for instance Rose Buckner, *Design for Selling for Bakers and Confectioners* (London: National Association of Master Bakers, Confectioners and Caterers, 1959), 68–81; Ruth Leigh, *The Human Side of Retail Selling* (New York:

D. Appleton and Company, 1923), 110–28; S.A. Williams, *Teach Yourself Salesmanship* (London: The English Universities Press Ltd., 1944), 38–47.

3. *The Spectator*, ed. Gregory Smith (London: J.M. Dent, 1906), vol. III No. 336 (Wednesday March 26, 1712), 62. The author of the piece is Richard Steele.

4. On this warning against female company for the nineteenth-century (male) *flâneur*, see Rachel Bowlby, 'Walking, Women and Writing', in *Still Crazy After All These Years: Women, Writing and Psychoanalysis* (1992; London: Routledge, 2010), 6.

5. The marketing of Wedgwood china, including a well-appointed London showroom, is the classic eighteenth-century example of this phenomenon. See Neil McKendrick, 'The Commercialization of Fashion', in McKendrick, John Brewer, and J.H. Plumb, *The Birth of a Consumer Society: The Commercialization of Eighteenth-Century England* (Bloomington: Indiana University Press, 1982), 35–99.

6. Fanny Burney, *Evelina* (1778), ed. Edward A. Bloom (Oxford: Oxford University Press, World's Classics, 1982), 27.

7. Burney, *Evelina*, 27.

8. Burney, *Evelina*, 27.

9. Burney, *Evelina*, 27.

10. Burney, *Evelina*, 27.

11. Burney, *Evelina*, 28.

12. Wilfred Burns, *British Shopping Centres: New Trends in Layout and Distribution* (London: Leonard Hill (Books) Limited, 1959), 43.

13. Jane Austen, *Pride and Prejudice* (1813), ed. James Kinsley (Oxford: Oxford University Press, 2004), 117.

14. Austen, *Emma* (1816), ed. James Kinsley (Oxford: Oxford University Press, 1995), 179.

15. Austen, *Emma*, 179.

16. Austen, *Emma*, 179.

17. Austen, *Emma*, 179.

18. Austen, *Emma*, 180.

19. Austen, *Emma*, 159.

20. Austen, *Emma*, 160.

21. Austen, *Emma*, 209.

22. Austen, *Emma*, 209.

23. Austen, *Emma*, 210.

24. Austen, *Emma*, 211.

25. Austen, *Emma*, 209–10.

20

Shopworkers and Shopkeepers

From the local grocery to the department store in the city centre, to have a shop of one's own is the natural dream of every apprentice and counter assistant and market stallholder: so runs the romance and the wisdom of textbooks and talk, as they course through the nineteenth and twentieth centuries. Balzac put it perfectly in a story of 1840: 'To be a shepherd as Poussin would like is no longer our custom. To be a grocer...is one of the happiest human conditions.'[1]

Shopkeeping happiness is presented with everyday warmth in a Co-op publication around 1930 about salesmanship—this topic acknowledged to be a new kind of focus for an organization that had up till then stood apart from such promotional considerations:

> To be a shopkeeper is also the dream of every little boy and girl:
> When one notices with what obvious delight little children play at shopkeeping, one realises that there is something fundamentally attractive in the occupation of shopkeeping, and that both sellers and buyers may derive considerable pleasure from their transactions.[2]

The sentence about children's delight is delightful in its own right. Far from feeling the need to adopt a technical marketing language, the writer points to the pleasures all round. Children like playing shops, and grown-up shopkeeping and shop purchasing should be just as much a source of enjoyment. In the same spirit of enterprise and openness, the trade literature about shops almost always recommends shopkeeping as something that it is obviously desirable and feasible to try; it is the substance of numerous twentieth-century how-to books. In the words of a post-war 'Teach Yourself' guide to shopkeeping, 'Most people have a liking for buying and selling in its broadest sense; children love playing at shops, and this trait is clearly reflected in our national economic organisation.'[3] The suggestion is not that you are going to get rich, or would wish to; instead, the small shop of your own responds to modest but worthy ambitions.

Very different in tone—perhaps uniquely so—is the sudden stark comment in a government-sponsored report on British shopping futures that came out at the start of the 1970s. The context is a largely negative discussion of 'street-corner' shops', put like that. Slum clearance programmes are doing away with most of them, although—so the report loftily sniffs—'We can hardly say that there will be no shops of this type in the 1980s.'[4] The concluding thought is remarkable not so much for what it directly states as for the underlying recommendation:

> there will continue to be a certain type of person who prefers the independence and hazards of small shop-keeping to the discipline and security of being an employee.[5]

Against the background of small shops in steep decline at the time, the assumptions about 'a certain type' incapable of not taking the risk of starting a shop, and the value of 'discipline', are presented as if they go without saying. But in comparisons between the two, it is rare to the point of unheard of for a shopkeeper, not their employee, to be seen as being or having a problem. What is also striking today, when shops of all sizes are struggling to stay in business, is the 'security' granted here to having a job in one.

A minor moment in John Braine's novel *Room at the Top* (1957) shows the position of the shop assistant in its more usual frame, one of pity bordering on disparagement. The scene takes place in a small chemist's, where Joe Lampton has stopped on the way home from work to buy some razor blades. He is known there and greeted by name. A conversation about politics is going on between the chemist and another male customer, but Joe focuses on a third man:

> The chemist's assistant finished wrapping a large parcel for the woolman. 'That's right, Mr Robbins,' he said. 'And look at the income-tax...' He was a big man, as tall as me, on the verge of forty. I remembered him telling me once that he'd been at Robbins' for twenty years. He was obviously the unqualified general mug who did all the rough work and worked the most awkward hours. His pale face was set in a fixed smile; the habit of submissiveness had rounded what had once been a fine pair of shoulders. 'You're right, Mr Robbins,' he repeated. 'Dead right.' His smile widened, and he nodded his head to underline the point. The other two took no notice of him at all, though they were standing cheek-by-jowl.[6]

The smile and nodding and failed attempt to join the conversation become further signs of subordination. Joe goes on to speculate about the assistant's low pay ('perhaps seven pounds a week') and lack of job security, but then realizes that his concern has arisen out of an unacknowledged similarity to his own situation at work (in local government), even if at a higher level. Once again, the man (whose name he does not give, perhaps does not know) is not regarded as an individual.

With the dominance of self-service in the last part of the twentieth century, the figure of the exploited worker without any future migrates from the counter to the checkout. The checkout cashier is doing a relatively simple, repetitive job that resembles working on a factory production line, as goods arrive in front of her requiring the same treatment and actions on her part. Unlike the assistant behind the counter, the cashier is not fetching or finding or packing up anything for the customers, and has no reason to talk to them. The goods have already been picked out, and all that remains is to get them scanned through and paid for, at a price now so far beyond negotiation that it is not even marked directly on the item. Moving the things as fast as possible along the conveyor belt, the cashier is an operative using a machine rather than a salesperson in active conversation with a customer. As a seller, she is redundant: unlike the pedlar or the grocer, there is nothing to be gained by her being able to talk about the commodities with knowledge or persuasiveness. Few words, if any, need to be said; the process is contactless in every way.

The checkout operator, without any powers of initiation, is seen as the antithesis of mobility. Unlike the pedlar, who moves about all the time, the person is stuck there in one place, socially and actually. The pedlar, in perpetual migration, is from elsewhere; the checkout girl is the one who has never gone anywhere else. The closing scene of a memoir by Annie Ernaux, *La Place* (1983) stages this situation with subtle force. The narrator is a teacher who moved into a different class to that of her parents, who had themselves moved away geographically and socially from their own origins, becoming the owners of a small grocery with a café attached. At the start of the book, Ernaux recalls the tension of the moment when she passed her teacher-training exam just before her father died. At the end, she is in the supermarket—that is, in the type of store that has put out of business many of the small, traditional kind that her parents ran. At the checkout she recognizes a young woman she had taught at school, but can't remember any details about her. She wants to say something all the same and so, 'when my turn arrived, I asked: "Are you well? Do you like it here?"' The girl rings up the things (which are specified, drinks and jam), and then replies, 'embarrassed', that 'it didn't work out, the technical college.' 'She seemed to think,' continues Ernaux, 'that I still remembered her study plans. But I had forgotten why she had been sent to technical college and which section.' Whether she can't or she doesn't want to, the girl then takes no more notice of her once teacher. She gets on with her fiddly and meticulous work; this being before barcodes, she is inputting the price of each item herself. The customer who comes after Ernaux is not mentioned, only the manual work: 'I said goodbye to her. She was already taking the next lot of things with her left hand and was typing without looking with her right hand.'[7] Nothing is stated explicitly of what is not known—is understood as not known—about the person or her thoughts or her history. But these are the very last words of the book. The anonymous shopworker, story untold, is given that place.

In 2008, a blog written by another French supermarket cashier, Anna Sam, became a bestseller as a book.[8] It documents the daily frustrations, boredoms, and amusement of being at the till—including, on one occasion, the humiliation of hearing a cross parent say to a child, about her but not to her, you'll end up like that person if you don't behave. Like Ernaux, Sam had a degree in English literature; her job in the supermarket had begun when she was a student. Writing about it brought it to an end, after eight years. Sam does not go against the picture of the checkout cashier as the epitome of exploitation. She has no patience with suggestions that an interviewee for the job might claim it as some sort of active choice or ambition: it's always been my dream to be a till operator! There is no redeeming surprise to be found in the work itself that might change the public view of it, as seen and imagined from the queue—or as Sam takes it to be imagined if customers even think of it, which she assumes that they generally don't. Instead, what she offers from the other side of the checkout is the thinking, observing cashier, whose retort to the mis-constructions or rudeness of customers who pass by her and whom she serves is to pay them back with her countering cartoon versions of them.

In Britain, the cashier's-eye view had its moment too, in the form of deliberate experiment rather than long-term working life. As part of a broader exposé of supermarket culture, Joanna Blythman went to work on the till at Tesco—but for just a week. Another journalist, Tazeen Ahmad, spent six months at Sainsbury's for the purpose of writing about that experience; her book, which came out shortly after Sam's, also follows a day-by-day diary style. Like Sam's, these accounts are relentlessly negative (with jokey alleviation), documenting the tedium and often physical strain of the work.[9]

The disparagement of shopworkers is not only directed towards employees. In *New Grub Street* (1891), George Gissing's novel about the London world of books and literary journalism in the 1880s, one character is writing a novel called 'Mr Bailey, Grocer'. It is a labour of loving authenticity, meant to lay out the particulars of a modest but worthy day-to-day existence in which no significant events occur. The book is destined for unsuccess in modern commercial conditions, but this is of no concern to its also modest and worthy (fictional) creator, who (in the most spectacular incident of New Grub Street itself) risks his life to rescue the just completed manuscript from a fire. But why should a grocer's life be seen as an object of mockery or amusement: as boring to live, and boring to read about? Mr Bailey, like his author, goes about his business far removed from the entrepreneurial energies that power up the various types of creative ambition to be found in the new literary marketplace that Gissing portrays. With the grocer, it is implied, there is barely a story at all—though his would-be author, explaining that he is based on a real-life equivalent near where he lives, does mention a significant life event: the woman he married whose money enabled the place to be bought:

> Well, Mr Bailey is a grocer in a little street by here. I have dealt with him for a long time, and as he's a talkative fellow I've come to know a good deal about him and his history. He's fond of talking about the struggle he had in his first year of business. He had no money of his own, but he married a woman who had saved forty-five pounds out of a cat's-meat business.[10]

This is the novelist (in a novel) practising oral history.

But it is not just the repetitions of his daily existence that makes the grocer appear as a stock-in-trade stupid type, barely worth a literary glance. He suffers from another form of distancing too, which is to do with where he stands socially, behind his own counter, graciously serving, politely conversing as he weighs and bags, somewhere between a worker and a gentleman but not really belonging as one or the other. This aspect comes to the fore in the grocer novel that Gissing himself then really did write some years after New Grub Street. In Will Warburton: A Romance of Real Life, a cultured middle-class

gentleman is desperate not to reveal to dependent relatives the financial hardship that has come upon him, and sets out to make a
moderate, stable income by taking over a small grocery. From then
on, his shame transfers to the fear of being found out by friends in his
adopted identity as an apron-wearing tradesman.

The condescending dismissal of the man in the shop seems to go
without saying—without further elaboration. In Virginia Woolf's *Mrs
Dalloway*, a generation later than Gissing, the grandest of guests arrives
at the evening reception—but is cut down to class size:

> 'The Prime Minister,' said Peter Walsh.
>
> The Prime Minister? Was it really? Ellie Henderson marvelled. What a
> thing to tell Edith!
>
> One couldn't laugh at him. He looked so ordinary. You might have stood
> him behind a counter and bought biscuits—poor chap, all rigged up in
> gold lace.[11]

Here the double disparagement, of both Prime Minister and grocer—
the grandeur of the first being plainly silly while the stupidity of the
other is obvious—occurs in the thoughts of an impoverished but still
genteel relative of the hostess, someone who had received only a
reluctant, last-minute invitation to superior party. A sighting of the
Prime Minister is a significant occurrence—something 'to tell Edith',
whoever she may be. But he is stripped of his decorations and reduced
to the image of 'ordinary', which is the type of man who weighs out
your biscuits. Passive and obedient: 'You might have stood him behind
a counter.' At an earlier point in the novel, a second high-ranking
character, the psychiatrist Sir William Bradshaw, is linked to the
shopkeeper he might have been but is not—in this case not because
he essentially is one, as with the Prime Minister minus his costume,
but because that is what his father had been, hence the spur to be
something else: 'He had worked very hard; he had won his position by
sheer ability (being the son of a shop-keeper)'; or again, his 'father had
been a tradesman'.[12] A shopkeeper (or a shopkeeper's son) is what not

to be, an origin to move away from but which will cling to your biography with its taint of trade, and its confirmation that your place in higher society has only the provisional status of one who has worked their way up and out—'worked very hard', as it happens.

The shopman imagined by Woolf's character as she stands in the presence of the Prime Minister is selling an 'easy' product (no expertise or preparation required) and one presented as being of blandly indifferent origin—'biscuits'. But the implied lack of skill and the absence of product specification have little in common with the likely work environment for the kind of person that Ellie Henderson wants to put down. At this time factory production and pre-packaging as yet affected only a few of the commodities sold in shops; grocers' lengthy apprenticeships, with a formal system of accreditation, were designed to teach them in detail about the preparation of goods prior to selling. Even a small shop would sell different grades of tea, for instance, with complex names and features to be mastered. Biscuits themselves were anything but just plain 'biscuits'. An example, almost at random: in 1881 a prominent Rochdale grocer, James Duckworth, had a substantial front-page advertisement in a local paper; it stated that he was the 'agent' for a particular make of biscuits, Powell's. This Duckworth—his stores were known as 'Jimmy Duck's'—was an alderman and later an MP; he was also, long-term, a friend and mentor of the younger Jesse Boot, from the time when Boot opened his first chemist's shop in Nottingham. No fewer than fifteen kinds of biscuit are listed in Duckworth's advertisement, in ascending order of price per pound, with plain or fancy names to match: Butter, Tea, Sugar, Fruit, London Mixed, Milk, Lemon Rings, Plain Arrowroot, Kinder Garten, Sponge Drops, Iced Rings, Celebrities, Lead Rings, West Ends, Ginger Nests.[13] Any one of these varieties would have been available for weighing out when asked for.

Gissing, unlike Woolf, knew something about the realities of working in a shop, as well as about the prejudices; he was born (in 1857) above his father's chemist in Wakefield (it was later a branch of Boot's for many years). Here is his Warburton, reflecting on the situation of the grocer:

Why, he was the slave of every kitchen wench who came into the shop to spend a penny; he trembled at the thought of having to please her, and so losing her custom. The grocery odours, once pleasant to him, had grown nauseating. And the ever repeated tasks, the weighing, parcel making, string cutting; the parrot phrases a thousand times repeated; the idiot bowing and smiling—how these things gnawed at his nerves, till he quivered like a beaten horse.[14]

Once upon a time, towards the end of the twentieth century, the daughter of a grocer in a provincial English town grew up to become a real Prime Minister—but that's another story.

Notes

1. Honoré de Balzac, 'L'Épicier' (1840) in *Les Français peints par eux-mêmes: Encyclopédie morale du dix-neuvième siècle*, tome 1, Médiathèque André Malraux de Lisieux, 4; ellipsis mine.
2. T. Ellison, 'The Art of Salesmanship', in T. Ellison, W. Eason, and J. Johnson, *Salesmanship in the Grocery Department* (2nd edn Manchester: The Co-operative Union Ltd., n.d.), 31.
3. V.G. Winslet, *Shopkeeping* (London: The English Universities Press Ltd., 1958), 11.
4. Distributive Trades EDC [Economic Development Council], *The Future Pattern of Shopping* (London: Her Majesty's Stationery Office, 1971), 57.
5. *The Future Pattern of Shopping*, 57.
6. John Braine, *Room at the Top* (1957; Harmondsworth: Penguin, 1972), 146–7.
7. Annie Ernaux, *La Place* (1983; Paris: Gallimard, 1991), 114. The book is translated by Tanya Leslie as *A Man's Place* (New York: Seven Stories Press, 2012).
8. See Anna Sam, *Les Tribulations d'une caissière* (2008; Paris: Livre de Poche, 2009). The book is translated by Morag Young as *Checkout: A Life on the Tills* (London: Gallic Books, 2009).
9. See Joanna Blythman, *Shopped: The Shocking Power of British Supermarkets* (2004; London: Harper Perennial, 2005), 125–32; Tazeen Ahmad, *The Checkout Girl: My Life on the Supermarket Conveyor Belt* (London: The Friday Project, 2009).
10. George Gissing, *New Grub Street* (1891; Harmondsworth: Penguin, 1980), 243–4.

11. Virginia Woolf, *Mrs Dalloway* (1925), ed. David Bradshaw (Oxford: Oxford University Press, 2000), 146.
12. Woolf, *Mrs Dalloway*, 81, 83.
13. *Rochdale Gazette*, Saturday 8 January 1881, 1.
14. Gissing, *Will Warburton: A Romance of Real Life* (1905), ed. Colin Partridge (Brighton: Harvester Press, 1981), 162.

PART III

SPECIALITIES

21

Bakers

'Give us this day our daily bread', in the words of the Lord's Prayer. In the Middle Ages, bread and ale (which was safer to drink than water) were the two staples of daily consumption whose price and measures were set by law in England.[1] Symbolically, bread is the original everyday food, a generic term for the sustenance that must be there for physical and social life to go on. It is the minimal 'food on the table' that is what a provider provides. More broadly, the *breadwinner* was supposed to be the primary if not the sole earner in a household, the word implying that money and bread are as if equivalent; he is not much mentioned now, thanks to changed household and gender norms. Theodore Dreiser's novel *Sister Carrie*, set in the 1880s, depicts a formerly well-to-do family man, once manager of an upmarket saloon bar in Chicago, who has fallen so far in status and means that he finds himself reduced to joining the midnight queue for free loaves from Fleischmann's bakery in downtown Manhattan.[2] This is to be on the bread line. And if bread is what needs to be earned or found in order just to live, at the other metaphorical extreme, *dough* can just mean money, including a lot of it.

In substance, then, bread is not really a buying choice so much as an expectation of constant supply, what should always be there at home. Bread was not always bought. Back in the baking day, even though most dwellings had no oven, much of the bread consumed was home-made. The local baker's oven operated as a shared facility, in the same way as the later laundrette. Mixed and proved at home, the dough would then be taken for baking in the baker's oven, for which a small charge was made. This was also the place to cook a pie, or the Sunday roast. Meat was bought at the butcher's or market and taken round to the baker's. As late as Elizabeth Gaskell's novel *Cranford*, set in a small town in the middle of the nineteenth century, a charitable 'captain' assists a 'poor old woman' one Sunday when she is 'returning from the bakehouse' with her 'baked mutton and potatoes'.[3] Which is to say that what bakers did was bake; *what* they baked was not necessarily bread, and not necessarily of their own making.

Bread is the ultimate basic food, the permanent need or potential lack. In Britain, unlike in France, there is no culture of bread needing to be so fresh that you would go out two or three times a day, not long before the next meal, to pick up a new supply from the baker's, just out of the oven. But even so, because it is so much a part of daily consumption, the fetching of bread (or the not running out of it) is always a ready reason for a short domestic absence, an excuse to get out of the house for a breath of open air. At the bakery or the corner shop a few words will be exchanged; the person who is on their own for most of the time is momentarily not. In the British election campaign of 2010 a disparaging comment by the then Prime Minister, Gordon Brown, was accidentally broadcast after he had briefly talked to a woman in Rochdale on her way to the local shop. As the background to a momentous turn of events, it was the perfect casual setting of the scene. What could be more ordinary? In the words of newspaper headlines the following morning, *she just popped out for a loaf*. The phrase suggests a remaining vestige, a crumb left over from when the housewife's buying of food was mainly on a daily basis: homes had no refrigerators (nor did shops), and the shops were not many steps away.

The word *bakery* is firmly locked now to the sale of bread and cakes (or 'flour confectionery'), even when the specific shop that goes by the name bakes nothing, and is many miles from the factory where what it sells is made. Since the middle of the twentieth century, the common-est kind of loaf for sale in all kinds of shop has been packaged—or *pre-packaged*, to use the more cumbersome term of those largely pre-packaging days. Factory production and standardized packing materials brought bread into line with many other foodstuffs that also began to be sold in this way in the 1930s. Chain stores sold their own factory-baked loaves, both the sliced and the non-sliced. But independent bakeries remained in large numbers, with most of them delivering directly to customers' homes. In the golden age of home deliveries—that is, in the motor-van middle decades of the twentieth century—the baker had a round, and customers had regular orders for bread in the same way as they did for milk and newspapers. All three items were supplied each day, to or through the door.

A different kind of mass-market bakery emerged in the 1990s, when local chains such as Thomas the Baker in Yorkshire took off with a large trade in takeaway snacks: cakes, sandwiches, and above all sausage rolls. In early 2020 Greggs, which used to be 'Greggs of Gosforth', a small chain based in a suburb of Newcastle, had over two thousand branches. Their launch of vegan sausage rolls at the end of 2019 attracted extensive media comment.

The quality of bread itself, in the pre-war decades when packaging and pre-slicing came in, was not the primary issue. Changes in the method of bread production are vaguely evoked with every reference to the greatest thing since sliced bread, as if that pre-cut feature could be likened to a new labour-saving convenience. Not just every loaf the same, but every slice as well, and the final preparatory work before consumption all done in advance. But if there can be a greatest thing since sliced bread—or if anyone ever really used that phrase, before it became the most stale cliché since its own invention—then the underlying suggestion is that bread itself occupies a major but some-how labour-intensive place in daily life. That is the opposite of a different representation, which makes bread and its distribution the very image of rustic authenticity. Thus non-sliced bread, not made in a factory, is retro-raised to a newfound twenty-first-century status as *artisanal*, but at the same time some mass-produced brands are mar-keted as if they were preserving all the warmth of an old tradition.

A 1973 TV commercial showed a delivery boy with his basket labouring up the hill with his Hovis loaf in a picture-book Dorset village. To compound the initial fabrication, later advertisements reference the first one as though it were itself an image of historical authenticity: when fake nostalgia really was fake nostalgia.

Does this usurping of tradition do harm to the really traditional businesses? The problem is itself an old one, to which a book for bakers published in the late 1950s had a surprising response, already. The author raises the question of national advertising: 'Smaller bakery shops have so far ignored advertising. Not so the combines. They are making the public bakery-minded every time the people see bakery advertisements in newspapers and magazines and on posters and televisions.'[4] The word 'bakery-minded' as a conception of the public response to an ad is pivotal here. Instead of fearing the big companies or trying in vain to compete with them, says this writer, an independent bakery should go along with the advertising flow, offering more and better of what is being promoted. It is a beautifully ingenious argument:

> Bakers should welcome the sight of every bakery advertisement as an advertisement for the products of their own shops. That is why the small baker would do well to cash in on the publicity and draw it towards his own shop. If sponge lines are nationally advertised, he should run special displays of his own sponge lines and rely on their quality to make the public in the neighbourhood think of his when they see any advertisement for sponge lines.[5]

Far from suffering, the business will positively benefit, on the back of the mechanized competitors' campaign.

There is a more fundamental reason for the success of the old-fashioned images in the marketing of modern bread. Aside from the specific history of how it has been made or sold, in reality or in advertising imagination, the sale of bread is able to draw on profound associations with an elementary sense of well-being: the smell and warmth of the loaf just out of the oven. Unlike the dutiful, manly associations of the breadwinner, here are the sensory comforts of maternal warmth, away from the rigours of the commercial world. It is as if the marketable memory were baked in from the beginning, part of the product's natural ingredients, and it may be the baker's special selling capacity, to be able to summon up a time of childish plenitude in the atmosphere of the shop. In a memoir, the cultural critic Richard Hoggart, who was born in 1918, recalls, from his time growing up in Leeds, a neighbour and small-scale baker who sold cakes from home on Saturdays; 'The smell in the yard', he says, 'was then all warm, yeasty, curranty and sugary.' When there were some cakes left over at the end of the day, they might be given to the Hoggarts. 'Even now, the smell and taste, the cushiony butteryness of a toasted teacake, not only seem marvellous but instantly bring back, with warmth, life in Potternewton Lane, even if I am having tea in a posh hotel.'[6] This remembered moment of consuming pleasure is primal and Proustian with its cake and its grandmotherly figure. It is homely in every way. The shop is more or less next door, it is part of someone's house, and in any case it is not like an ordinary shop with regular hours.

In the chronology of Richard Hoggart's life as told, this story is the very first instance of anything to do with buying and selling as a part of life. But while it does come from a sort of shop and was baked to be sold, the teacake has not been bought; it has been given. Given to a family known to be 'hard-up' (Hoggart's word), but also, you infer, given out of kindness and neighbourly hospitality, and consciously against the grain of monetary considerations.[7] As if naturally, baking is bound up with human sharing.

Notes

1. See Dorothy Davis, A *History of Shopping* (London: Routledge & Kegan Paul, 1966), 10–12.
2. See Theodore Dreiser, *Sister Carrie* (1900), ed. Lee Clark Mitchell (Oxford: Oxford University Press, 1991), 446.

3. Elizabeth Gaskell, *Cranford* (1853), ed. Peter Keating (Harmondsworth: Penguin, 1976), 40.
4. Rose Buckner, *Design for Selling for Bakers and Confectioners* (London: National Association of Master Bakers, Confectioners and Caterers, 1959), 99.
5. Buckner, *Design for Selling*, 99–100.
6. Richard Hoggart, *Between Two Worlds: Essays* (London: Aurum Press, 2001), 213.
7. Hoggart, *Between Two Worlds*, 213.

22

Butchers

Towards the end of *Pride and Prejudice*, a tiny scene takes place. Mrs Bennet has been wondering if it is really true that Mr Bingley will soon be back, and her sister has definite information, straight from his housekeeper: 'She was going to the butcher's, she told me, on purpose to order in some meat on Wednesday, and she has got three couple of ducks, just fit to be killed.'[1] Jane Austen repeats the over-fullness of Mrs Phillips' knowledge, and in the local excitement of it all it is easy to miss something much more mundane, which is simply the presence in this little town of a butcher's shop that is open, at least for orders, into the evening, and where a woman planning a special dinner might expect to be getting supplies. Or some of them: the ducks that are ready—'just fit to be killed', as she vividly says—have been raised on the estate.

Butchers' shops were always to be found in places where there were shops at all. Every village had one, or more than one. In populous town neighbourhoods, they were on every street. In the great market halls built in the nineteenth century, there were rows of up to forty or fifty stalls for butchers. The mixed consumption of home-reared and bought-in meat was not only for the wealthy or landed. Before most of the population lived in towns and cities—and often within them, too, right into the twentieth century—it was common for families to keep some poultry and perhaps a pig, its meat to be cut up and preserved for eating through the winter. Writing much later about her childhood in the East End of London, a woman born in 1855 explains that 'every house in that part of Bethnal Green had a large garden and nearly everyone kept either pigs or chickens or ducks—sometimes all three.'[2] There would also be meat to buy from the butcher, and in the country from local farmers, producer-retailers who sold at the weekly market. If the butcher had a shop he would buy 'on the hoof', again at a market, and slaughter the meat himself; until into the twentieth century, this remained the most usual arrangement.

Beginning in the last quarter of the nineteenth century, new facilities for refrigeration and steamship transportation led to the importing of low-cost frozen meat from distant countries, above all Argentina and New Zealand, and with the aid of a rise in average incomes, the new imported product contributed to a substantial increase in general meat consumption at this time. There were chains of 'foreign meat shops', so called, organized around its sale (traditional butchers had no use for it). When the Union Cold Storage Company took over various other companies involved in this industry in 1923, it had over four hundred shops. In some ways, the division of quality and price—between imported frozen and fresh domestic meat—was a forerunner to what happened when intensive livestock rearing methods were intro-duced in Britain after the war. The Argentinian beef was produced and distributed on an industrial scale, from rearing to refrigerated trans-portation to retail. It was simpler to handle, since no selection or slaughter of livestock was necessary; stated from the other side, it was meat that had been produced and treated under conditions that would not occur in the country of consumption.[3]

Despite the capacity for industrial levels of efficiency, with remote production, long-term storage, and long-distance transportation, meat production does however come up against distinctive natural limita-tions. Even if the demand is much greater for particular joints of meat, all the other parts of the animal are still produced at the same time. But just as the imported meat was largely sold in working-class areas, so sometimes the residential divisions for conventional butchers fol-lowed class lines of distribution: the superior bits of the beast went to one end of the town and the rest to the other. This testimony about a Brighton butcher in the early twentieth century also captures the combination of a fixed shop with door-to-door delivery:

> My father's theory was really good. If you sold your best parts to Hove, you'd make more money than what you could in this district, so what you got left you could lower—so we had big trays with anything from 4d to £1 upwards cut up of a morning. He'd start at six, he was never late, and the staff—no messing around—we'd go on till ten at night.[4]

This was especially the case on Saturday nights, when everyone was buying for their Sunday dinner, and the prices came down to make sure that all was sold (no refrigeration as yet in either the shop or the home).

It is easy to pass by the *Pride and Prejudice* butcher's without noticing its momentary presence. Even more than most other local shops, ubiquitous staples of small-town life, butchers are thin on the novelistic ground. Unlike more glamorous retail establishments, they do not provide a diverting or romantic setting for a scene. Nor will they have been places that most readers of novels even went into, if that was the job of the servants or the meat was delivered by the butcher's boy. Mrs Bennet is shown talking menus with her cook but is not seen venturing out to buy food. When a butcher's shop does show up in a novel, it is unlikely to be because of the pleasure or interest of visiting the place. The following passage, from George Orwell's novel *A Clergyman's Daughter* (1935), describes a miserable morning when the downtrodden Dorothy, keeping house for her widowed father, had woken from bill-induced nightmares:

> Meanwhile, she had got to settle about the meat for today's dinner—luncheon. (Dorothy was careful to obey her father and call it *luncheon*, when she remembered it. On the other hand, you could not in honesty call the evening meal anything but 'supper'; so there was no such meal as 'dinner' at the Rectory.) Better make an omelette for luncheon today, Dorothy decided. She dared not go to Cargill again. Though, of course, if

they had an omelette for luncheon and then scrambled eggs for supper, her father would probably be sarcastic about it. Last time they had had eggs twice in one day, he had enquired coldly, 'Have you started a chicken farm, Dorothy?' And perhaps tomorrow she would get two pounds of sausages at the International, and that staved off the meat-question for one day more.[5]

The rector's studied obliviousness to the household's financial situation goes with a fussy naming of mealtimes, with or without their meat content. From the point of view of the history of consumption, what the passage shows too is the clear distinction, beginning to emerge, between food from the butcher's and food from a chain store, the International. In the rector's household, three cooked meals a day must be provided, and meat is the default main ingredient; eggs figure as a meat substitute, unacceptable more than once in a single day. Sausages are somewhere on a border between meat and not real meat. But they have the advantage not just of being cheaper, but also of being obtainable from a store other than the one where the personal service has become a source of embarrassment for the customer in debt and afraid to show her face.

Notes

1. Jane Austen, *Pride and Prejudice* (1813), ed. Tony Tanner (London: Penguin, 1984), 342.
2. Mrs. Leyton, 'Memories of Seventy Years', in *Life as We Have Known It, By Co-operative Working Women*, ed. Margaret Llewellyn Davies (1931; London: Virago, 1982), 2.
3. See James B. Jefferys, *Retail Trading in Britain 1850–1950* (Cambridge: Cambridge University Press, 1954), 187–96.
4. Neil Griffiths, *Shops Book: Brighton 1900–1930* (Brighton: QueenSpark Books, c.1978), 15, quoting Mr Stone.
5. George Orwell, *A Clergyman's Daughter* (1935; London: Penguin, 1988), 31–2.

23

Chemists

Figure 10. Gilbert Batting, chemist's, Tunbridge Wells, Kent, 1893
Image courtesy of The Amelia, Tunbridge Wells

C hemists' shops are beautifully hybrid, combining the mysterious
sense of secret arts with a show of white-coated medical expertise. Since the mid-nineteenth century, dispensing chemists have been
qualified professionals whose certificates prove they have undertaken

a long and regulated training. The move to this mode of validation was a confirmation of scientific knowledge, as distinct from the older arts of the apothecary. But as though not quite ready to let go of a pre-scientific past, the small chemist's shop long retained the mystique of potions and bottles and special preparations of all kinds. Patent medicines and cosmetic products were always pulling in different directions from the formulaic, engendering their own forms of potency, personal accreditation, and familiarity. Evidence-based the branded medicines were not; effective placebos they surely often were. They stood out not only for their colours and slogans and crazy names but also because they clashed with the dignified medical efficiency on view in the same selling space.

By any standard, chemist's shops sold the oddest assortment of things. There were the straight medical prescriptions, individually made up for the customer and put into bottles with their personal labels. There were the proprietary (or 'patent') medicines in their different bottles with their different labels. There were toiletries and cosmetics promising to maintain or add to the look or health of the visible face and body or treat its defects. There were perfumes (for women), by the 1920s with mass-market brands such as Yardley or Coty. Much later, there would also be skincare products and perfumes marketed to men—or to women, as gifts to give to men. In the French writer Annie Ernaux's memoir about her working-class father's life through the twentieth century, a poignant detail is her (unwanted) Christmas gift to him, in the 1960s, of a bottle of *aftershave*. She uses the English word, marking its status as a widely advertised product whose foreign allure was meant to enhance its prestige.[1]

Together with make-up and bodily soothers and beautifiers of every sort, chemist's shops also took on a new specialization towards the end of the nineteenth century, which was photographic goods. Photography was becoming a popular hobby, accessible through the affordability of the portable Kodak; for a while Kodak became the generic name for a camera, as would happen a few decades later with the Hoover (to mean any vacuum cleaner). In the middle of the nineteenth century, photography had initially developed as a small professional enterprise, with a studio on every high street, where family or individual pictures could be taken: it was no longer only the wealthy who could have family portraits to keep and pass on. Now, with the Kodak, the apparatus as well as the result was becoming available to all. The chemist also sold the rolls of film to be put in the camera to yield a set number of images. The shop would develop the film for the customer in its own darkroom—or send it away to the lab. With the advent of digital photography and smartphones in the early twenty-first century, all these complex and time-taking rituals of photography—from the purchase of the film to the tensely awaited prints—have vanished into a nearly forgotten recent history.

There is a clear rationale for the provision of photographic services in the pharmacy. Photography is itself a chemical process: fully scientific in its methods, but also with an aura of magic and wonder, as true images of departed moments and people are preserved into future times. But a real curiosity among the offerings of many chemist's shops until the late twentieth century was the presence of a library. For the many branches of Boots, this practice had a clear origin. The father of Florence Boot, wife of the founder, ran a bookshop in St Helier, Jersey, where Jesse first met and courted her; the Boot's Book Lovers Library was Florence's own initiative and then her special interest within the firm.[2] This library became a national network which lasted into the middle of the 1960s; an early scene in the 1945 film *Brief Encounter* shows the heroine, Laura, changing her books in Boots as part of her weekly shopping and cinema visit to the local town. Nor were chemists the only small shops to offer (mainly) small-scale private library services on their premises. Tiny libraries were also to be found in newsagents, where the print-matter logic is easier to see than for chemists. And also, delightfully, in sweet shops, where it isn't; although the availability of books and confectionery in the same place rather nicely reinforces the view of those who compared novel-reading to sweet-eating as mildly addictive ordinary treats. Perhaps the chemist's library was medicinal.

The pharmacy's blurring of modern science with mysterious arts is strikingly evoked in a story of 1902 by Rudyard Kipling, called 'Wireless'. It takes place in a chemist's shop open late on a Saturday night—as was the norm for all shops at the time. Kipling's imagined shop, in a south-coast resort with grand hotels on the seafront, has every stylish feature of the period. From details here and there we pick up that there is a mahogany counter, with a rail. There are glass knobs on the 'drug-drawers', which are 'explored' by the narrator, a visitor, in his half hour of minding the shop.[3] The window is plate glass, with the big glass jars of coloured liquid that were standard for chemists' displays at the time. Two modern features are the white floor tiles and the electric lighting, singled out not just for its power of creating distinctive hues, reflecting the colours of the jars, but also for its proud contrast with the still gas-lit shops nearby:

> Our electric lights, set low down in the windows before the tun-bellied Rosamond jars, flung inward three monstrous daubs of red, blue, and green that broke into kaleidoscopic lights on the faceted knobs of the drug-drawers, the cut-glass scent flagons, and the bulbs of the sparklet bottles. They flushed the white-tiled floor in gorgeous patches; splashed along the nickel-silver counter-rails, and turned the polished mahogany counter-panels to the likeness of intricate grained marbles—slabs of porphyry and malachite.[4]

The shop is evidently not part of a chain—though in its time it might well have been, with Boots just then expanding very fast, and various smaller regional groups in the picture, too. Boots had 250 branches in 1901 and more than twice that number by 1914. The assistant, along with his 'dreams of a shop in London', has a 'hate for the price-cutting Co-operative stores'.[5] (The Co-op did not cut prices of branded medicines directly; but the dividend paid to customers had the same effect, and was resented and legally disputed by other retailers.)

The title 'Wireless' refers to an experiment being conducted, in the here and now of the story, from a back room of the shop; it is an attempt to make remote contact with fellow amateur practitioners many miles away. This up-to-the-minute science borders on the fantastic, with shades of spiritualism in the air. Meanwhile, in the main part of the shop, the assistant, Mr Shaynor, who drinks a potion to ease his consumptive cough, is found to be compulsively writing out lines from a poem by John Keats, verbatim, as if they are being transmitted straight into him (and then out of him, onto the paper) by some equally remarkable process of science or *séance*. It is a further uncanny manifestation of a connection from afar, now bringing together two times, and perhaps two minds, as Mr Shaynor produces the very same words as did Keats.

An intercommunicative universe, at once otherworldly and super-scientific, is distilled into the few pages of this story. Kipling suggests at every turn the parallels between the borderline events that are currently occurring and the extraordinary phenomena that are part of the day-to-day business of this special kind of shop. A medicinal product that is meant to be soothing for Mr Shaynor's cough brings together the puffery of the branded product with an age-old whiff of ecclesiastical incense: 'He thrust his chin forward toward the advertisement, whereunder the last of the Blaudett's Cathedral pastilles fumed in its holder.'[6] Mr Shaynor is religiously devoted to the picture of a pretty girl on an advertisement placed in front of him, and this image at times becomes merged with the sight of a real girl he knows, who comes in and takes him out for a walk.

In the shop window is the display of large bottles containing coloured liquids. These are linked to a well-known old children's story, by Maria Edgeworth—so that a fiction that dates from a hundred years before this one partly becomes the basis for what is seen now:

> Three superb glass jars—red, green, and blue—of the sort that led Rosamond to parting with her shoes—blazed in the broad plate-glass windows, and there was a confused smell of orris, Kodak Wlms, vulcanite, tooth-powder, sachets, and almond-cream in the air.[7]

In Edgeworth's story, Rosamond begs her mother to buy her the beautiful purple jar instead of the shoes she needs—and is made to learn the moral lesson when she finds out later that the colour comes from the contents, not the glass. In the ongoing time and place of Kipling's story, no new Rosamond is present to confuse the effects of the liquid and the solid, but since her story is mentioned, the little girl is not *not* present, either; she is there, as it were, in spirit. 'The Purple Jar' is about a visual appeal that exceeds the functionality of shoes made for walking. Away from the shop and from the power of its display, the illusory attraction of the jar is gone. But fascinating jars, in the modern-day shop, are still a feature—three of them, and 'superb'!—and their beauty, deceptive or otherwise, is set alongside the upright medical functions of the pharmacy, equally noted: both are simultaneously part of this place. In the same vein, the matter-of-fact naming of the Kodak product might conjure up the way that any photograph conjoins the simultaneous presence and absence of its subject, fixed by a chemical process.

As a piece of old literature returning or entering into the here and now of this night in this place, Edgeworth's story floats in the atmosphere of the shop—and of *this* story, Kipling's, that we are reading. Keats' poem 'The Eve of St Agnes' is present even more directly, since its actual words are repeated, written down, and recognized, together with the question of how, scientifically or otherwise, to explain their appearance, on the evening that is being shown. There is also a connection to Keats' own real-life pharmaceutical background: 'Ah! Anybody could see he was a druggist from that line about tinctures and syrups', says Mr Shaynor, when one of the passages he has just written down in his own drugged state is quoted back to him.[8] In Keats' poem the hero, Porphyro, has penetrated into his lady's bedchamber, and various unguents and delicacies are taken right there from her own supply, which is like a little secret store:

> And still she slept an azure-lidded sleep,
> In blanchèd linen, smooth, and lavendered,
> While he from forth the closet brought a heap
> Of candied apple, quince, and plum, and gourd,

With jellies soother than the creamy curd;
And lucent syrups, tinct with cinnamon;
Manna and dates, in argosy transferred
From Fez, and spicèd dainties, every one,
From silken Samarkand to cedared Lebanon.[9]

Sweets and creams and 'spicèd dainties, every one' all combine and merge in this 'heap' of a magical shopping list. The exotic things come out of the special 'closet', the stock of things, but are also given far-off, fabulous sources. The wondrous connection then becomes comparable to the strange travelling airwaves back in the night of the main story, passing between here and far away, the scientific miracle of the chemist's shop.

Notes

1. See Annie Ernaux, *La Place* (1983; Paris: Gallimard, Folio, 1991), 98.
2. Stanley Chapman, *Jesse Boot of Boots the Chemists: A Study in Business History* (London: Hodder and Stoughton, 1974), 71–2, 88.
3. Rudyard Kipling, 'Wireless' (1902) in *The Oxford Book of English Short Stories*, ed. A.S. Byatt (Oxford: Oxford University Press, 1998), 116, 122; 114.
4. Kipling, 'Wireless', 116.
5. Kipling, 'Wireless', 112.
6. Kipling, 'Wireless', 122.
7. Kipling, 'Wireless', 112.
8. Kipling, 'Wireless', 125.
9. John Keats, 'The Eve of St Agnes', in *Selected Poems*, ed. John Barnard (London: Penguin, 1988), 150–1.

24

Florists

Figure 11. Florists in Westow Hill, Upper Norwood, south London. Photograph taken by Emile Zola, 1898 or 1899
© Association du Musée Emile Zola

'**M**rs Dalloway said she would buy the flowers herself.'[1] Virginia Woolf's novel begins enigmatically with a future purchase. What flowers, and why 'the' flowers, that somehow need to be bought? The next sentence indicates that it has to do with helping out on a busy day: 'For Lucy had her work cut for her.' Mrs Dalloway is in a position to make this call, to step in, graciously, on a servant's behalf, to buy the flowers 'herself'. It is a sign of the considerateness of an employer for an employee in the personal intimacy of a domestic setting. But it is also Mrs Dalloway's privilege to be able to offer her assistance with a task that someone else is paid to do for her. She doesn't have to. And the buying of flowers, in any case, is a pleasant enough kind of work. The sentence does not say, for instance, that Mrs Dalloway said she would sweep the doorstep herself, or clean the stove. Flower-shopping is a ladylike occupation that does not involve getting your hands dirty; it is about supplying the house with beauty, not scrubbing it clean. Yet there is still in some functional sense, a job to be done. For a grand party—which is what is in prospect—flowers are essential, not optional extras. She said she would buy *the* flowers: definite articles.

Above all, this opening sentence presents flowers as objects of purchase: *buy* the flowers herself. They may be the most natural things in the world, but grown or at any rate picked for sale, and given a price that makes them comparable to every other commodity, they become something else. In the novel that follows, any number of small incidents show flowers being bought, different kinds and grades, and for all sorts of different reasons. One character, pitying an impoverished street seller, buys wilting blooms when she herself has little money to spare. A court official buys roses for an unfeminine female aristocrat who has invited him to lunch. Mr Dalloway buys a bouquet and carries it home to show his wife he loves her. A shabby relative of Mrs Dalloway's buys 'cheap pink flowers, half-a-dozen' to take to the party.[2] Even pressed orchids from far away and long ago, preserved by the aged Aunt Helena when she was a girl growing up in Burma, have been imported and marketized. She once wrote a book about them which, so she proudly reports to other guests at the party, went into three editions. That is, Aunt Helena's Asian flowers were frequently bought.

In the beginning, the novel accompanies Mrs Dalloway into the shop in Bond Street 'where they kept flowers for her when she gave a party', a customer well known to the owner, Miss Pym, with whom she has a long-standing relationship of mutual respect and support.[3] Quite apart from the fact that the flowers do need to be bought, being in the florist's shop is a pleasurable and multi-sensual experience in its own right:

> There were flowers: delphiniums, sweet peas, bunches of lilac; and car-nations, masses of carnations. There were roses; there were irises. Ah yes—so she breathed in the earthy-garden sweet smell as she stood talking to Miss Pym...turning her head from side to side among the irises and roses and nodding tufts of lilac with her eyes half closed, snuffing in, after the street uproar, the delicious scent, the exquisite coolness.[4]

In this different space, the flowers are seen and smelled as real flowers, differentiated by names and by a profusion of colours and perfumes and a different atmosphere of 'exquisite coolness'; 'so she breathed in the earthy-garden sweet smell.' Therapeutically, the shop interior becomes a refuge for Mrs Dalloway from the turbulence of the 'street uproar' and from her own negative thoughts.

Flower sales are among the types that have a tendency to hover outside the classificatory boundaries. They crop up in many types of outlet and situation, from street to market stall to shop, and according to every type of selling mode, from the global network to the local and casual, one-on-one. Their product is highly perishable, but it is not food. Sales are specific to occasions and to seasons (and to seasonal occasions), perhaps more than with any other commodity type. Wed-dings and funerals are major occasions for ordering 'the' flowers, Trainee florists of the 1930s were advised to learn an art of tactful recommendation for each, beginning with the recognition that 'the prospective bride or the bereaved relative who enters a flower shop is on a different footing from the one entering a grocery store.'[5] Special days are assiduously marketed as occasions for giving flowers to women: Valentine's, Mother's Day, birthdays, and anniversaries. Also Sorry, Thank You, Get Well Soon—and any number of other emoti-conic thoughts that a person may feel the need to communicate florally.

Flowers can also be regular purchases. This is a feature pointed out in the interwar trade guide providing advice for prospective florists, but as something that does not go without saying, 'for there are many beautiful wares in other trades to compete for the "luxury penny" of the average purchaser.'[6] It must also be noted that these average purchasers come in different local varieties: 'Every florist's shop or prospective flower shop will have an individual character suited to the district in which it is situated and the class of customer it serves, and it will set its stage accordingly.' Mrs Dalloway, with her important purchase for the grand party and her attentive Miss Pym, is a floral world away from most other customers. The trade guidance continues:

> It is common knowledge indeed that many people are fearful of entering a flower shop because they think the goods may be expensive and because they are afraid that they will be forced to buy something they do not really want. There is a good deal of foundation for this fear.[7]

It is the opposite of the feeling of well-being that the shop interior provides for a confidently affluent customer like Mrs Dalloway, and this other mode of wary unease is what the florist must work to alleviate: 'Above all the saleswoman must be possessed of infinite patience.... Flowers themselves need keen understanding, and they should teach understanding of human nature.'[8]

In his different way the privileged but reticent Richard Dalloway is a walking example of the likely usefulness of this tactful philosophy. He purchases flowers for his wife, 'setting off with his great bunch held against his body to Westminster, to say straight out in so many words (whatever she might think of him), holding out his flowers, "I love you."' Why not?'[9] Richard is delivering the flowers (they are roses) in person, even *on* his person—'held against his body'—and like his wife, he is buying the flowers himself. But his thoughts might be voicing the catchline *Say It with Flowers*, the phrase long identified with worldwide floral marketing.

The flower-selling industry has been at the forefront of long-distance selling in all its developing forms for the past century. 'Say It with Flowers' came into the marketing world with the Florists' Telegraph Delivery Association, founded in Detroit in 1910. The British trade guide published in the 1930s stresses the power of these words and their variations: 'Members of the Association frequently amplify the slogan to read: "Say it with Flowers, by Wire," or "Say it with Flowers, Anywhere, Anytime."'[10] A British unit of the FTDA had been inaugurated in the same year, 1923, that *Mrs Dalloway* is set; by the mid-1930s there were 700 affiliated shops. The FTDA, which later became Interflora, pioneered a method of selling and distribution that could include distance ordering (by telephone) and national or even international coordination of deliveries by telegraph. It was thus a direct precursor of online delivery services:

> A lady or gentleman may go into a florist's shop where the Mercury sign is displayed, say, in London, or Manchester, or Glasgow, or Belfast, and place an order for flowers to be delivered the same day in New York, Paris, Toronto, Southampton, or Edinburgh, and the flowers will be delivered as safely and as surely as if the customer's friend lived just round the corner.[11]

It is also tactfully noted that if the delivery is not urgent, so that the regular postal service can be used instead, the customer will be spared the cost of the cable or telegram.

With Richard Dalloway, no details are given of the actual purchase of the flowers he does buy for Clarissa, but across the space of a sentence the deed has been done: 'The time comes when it can't be said; one's too shy to say it, he thought, pocketing his sixpence or two of change.'[12] What was the price of the flowers? And how many sixpences in the change, exactly? These are not questions that Mr Dalloway needs to bear in mind.

Florists have an obvious relation to the much more recent phenomenon of garden centres, but the two rarely share space. Garden centres tend to be out of town, florists in shops on the high street or on market stalls. Garden centres flourish near places where people have gardens, florists where they don't. Another place, different again, where flowers are sold is on garage forecourts. Petrol and flowers: it is one of the stranger commodity juxtapositions, worth comparing to other odd pairings, such as when chemists and sweet shops had their little lending libraries at the back. The garage logic is one of situation—the driver is on the way somewhere, and the somewhere may be one of the heterogeneous types of social occasion, from the dinner party to the hospital visit, when a bunch of flowers can be something appropriate to bring, and when something to bring is a thought that may have escaped the visitor until they are on the way. Garage flowers are notoriously nasty, a last resort; since they began to be seen, around the 1990s, they have been substantially superseded by generally superior supermarket offerings, also placed near the entrance. They are there to attract and appeal to the customer coming in. But without any sign of a florist on hand to try out a gently persuasive understanding of human nature.

Notes

1. Virginia Woolf, *Mrs Dalloway* (1925), ed. David Bradshaw (Oxford: Oxford University Press, 2000), 3.
2. Woolf, *Mrs Dalloway*, 143.
3. Woolf, *Mrs Dalloway*, 10.
4. Woolf, *Mrs Dalloway*, 11, ellipsis mine.
5. W.B. Shearn (ed.), *The Practical Fruiterer and Florist* ((London: George Newnes, 1930s [n.d.]), Vol. I, 206.
6. Shearn *The Practical Fruiterer and Florist*, I, 205.

7. Shearn, *Practical Fruiterer and Florist*, I, 207.
8. Shearn, *Practical Fruiterer and Florist*, I, 207.
9. Woolf, *Mrs Dalloway*, 97–8.
10. Shearn, *Practical Fruiterer and Florist*, III, 212.
11. Shearn, *Practical Fruiterer and Florist*, III, 213.
12. Woolf, *Mrs Dalloway*, 97.

25

Furniture Shops

Fashion demands repeated updating, via the purchase of new things—and by the discarding or handing on of old ones, now deemed 'out of date'. It applies, most evidently, to clothing, and initially to the upper classes; the story of the expansion of consumer culture over the past two hundred years is inseparable from the extension of fashion beyond those grand and expensive heights, as mass production made possible the purchase of ready-made new clothes.

But fashion's demand to switch and show new does not apply only to clothes. Not only the body but also the room was destined to become a site of fashionable adornment. As with clothes, the movement—the idea that there is movement and change to be sought and bought—begins with the aristocracy. In the case of furnishings, though, the surprise is that such change should displace the valuable things that are there before. A passage from the novelist Fanny Burney's journal in the 1790s describes a visit to Powderham Castle, near Exmouth in Devon, where there have been, she discovers, sub-stantial changes to the décor. Burney gives a wonderful sense of the questions of class and taste that entered into the difference between, on the one hand, fixtures and fittings newly bought and conforming to current fashions, and on the other, older things left in the background and not thought worth looking at:

> The House Keeper did not let us see half the Castle; she only took us to those Rooms which the present lord has modernised, & fitted up in the

sumptuous french taste: The old part of the Castle she doubtless thought would disgrace him; forgetting—or rather never knowing—that the old part alone was worth a Traveller's curiosity, since the rest might be anticipated by a visit to any celebrated Cabinet-Maker.[1]

It seems that the lord has had a refurb; or in Burney's own word, which is as new as what he is doing, he has *modernised* the old place. But heritage—'the old part'—has its value as a tourist attraction, for Burney if not for the housekeeper: it is 'worth a Traveller's curiosity'. Burney does not quite say that the new styles are not to be seen at all— only that in a castle context this is not the point. Why visit a stately home when you could see the same display in a furniture shop? By saying 'any celebrated Cabinet-Maker', she manages to imply that such places are both ordinary and exclusive: for sure, you would be going to one with an outstanding reputation, but at the same time there might be such a one on every corner: 'any' of them will do. The phrase is also like an invitation: if you want to get an idea of contemporary interiors, then don't go to a castle, go to a shop. Thus another notable aspect of Burney's remarks is the pairing of the castle and cabinet- maker's as two kinds of venue for seeing furniture. Whether old or contemporary, furniture is not just for using or possessing; it is also for looking at.

The tour of the stately home is not being paid for (any more than it is when Mr Darcy's housekeeper shows some chance visitors round the impressive rooms of Pemberley in Jane Austen's *Pride and Prejudice* (1813), written not long after Burney's time). Nor, presumably, is it open to any random caller of whatever social class. But Burney presents such a showing as an accepted practice on both sides, an outlet for the 'curiosity' that is natural to the 'Traveller'. Shops, increasingly, would come to adopt an equivalent role as sites for the display of different styles: for pre-selling as well as for selling. Satisfy- ing a curiosity or learning about what is available, the viewer takes on a new role which will govern a great many future ways of being in the world: the role of *prospective* customer. This is no eighteenth-century

IKEA, and there is no self-assembly: production will likely be taking place on the same site, with the workshop adjoining if not continuous with the area where customers come. But like IKEA and other later furniture stores, the cabinetmaker's is a place where you may go to have a look at what's there—and *just* to look, not necessarily to make a purchase or place an order here and now. And it is a place where a furnished room is not, as such, a room—for use and for living in—but an advertisement for itself: a *show* room.

The furniture shop itself is primarily a showroom, like a living catalogue; in the same way kitchen and bathroom shops display sample items only. What you see (or sit on, or lie on) is what you will get generically—but not this particular sofa or bed or shower. IKEA—until well into the twenty-first century primarily a furniture store without a delivery service—operates its own idiosyncratic fusion of the catalogue with the showroom. The customer probably peruses the catalogue in advance. They are guided in a particular order through the store, a series of full displays of the merchandise in room settings. In a final featureless section they seek out the desired items in flatpack form (that is, in pieces); put them in a trolley; and pay for them at a checkout. The furniture is then—final part of the total self-service plan—assembled at home.

Catalogues display images of merchandise, generally for mail or (now) online order. In the exceptional case of Argos, the catalogue for summoning from the shop's own store is on the same physical site, here and now. In this high street chain, shoppers browse the book and then go up to a counter to order what they want, which is swiftly produced from elsewhere in the building. Unlike the time delay for delivery of other catalogue orders, there is only a few minutes' wait; and unlike the displays of goods in other shops, there is only the book.

In the second half of the nineteenth century, city department stores had their furniture sections on upper floors—away from the traffic of more frequented departments lower down, with space to spread out all the beds and tables and sofas: these stores were meant to stock *everything*. In the mid-twentieth century, especially after the war,

furniture shops went mainstream and downmarket, and also downstairs; selling factory-made products, they were aimed at working-
class couples who, with the offer of long-term hire purchase arrangements, could embark on the payments for a bed or a 'three-piece suite'
(that is, a sofa and two chairs). A passage from the cultural critic
Richard Hoggart's *The Uses of Literacy*, published in 1957, captures the
feel of such a place for a uniquely reflective and observant customer.
This is the beginning of it:

> The louder furniture stores are of unusual interest, especially because of
> an apparent paradox. At first glance these are surely the most hideously
> tasteless of modern shops. Every known value in decoration has been
> discarded: there is no evident design or pattern; the colours fight with
> one another; anything new is thrown in simply because it is new. There
> is strip-lighting together with imitation chandelier lighting; plastics,
> wood and glass are all glued and stuck and blown together; notice
> after blazing notice winks, glows or blushes luminously. Hardly a
> homely setting.[2]

In this first glance first stage, Hoggart presents a wholesale abolition of
both taste and familiarity, with 'Every known value' thrown out. It is
now all fake, 'imitation' lighting, flashing away, newness for newness's
sake—the standard objection to lack of substance in mass-produced
consumer goods. 'Hardly a homely setting', comfortably rueful and a
bit sarcastic, then comes back to soften the initial screech at 'surely the
most hideously tasteless of modern shops'. Still, the implication is that
home is what a furniture shop should feel like.

Yet this is only the preamble, as there are second and third glances
to come. These turn on the salesmen who come across to begin with
as a continuation of the general alien environment:

> Nor do the superficially elegant men who stand inside the doorway, and
> alternately tuck their hankies up their cuffs or adjust their ties, appear to
> belong to 'Us'. They are not meant to. With their neat ready-made
> clothing, shiny though cheap shoes, well-creamed hair and ready smiles

they are meant (like the equally harassed but flashier motor-car salesmen) to represent an ethos.[3]

All show and surface, just like the goods they are selling. On the one hand, there is no substance beneath. And on the other, this is a performance. The salesmen are standing for something (they 'represent an ethos'): this is a show with a meaning. But also, quite simply, they are acting, putting it on, smiling to order.

But then, in a third glance (or perhaps after a longer listening) these men of unsubstance turn out after all to be decent underneath, to be just like you and me; the sound of them is familiar where the look of them is not:

> The proprietors realise that working-class people will be dazzled by the exuberance and glitter of their display, will be attracted and yet a little awed. The manner of their salesmen is usually, therefore, understandingly colloquial... 'I know what it's like, madam,' or, 'I had a young couple just like you in only last week'; all in the tone of an understanding son who has done well and become cultured.... this type of shop—the huge, glossy affair aiming specifically at working-class customers—specialises in this approach.[4]

Hoggart's portrayal both is and is not an indictment of 'this type of shop'. For all the apparent turn or return to the sense of a relatably local boy who can after all be comfortably found inside the smart suit, the subsequent sentences are clear about the decisive agency of 'Those who direct' and the way that the appeal of 'the personal' is a deliberate and deceptive ploy; it's described as 'a pretty Trojan horse'.[5] But most striking in the passage are the many levels of the description. There are the superficial presentations, of the décor and the stuff for sale and the salesmen's outfits. There are the likely phrases to be used. And behind these there is the analysis of customer expectations, of how the 'understandably awed' are at the same time 'attracted'. On the part of the understated observer, who listens to the patter with a placing ear, there is an identification with each one of these always at least double parts. Hoggart puts himself in the place of the customer reacting to the new kind of shop; of the entrepreneur considering the customers' likely reactions; and implicitly, of the youngish salesman who is in one way part of the new furniture and in another a representative of home.

A few years later, another big furniture store is described, this time from its outside, by another male observer, this one fictional and on his own. In *The Unfortunates*, B.S. Johnson's experimental novel of 1966, the narrator—a football reporter—is walking about on a Saturday morning in the centre of a city he knows he has been in before, but cannot identify. He recognizes one particular store:

> Downhill, this must lead to the square, I remember this big furnishers, yes, it lies directly the other side, a whole block, follow it round, follow it round, to the front. These curved windows were modern, now seem dated, but there are no reflections, still, they take up space, a four-feet-wide strip round the perimeter of your showroom, that much out of your floor area, selling floor area, too. Can we afford it?

As he rounds the corner he starts to imagine what could lie behind the thinking of the store management in making their choices. He doesn't so much describe the unusual windows as translate them obliquely into hypothetical calculations of cost-effectiveness. But his internal invention then shifts its position—into the store, and now into the minds of the buyers not the vendors, the 'couples' who come in to purchase:

> Not that the sort of stuff they stock needs selling, anyway, it is that kind which is so presented that it appears to offer a complete range of choice, indeed, I should not be surprised if there were to be notices inside claiming something to that effect, if not for the whole country perhaps for the biggest range, most complete choice in the Midlands, certainly in this city: so that almost all couples coming here for their bedroom suite, their sofa and easy chairs, their carpets and kitchen cabinets, will feel that what they see does indeed represent all that there is to choose from, and therefore limit the area of their own choosing merely to colour and price and simple availability.

This whole interior scene takes place in the narrator's head as he stands on the pavement outside. It is an imagined encounter between the customers and the presentation of what they can see, complete with promotional notices inside the store.

In a final flourish of the fiction (that is, of the fiction within the fiction), the couple or couples are at home at some indeterminate point in the future, in the not enjoyment of what they bought in the first imagined moment:

> Then they wonder at the ordinariness, the sameness, the dissatisfaction they vaguely feel, the resentment at each instalment payment, for thirty months or more a weekly reminder of the moment of non-choice. I am so cynical. And besides, how do I know any of those things? I do not.[6]

Cynical and ignorant that he is, or claims to be, Johnson's narrator is sociologically sharp in his identification of a newly couple-oriented mode of Saturday shopping. Johnson supposes not only that the couples will not be happy—'the ordinariness, the sameness, the dissatisfaction they vaguely feel'—but also that the moment of purchase will linger as a bad memory, to be triggered whenever they have to make a payment for the furniture that has failed to bring them the pleasure they hoped it would.

There is no sympathetic identification here—as there is when Hoggart, in his own observations of the psychology of the modern furniture store, moves between the imagined minds of salesmen, management, and customers in his big new furniture store.[7] But Johnson, despite the persona of wilful disengagement, has nonetheless developed an absorbing account of the shopping environment he finds himself standing in front of. Both narratives, his and Hoggart's, testify to the power of new kinds of shop to elicit new stories of likely behaviour and disposition, with all concerned, the various grades of customer and vendor, being cast in new roles, each with particular kinds of dialogue. The furniture store, with its stage-set reality, is perhaps the ideal home for such inventions.

Notes

1. Fanny Burney, *The Journals and Letters of Fanny Burney (Madame d'Arblay)*, Volume I: 1791–1792, Letters 1–39, ed. Joyce Hemlow with Curtis D. Cecil and Althea Douglas (Oxford: Clarendon Press, 1972), 29; entry for Tuesday 16 August 1791.
2. Richard Hoggart, *The Uses of Literacy: Changing Patterns in English Mass Culture* (1957; Boston: Beacon Press, 1961), 90.
3. Hoggart, *The Uses of Literacy*, 90.
4. Hoggart, *The Uses of Literacy*, 90.
5. Hoggart, *The Uses of Literacy*, 90–1.
6. B.S. Johnson, *The Unfortunates* (1969; Picador, 1999), 5th section, 1–2.
7. See Hoggart, *The Uses of Literacy*, 90–3.

26

Haberdashery

This crazy word—*haberdashery*—somehow holds together the abstraction appropriate to a very long noun, along with a ratatat string of little not quite words running around inside it—the run-up to the *dash* and the slide down after. Have-a-dash-at-it! It is delightful to discover that not only are the origins of the word unclear—though it has a long and sometimes noble history, going back to the early Middle Ages—but also that it apparently has no particular meaning. Like the jumble of its own syllables, it is sort of all the bits and bobs, the odds and ends and little thises and thats' that don't belong anywhere else. Since about the middle of the nineteenth century, this assortment has mostly meant sewing materials, from thimbles and needles to thread and scissors: that is, everything you need for making something except the fabric itself. More or less well-stocked inventories of haberdashery would be and often still are present in shops of many varieties: in department stores, most noticeably and by (departmental) name, but also in village shops, and ordinary local general stores, as well as (in earlier centuries) the mercers who sold the materials for making clothes. Today, small hardware stores may also stock this stuff under the sign of 'sewing materials'—the so much more colourful *haberdashery* having sadly been tidied away.

In department stores, once upon a time, but not so long ago, haberdashery was always to be found on the ground floor, along with cosmetics and also, quite likely, menswear. This seemingly unlikely positioning of men's clothing and accessories deserves some comment as part of a curious corner of the history of layouts of large stores. Menswear was put in this prominent place on the grounds that if the man was buying for himself (as opposed to being bought for by some ancillary female) he would not want to be troubled by having to seek out the appropriate department at any significant distance from the entrance. To find what he needs he must be able simply to drop in and out, to dash but not haberdash, and then—after obtaining his requirements—to get on with the many other pressing demands on his time and attention.

In the early 1980s, a marketing agency proposed to one Paris department store that one way to increase the number of male customers would be to have topless women assistants in the mens-wear department. This was not implemented, but the very suggestion shows what could be presumed, in one quarter at least at this time, about men and shopping. The embarrassment or unlikeliness of a man shopping at all might be overcome if he was visibly doing it for a more basic reason. Whereas if women want to buy clothes—as they so much more often do than men—they will willingly, so the theory implies, go upstairs to the next floor. The entrance-level department store experience for ladies is much more recognizable as a manifest-ation of ordinary feminine occupations and preoccupations: make-up and toiletries for body and face are adjacent to haberdashery and often to fabrics too, supplying those things for the always ongoing work of sewing, both mending and making. These are all small items, not heavy in weight or price; they are sited accessibly for a swift planned purchase; they are also there because it is the area that everyone has to pass through on the way to or back down from upper floors. Like the little items put on a counter next to the till, they are meant to catch the passing eye and suggest the 'impulse' addition of something else.

In H.G. Wells's novel *Kipps*, published in 1905, the young hero grows up living above a high street shop in a small town on the south coast of England. He becomes best friends with the haberdasher's son next door. He gets a job in a department store big enough to have a 'ribbon department' and 'glove counter' separately named.[1] Years later, after he and his wife have experienced both a sudden rise and then a sudden fall in their material fortunes, Kipps is all ready to set up a branch of a new style of bookshop. Its smart fitting out is described with loving detail, down to the pleasure of inscribing name and figures in the beautiful new accounts notebook. But out of the blue, while he is basking in anticipation of the shop that is about to be, it suddenly turns out that there would have been something even better: 'Next to starting a haberdasher's shop I doubt if Kipps could have been more truly happy than during those weeks of preparation.' And it ought to be obvious why:

> There is, of course, nothing on earth, and I doubt at times if there is a joy in heaven, like starting a small haberdasher's shop. Imagine, for example, having a drawerful of tapes (one whole piece most exquisitely blocked) of every possible width of tape, or again, an army of neat large packages, each displaying one sample of hooks and eyes. Think of your cottons, your drawer of coloured silks, the little, less, least of the compartments and thin packets of your needle-drawer! Poor princes and wretched gentlefolk, mysteriously above retail trade, may taste only the faint unsatisfactory shadow of these delights, with trays of stamps or butterflies. I write, of course, for those to whom these things appeal; there are clods alive who see nothing, or next to nothing, in spools of mercerised cotton and endless bands of paper-set pins.[2]

This eulogy comes out of nowhere, 'and as I write', says the mock-embarrassed narrator, 'I wonder that Kipps resisted haberdashery. He did.'[3] The pleasure is all for the careful keeping and consequent contemplation of the tiny and infinitely differentiated articles of the haberdasher's stock. It is a collection to be curated—as with the private 'museum' of sample spices and tea leaves which a grocer's apprentice of this period is instructed to send for and study, as a preliminary to conducting real trade with such things in a shop.[4] And as such—as a specialized gathering together of all the varieties of one kind of thing—it is an excuse for a moment of gentle class satire: each to their own tray of beloved objects of devotion and knowledge, but the shop offers so much more.

In this early twentieth-century iteration, in the form of the little items of sewing kit, haberdashery seems to be edging towards the old-fashioned; a century later, the shops had gone. But in the third decade of the twenty-first century, crafts and making are returning to the shopping picture. This is part of the emerging resistance to fast fashion, with the recognition of the environmental damage done by cheap ready-made clothes and the frequent purchase and discarding of them. But the handiwork of knitting and sewing is also popular because of what it can do for the heart and soul of the maker, here and now, as the hand moves the needle in and out of the material. No rush—no needless haberdash—but a slow time set against the speed of the fashion cycle and the habitual distance, both physically and in terms of knowledge, from the manufacturing sources of what we buy and wear and throw away. Even without the long name (the word itself isn't really back on the table), haberdashery may be said to be having a moment fit to gratify *Kipps'* narrator.

Going further back in time, haberdashery was something else again. In the Middle Ages, the haberdashers were one of the fourteen merchant guilds. They were second only to the mercers; a haberdasher features among five tradesmen in the General Prologue to Geoffrey Chaucer's *Canterbury Tales*. The mercer, in many ways complementary to the haberdasher, is another now virtually abandoned character who was common in earlier times. As a word, it may be less immediately attractive than the dapper haberdasher but at one time the mercer's place among the basic shops of any small town was equally essential, and he or (often) she has distant successors in any shop now that sells clothes. *Mercery* referred (at least) to the cloths and fabrics to be bought and then made into garments and domestic drapery, but might well include non-perishable food items as well. *Mercer* comes from a Latin root, the same as for *merchant* and *mercenary*—two roughly trading words that have survived their meandering journeys through the centuries with more success than their more settled selling brother, the mercer. In the seventeenth and eighteenth centuries the terms *mercer* and *milliner* were practically interchangeable—with milliner not yet having fixed its later specialization to mean only what ladies put on their heads; there was also an overlapping of meaning (and of commodities) between *mercer* and *grocer*, the latter not selling just food and the former not just *not* food. Such a rudimentary binary division of portable goods may seem crude—either hand to mouth, or not—as though in need of some superior system of classification; but present-day all-selling superstores have found no better way to separate their products than by means of this would-be primordial differentiation between food and non-food.

Both the prosperity and the public service of the members of medieval guilds are evident in their endowment of educational insti-tutions; Haberdashers' Aske's school, founded in the late seventeenth century, is probably better known now than the organization that began it. But haberdashery's own beginnings, before this later bricks and mortar time, are more varied and more simple. The word was first known in the context of the multiplicity of small items to be found in a pedlar's pack. These included not only the useful—the pins or needles—but also the pretty—the ribbons or brooches. Of course, a distinction between the pretty and the useful is both needless and wrong (all else being equal, why would you not choose the more attractive ribbon?). But since pedlars were, in their time, a main source of such goods as were actually bought—as opposed to being made or grown or swapped—then haberdashery's packing in of objects of both use and pleasure in one long capacious word seems exactly right.

For if haberdashery has one true identity it is as a (charming) name for any little commodity: something that has been bought and sold, but also, within that minimal definition, anything at all. In the all but thingless world of Samuel Beckett's novel *Malone Dies* (1951), there is left on a table 'the crumpled paper-bag containing a few little articles of haberdashery'.[5] That seeming precision without really any at all encapsulates the beauty of the word: its very length implying author-ity but also, given the contrast with the small things it refers to, a kind of linguistic absurdity. We can't see and aren't told what is in this bag—but paper bags do come from shops, and so does haberdashery.

Someone some time bought something. Curiously, haberdashery doesn't really belong in a house; once out of the bag and into a drawer, separated into its different items, it stops being known by that name.

So perhaps after all, through all its variations, there is some stability of haberdasher meaning, as one little thing or another makes its way round the fairs, through the shops, and finally into the drawers and boxes at home where useful or pretty oddments may be kept. Whatever else it may be, haberdashery is something that has been or will be bought and sold in and for a small amount: for *pin* money, perhaps. Samuel Johnson's dictionary, from the middle of the eighteenth century, says this of the haberdasher:

> This word is ingeniously deduced by *Minshew* from *habt ihr dass*, German, *have you this*, the expression of a shopkeeper offering his wares to sale. One who sells small wares; a pedlar.

Johnson's definition encompasses both shopkeeper and pedlar, both bricks-and-mortar and mobile shopping modes; and both ancient and (in his day) newer practices. The etymology he offers, whether or not it has any validity, perfectly summarizes the essence of every pre-purchasing encounter. Have you this? It could be anything—any thing. Notably, too, that question moves across the counter to switch to the other role. Here it is the shopkeeper making a suggestion (and if you don't already 'have' this, you may want or need this); on the other side, it can be a customer who already knows what they want and asks if it is in stock—or in the pack. This would surely make haberdasher or haberdashery the perfect portmanteau shopping word, including both buyer and seller in their likely verbal interchange, and including also the shifting boundary between needed and newly desirable commodities: what must be bought, or what it is nice to buy.

Haberdashery, then, has undergone some mutations in its long slow movement through retailing history. But as if to throw a further spanner into the works—or a random hook into the fabric—the American use of the term is different again. It refers to a store or department specifically selling men's clothes—and so the *dash* within the word can take on a more smartly masculine sound or appearance, while the initial *haber*, a little like Latin, suggests something almost preppy, a sense of the upstanding and dignified, perhaps, to team with the dashing exterior. No more trivial little things, no more bits and pieces of sewing stuff; those items, in America, are usually called not haberdashery, but *notions*. And so it could happen that in the 1970s a male American editor of the works of Chaucer, succumbing to a sort of reverse anachronism, glossed the General Prologue's HABERDAS-SHERE as a 'dealer in men's clothes and sewing notions'.[6]

But finally, could it be that haberdashery, with all of its pretty and useful little things, might hold the key, or the pin, for a smaller and slower future for fashion. Before clothes were bought ready-made or new, every garment was different from every other to begin with. Clothes might be passed on to someone else, but they would not be thrown out (they would probably be handed on or down). On the other hand they could be endlessly altered to fit with styles or seasons or sizes, at the pleasure of the present owner. Haberdashery could make them different for the new wearer or the new year: threads and ribbons and bits of lace here or there could alter or remake a gown or a bonnet at any time. In the many centuries before the factory pro-duction of identical garments, this was what happened as a matter of course—thanks to what could be bought from the mercer's or draper's shop in the town or village; or else, before there were shops at all, from the pedlar or market trader. Haberdashery, with its modest assortments of pretty and useful wares, offered the means for these individual touches and occasional transformations of one thing or another.

Notes

1. H.G. Wells, *Kipps* (1905; Harmondsworth: Penguin, 1946), 95.
2. Wells, *Kipps*, 336.
3. Wells, *Kipps*, 336.

4. C.J. Elliott, *The Retail Grocery Trade: A Book of General Guidance for Apprentices and Assistants* (London: Methuen & Co. Ltd., 1938).

5. Samuel Beckett, *Malone Dies* (1951; Harmondsworth: Penguin, 1962), 38.

6. 'General Prologue', *The Canterbury Tales*, The *Complete Poetry and Prose of Geoffrey Chaucer*, ed. John H. Fisher (New York: Holt, Rinehart and Wilson, 1977), 16, referring to line 361 of the *Prologue*.

27

Household Goods

In the second national Census of Distribution in 1961, the commodities sold by more than sixty thousand of Britain's shops are placed inside the broad category of 'household goods'. At that moment in time, four subdivisions are chosen; they include (with perhaps a speck of classificatory despair) 'Radio and/or electrical goods', but also 'Cycle and perambulator shops (including cycle & radio shops)'.[1] 'Household goods' covers an evolving mix of things that at any one time provide the tools and tech and machines of the home; in 1961 it is surely television sets that have prompted the confusing hybridity of that 'radio and/or electrical' box. Once superseded, most of these one-time state-of-the-household brand new things will be consigned to the collective basement of oblivion or nostalgic memory. There they keep the associations of an earlier moment when the item in question was part of the fabric of future (desirable) then of ordinary life: the movement from the publicity of 'every home should have one' to the dull fact that every home has one. When it's gone, it's gone.

But that isn't then the end of the story. Some of these relatively short-lived commodities and the shops that supply them, closely bound up with particular times, may come to have a far more active presence in conversations and representations of every kind than they did during the period when they were just part of the furniture, ordinary objects in regular use. Who (if they ever went into one) does not have memories of the video rental store, which came and went in a few short years from the start of the 1980s—to be seen no more on the high street, but to be lovingly reminisced about until the end of time?

One source of household goods whose stock and stability have changed little over the course of the past century is the ironmonger's or hardware store. Against the odds, this has survived the competition from DIY superstores, which arrived in the1980s alongside the big new supermarkets that often shared the same out-of-town sites. The ironmonger's has a presence in every row of local shops, but it is not a common subject of written reflection, and fictional appearances are few. So it is all the more surprising to find one in Aldous Huxley's *Brave New World*, of all unlikely places. In the blandly futuristic environment of this novel, in which easy going and happy feeling are the only ways to be, 'John the Savage' is the natural-born character unconditioned by the standard methods of socialization, and deployed within the narrative as a voice of authentic protest, come from afar. His fortunate childhood reading of the complete works of Shakespeare (a volume encountered by chance) later stands him in good critical stead when he is transported to the world of modern civilization. But the change does not work and it does not take long for John to have to be billeted off to a retreat well away from everyone else's world, in the depths of rural Surrey (as such retreats always are in Huxley's novels). Prior to going there, John makes some practical preparations, which are detailed (very fully detailed) as follows:

> Before leaving London he had bought four viscose-woollen blankets, rope and string, nails, glue, a few tools, matches (though he intended in due course to make a fire drill), some pots and pans; two dozen packets of seeds, and ten kilogrammmes of wheat flour.[2]

What universe are we suddenly in? It is as if the smoothly modern techno-world of the rest of the novel had momentarily disappeared into thin air while the narrative reverts, for a moment, to a good old-fashioned shopping list for some practical camper carefully getting himself ready for a trip to the pretty Surrey hills. And where on earth— or where in the world of *Brave New World*—does John get this stuff? There is, just about, a hint of some sort of actual store in which, like the object of a marketing textbook discussion, 'he had not been able to resist the shopman's persuasion' and had succumbed, against his better intentions, to various unnatural food products; 'looking at the tins now, he bitterly reproached himself for his weakness. Loathsome civilized stuff!'[3] Yet in the rest of the novel, for all its preoccupation with the hedonistically consuming lifestyle of the inhabitants of the new world, there is not a word about shops or shopping of any kind. What is remarkable, then, about the half acknowledged episode is not this rejection of weird new things, the Savage's trademark attitude, but instead the implication, given the list of purchases, that he simply dropped into some good old local hardware store to pick up a few bits and pieces.

Brand new shops selling brand new machines for the home, along with all the accessories to go with them or play on them, were the stand-out high street newcomers of the decades before the war. Such things were noted as especially suited for sale in smaller, local shops because of the service aspect: someone to explain how it works, set it up for you, and maintain it after the purchase. For this purpose most shops had their own workshop. Once, such a place attached to a sales area would have meant that the goods were made on site. This later kind was only for repairs. But aftersales service in all its forms brought back an element of manual workmanship to shops, at the same time as they became the primary outlets for products associated with technical innovation and factory production. A book of the early 1930s draws attention to this rare double advantage of the modern appliance store (rare in that generally, for these economists, there are far too many small shops for the good of either their keepers or their customers). In the traditional ways, the shopkeeper is close to his customers: on hand to assist both before and after the purchase. And 'if he is of an adventurous turn of mind, he can pioneer the sale of new commodities—radio sets afford a recent striking example— and hope with luck and judgment to do very well for himself.'[4]

Stan Barstow's novel *A Kind of Loving* (1960) has a nice example of just such a quietly enterprising small-town store. The history of this shop is like a textbook case of the successful local business adapting to changing times and newly promoted demands for household tech. Before the war it was selling the then current domestic entertainment goods, including gramophones and radio sets. More mundanely and practically, there is mention too of packets of needles, and older equipment brought in for repair. Now, in the 1950s, TV sets are the vital new object, and the shop also sells (vinyl) records. These include the singles from the weekly 'Hit Parade', which the owner, Mr Van Huyten, doesn't pretend to understand—or makes a show of not understanding. Hire purchase payment is standard for major purchases: one customer astonishes by handing over the cash—all of seventy-four guineas—for the radiogram he is buying. Speaking outside the shop to a potential customer, the novel's main character Vic smoothly refers to its interior as 'our inside showroom', to be seen as an amplification of the external display in the windows. True again to the standard picture, there is a workshop for the repairs onsite, in a room behind the main selling space. Mr Van Huyten has recently invested in a smart new motor van, with the shop's name on it, for deliveries of heavy appliances and for picking up those to be taken in for repair. It replaces a battered pre-war vehicle that had been doing the job before.

Vic has his own bright ideas for modest innovation. One is to stagger staff lunch hours on the busy day, Saturday, so that the shop does not need to shut; another is to make it possible for customers to browse through the records in stock, rather than have to know in advance what they want, and ask for it. It is as if he is following the advice of a salesmanship manual and taking a conscious interest in psychology:

> One day, towards the back end of June I'm leaning on the counter in the shop, feeling a bit cheesed. Mr Van Huyten's doing his accounts in his little glass cubby-hole and Henry's busy in the back. Things are a bit slack

this morning and by ten o'clock we've had a woman in for a record catalogue, another woman with an electric iron for repair, and a bod who's wandered round looking at TV sets and radiograms and wouldn't let me tell him anything about them. 'I'm just looking,' he says. I know his type. He'll go home and tell his family that the assistants at Van Huyten's are too pushing. And if you take no notice of people when they come in they go away and say we don't give them service and attention.[5]

Turning the non-purchaser into a 'type' is a way of getting a distance on him—just as Vic also imagines that the customer does the same with him ('the assistants...too pushing').

Such details about the running of the shop, or sample scenes, emerge here and there in the course of the main story of *A Kind of Loving*, which otherwise follows a familiar pattern for novels by men about northern industrial towns in the 1950s and early 1960s. That is to say, a more or less disaffected local young man with a solid but boring job thinks of breaking away, but his on-off girlfriend gets pregnant and so they marry and that is the end to his dream of a different life. At the start of the novel, Vic works for an engineering firm as a draughtsman; he also has a Saturday job in the music and electrical goods shop. Then Mr Van Huyten, who is getting on in years and wants to step back, offers him a full-time post. The shop remains the constant in his life when Vic has to move from his parents' house to his in-laws', after the wedding. The two other men in the shop, both of them quite content with their lives, represent opposite models of male existence. Henry, who does the repairs, has a wife and five children. Mr Van Huyten is the cultured older mentor who introduces working-class (but grammar-school) Vic to classical music. The suggestion is that with no near family of his own, he is going to leave the shop to Vic as a surrogate son.

Mr Van Huyten is oblivious, or pretends to be, to the turmoil that leads to Vic's sudden need for a week off to go on a honeymoon. In the shop, the only kind of exceptional hurry comes with the wanted and expected 'week-end rush', which brings numbers of younger customers into the shop on a Saturday morning ('the rush starts and the fans are crowding me at the counter'), a sign that the place is doing well.[6] When the distresses of his new wife's miscarriage and rows with the mother-in-law take hold of Vic, the shop owner's initiative in adopting him as his successor is a significant story in its own less dramatic way, combining a mutual fit between two individuals with an informal piece of intercultural integration (Mr Van Huyten is Dutch). In a similar way the shop itself, through the easy-going personality of its proprietor as well as in what it sells, creates a friendly coexistence of old and new musical tastes.

Mr Van Huyten makes an imaginative choice for the future of his shop, one that departs from conventional stories of the commercial marriage of convenience and its household histories. The traditional small-shop story involves a business passing from father to son or sons—or failing that, to a daughter's husband who would typically have worked his way into becoming part of the family, via an appren-ticeship. The living quarters were usually above or behind the shop, and the wife and the rest of the family shared the work as well as the space. In the absence of a son (who would also learn the trade himself), a decent apprentice becoming the son-in-law was a natural alternative. There are plenty of literary examples of this second plan, generally when it goes wrong in some way: that is, if either the daughter or the apprentice is attracted to an outsider instead. In a short story by Balzac, 'La Maison du Chat-qui-pelote' (1830), the daughter in a small draper's is expecting to marry the apprentice—as he is her. But then she falls for a painter who has fallen for her—and whose picture of her in the tenderly old-fashioned setting of the family shop is the cause of his sudden success. His fame moves him into superior social circles, and the rest of the story is then a case study of the young wife's attempts to overcome her inadequacy in the face of a new sort of class divide. But it is too late for her to go back to the shop that is now an image of endearing anachronism—as it is in the story itself, which is set some decades before the time of its writing.

Zola's novels include both versions of the thwarted succession-by-marriage story. In *Thérèse Raquin* (1867) the shop, in a dingy Paris arcade, belongs to a widow who has a delicate son and a feisty adopted daughter, her brother's child. In a perversely excessive project of matriarchal control, keeping everything in the (micro-)family, she has always intended for them to marry. Which they do, only then for Thérèse to begin a passionate affair with a brawny long-standing friend of the family, leading first to the husband's murder and then to an aftermath of guilt for both parties—the shop in its small way keeping going all the while.

In *Thérèse Raquin* the scene rarely leaves the confining space of the shop and its upstairs living quarters; its limited, unenterprising trade is not a source of either interest or preoccupation for any of the characters. But in *Au Bonheur des Dames*, written ten years later, it is the contrast between two different types of shop, one brazenly modern and the other hopelessly stagnant, that underlies the fateful attraction of Colomban, the dull apprentice, to a female assistant from the brash new department store which is putting his master's small local shop out of business. Colomban's transgressive adoration continues in its sad, unrequited way while the daughter's health declines, as does her parents' income from their shop. His desertion, and the halting of the simple marriage story, is presented as one more indication of an inexorable economic process, as the helpless little shop succumbs to the dynamically predatory new one. The marriage with which this novel ends is the fairy-tale cross-class union of Octave Mouret, the owner of the big store, to the penniless Denise Baudu, an orphaned niece of the declining shopkeeper; Denise has been working at the rival establishment in order to support two younger brothers. In a mythically satisfying way, Denise thus represents a unifying bridge between the two worlds, as well as being given an updated role as a sort of socially conscious saint. She is maternal with her little brothers but also in relation to her job, where she uses her influence with the boss to press successfully for a whole raft of welfare measures: a pension scheme, paid holidays, and an end to the practice of seasonal redundancies. But she also appreciates the creative energy of the new way of doing things, and is swiftly promoted to run a new department (children's goods, of course). In her job, and then through her marriage, Denise's feminine niceness is seen to domesticate the ruthlessness of the hitherto unrestricted entrepreneur. With a modern updating, this is thus a version of the classic plot of the virtuous woman tempering the naturally amoral male. Denise is an upwardly mobile employee with a responsible job of her own; at the same time she is a well-behaved advocate of workers' rights, in the spirit of late nineteenth-century reforming times.

The household story in *A Kind of Loving* is different from any of these diverse small- and large-shop marriages, as seen by Balzac and Zola. In Barstow's novel there is an assistant and there is a wedding, but this happens for reasons of moral necessity rather than commercial convenience; it has nothing to do with the shop. Or to put this the other way round: there is a plan for a quasi-filial inheritance for the shop, but here it has nothing to do with the marriage. With its sense of a past and future of solid transmission and continuing innovation, this commercial hopefulness quietly makes up for the other kind of loving.

Notes

1. *Report on the Census of Distribution and Other Services 1961* (London: Her Majesty's Stationery Office, 1963), Part I, Establishment Tables.
2. Aldous Huxley, *Brave New World* (1932; Harmondsworth: Penguin, 1970), 191.
3. Huxley, *Brave New World*, 191.
4. Dorothea Braithwaite and S.P. Dobbs, *The Distribution of Consumable Goods: An Economic Study* (London: George Routledge & Sons Ltd., 1932), 245.
5. Stan Barstow, *A Kind of Loving* (1960; Harmondsworth: Penguin, 1962), 166.
6. Barstow, *A Kind of Loving*, 59, 154.

28

Jewellers

'**D**ame Roase, buying many things in the shop, drank tea with me'; 'Dame Vallow and daughter, buying some things in the shop, drank tea with me.'[1] Regular customers of Thomas Turner's village shop in the eighteenth century might be invited into the private accommodation at the back for a drink or a game of cards. The sitting room enabled Turner to speak or relax with customers and other commercial connections, such as the reps who called to take and deliver his diverse orders. This room behind also suggests the continuity of the shopkeeper's position as a part of the community in both his selling and his social capacity. Relations with customers and with other tradesmen are fostered by the sharing of a meal or drink, but there is no rigid divide in the first place between the personal and the professional roles, any more than the further room is radically cut off from the main selling space of the shop. The memory of this indistinction may remain in the generic designation of a shop or trading business as a 'house'—as in 'House of Fraser', 'house style', or 'in-house'; the usage is even more standard in French, where a business is regularly referred to—like home—as *la maison*.

For purchases of jewellery or other luxury goods at the top end of the market, the whole shop may be a private, exclusive space, with uniformed bouncers on the door to ensure that only the right kind of person is allowed to enter. This arrangement goes against the modern shop ethos of open access, whereby anyone is free to come in and look around; by the same token it reinforces a sense of the special distinctions of the jeweller's. There is a rich example of this overlaying of the exclusively private and the discreetly commercial in Madame de Lafayette's novel of 1678, *La Princesse de Clèves*. This features one of the earliest scenes in literature to take place in something like a shop, meaning a fixed indoor place (not a market stall or an opening onto the street) where customers enter to look and be shown and to choose. The scene is very brief: it is over in the blink of an eye and the turn of a page. But for the plot of the novel it is vital: love at first sight! The setting is the French court of the sixteenth century (a hundred years before the date of the novel), and Mlle de Chartres is as yet unknown in Versailles:

> The day after her arrival, in order to match some precious gems, she went to the house of an Italian who traded in them throughout the world. This man had come from Florence with the Queen, and his trade had made him so wealthy that his house looked more like a great lord's than a merchant's. While she was there, the Prince of Clèves turned up. He was so surprised by her beauty that he could not hide his surprise; and Mlle de Chartres could not stop herself from blushing when she saw the astonishment she had given him. She pulled herself together all the same, without showing any other attention to the prince's actions than what politeness required her to give to a man of the kind he appeared to be.[2]

The focus shifts from one to the other, and what each was unable *not* to do (be surprised, or blush). There is no formal introduction. He falls for her, and there is a mutual sizing up much like the kind of knowledgeable appraisal and valuation that would occur with the jewels. As with her reading of him, he can see that she must be someone important, and he also speculates about her age. This being a highly enclosed court society, he is indeed properly introduced to her the very next day. Meanwhile the merchant's house offers a rare opportunity for an encounter which is anonymous, while at the same time both parties can appreciate each other's status, their likely credit-worthiness as potential partners.

From a later perspective, what can be seen is that this is an intermediate kind of space, not fully a shop after all in the modern sense,
since there seems to be no separation between living quarters and
selling space. That it should be at a jeweller's establishment that the
sighting and not quite meeting take place is exactly right for the
choosing of such a uniquely priceless woman—and draws on long
religious and mythical traditions likening beautiful young girls to
matchless gems. But frustratingly, apart from the general appraisal of
its grand appearance, the novel provides not a single detail about the
house-shop's interior, or the jewels that are available, or whatever
discussions and showings have already taken place between Mlle de
Chartres and the merchant before the disruptive arrival of M. de Clèves.

On the other hand, that the merchant is an Italian who came to
France with the queen is precious information. This novel is historical:
it is set a century before its own time, specifically at the court of the
French king François II, whose queen was Catherine de Medicis,
famous as a patron of artistic work in Florence and then in France.
Mlle de Chartres and the Prince de Clèves were not actual historical
people, but most of the characters in the novel were, and it is irresist-
ible to wonder whether there was such a cosmopolitan jeweller as this
one in the environs of the court. Unlike his distinctive client, who will
be at the centre of the story that follows, this merchant remains
without a name, whether fictional or real, and is never seen again in
the novel.

Some centuries on, Virginia Woolf's Mrs Dalloway (1925) shows a
glimpse of an early twentieth-century London version of the upper-
class jeweller's. After their (very slightly) working luncheon in the
Mayfair home of the grand Lady Bruton, Richard Dalloway and
Hugh Whitbread drift away together and find themselves semi-
shopping in the post-prandial aftermath of their meal. 'They looked
in at a shop window; they did not wish to buy or to talk but to part.'[3]
After this curt assertion of a negative motivation shared—even in its
division—by both, there is a mental rather than physical separation
between them. Hugh starts to take an interest in a possible purchase

for his wife, while Richard gives inner vent to a contempt for the pampered privilege of Hugh and Evelyn. And for what it's worth, this passage is a very rare picture, whether in literature or any other medium, of two men, even if accidentally, out shopping together:

> Aware that he was looking at a silver two-handled Jacobean mug, and that Hugh Whitbread admired condescendingly, with airs of connoisseurship, a Spanish necklace which he thought of asking the price of in case Evelyn might like it—still Richard was torpid; could not think or move. Life had thrown up this wreckage; shop windows full of coloured paste, and one stood stark with the lethargy of the old, stiff with the rigidity of the old, looking in. Evelyn Whitbread might like to buy this Spanish necklace—so she might. Yawn he must. Hugh was going into the shop.[4]

Hugh and Evelyn's specialized knowledge of valuable old things also features earlier in the novel in the thoughts of another character, Peter Walsh. The earlier passage involves a memory of being given a tour of the Whitbreads' house as if it were a museum. Peter remembers being shown a series of carefully preserved or collected features and things: 'you had to spend a great deal of time always admiring whatever it was—linen cupboards, pillow-cases, old oak furniture, pictures, which Hugh had picked up for an old song.'[5] So Hugh bargains or bids on occasion—with the knowing cliché of getting it for a song also suggesting that this is the way that he likes to talk about it himself: that how he acquired the things and how little he managed to get them for is part of the story he tells about what they are and when and where they come from.

At the jeweller's, though, there is no mention of a deal or even a discussion about the money. Hugh goes in to find out more about the necklace since 'he thought of asking the price in case Evelyn might like it'. This sounds like a possible present, but is soon clarified as meaning that 'Evelyn might like to buy this Spanish necklace': Mrs Whitbread would buy the necklace herself! But the consuming question, once inside the shop, turns out to be not the object that Evelyn might hypothetically want, but instead the absence of a particular member of staff (or perhaps he is the owner):

> 'I should like to see Mr Dubonnet,' said Hugh in his curt worldly way. It appeared that this Dubonnet had the measurements of Mrs Whitbread's neck, or, more strangely still, knew her views upon Spanish jewellery and the extent of her possessions in that line (which Hugh could not remember). All of which seemed to Richard Dalloway awfully odd.[6]

Hugh's relationship to this shop is about the particular persons involved as seller or potential owner, as much as about the possible objects of purchase. Mr Dubonnet's special qualifications include his knowing what it is that his (Hugh's) wife both thinks and has—and also knowing the relevant measurements of the relevant parts of her body. If Mr Dubonnet, with his unique expertise in relation to the unique Evelyn, is not available, then Hugh is not going to think of buying—a scenario which is filtered, again, through Richard's decoding and distancing from it:

> But Hugh was on his feet again. He was unspeakably pompous. Really, after dealing here for thirty-five years he was not going to be put off by a mere boy who did not know his business. For Dubonnet, it seemed, was out, and Hugh would not buy anything until Mr Dubonnet chose to be in; at which the youth flushed and bowed his correct little bow. It was all perfectly correct. And yet Richard couldn't have said that to save his life! Why these people stood that damned insolence he could not conceive.

Hugh's indignation combines the demand for the familiar service of one individual with contempt for a junior blamed for being in his place. It puts Richard into a doubly negative position, finding himself unable to imagine acting as either man just has, on either side of the counter and class divide.

But at the same time, for all Richard's general scorn for Hugh and his ways, the other man's uxorious interest in the possible piece of jewellery for Evelyn also begins a thought about finding a gift for his own wife, Clarissa; and here the novel just touches on a paradox about two kinds of shop whose commodities, while entirely different from one another, are commonly used for a similar gift-giving function. Richard thinks he will buy for Clarissa not jewellery but flowers. 'Flowers? Yes, flowers, since he did not trust his taste in gold; any number of flowers; roses; orchids.'[7] Jewellery and flowers are interchangeable, since both will do the job or give the pleasure of expressing to their recipient how he feels about her. Two types of beautiful thing, one that lasts for ever and the other whose brief short blooming is a traditional emblem of ephemeral youth and beauty, or ephemeral human life. Both freighted with cultural associations since time immemorial, both part of an elaborate commodity network but also natural in some fundamental sense: they come out of the ground.

And both jewels and flowers are also sourced—that is, mined or cultivated—in complex and often exploitative ways that are generally obscure to those who ultimately buy them or enjoy their possession. Flowers, bought and given with more or less love and with more or less cash to spare, may cost little, but jewellery is bound up with prestige and enduring value: the long term of personal commitment and rock-solid investment, as well as the sparkle of a special moment. 'Jewellery is a luxury and yet impulse merchandise', it was aptly said by an architect writing in the 1950s.[8] Jewellery chain stores such as H. Samuel—still a presence on the British high street—appeared from the beginning of the twentieth century, offering a quite different product and buying experience to that of the exclusive type of shop patronized by a Hugh Whitbread. Stock was mostly on display in the windows, often in arcade form on either side of a recessed door, to provide more space; and the price was clearly marked. In that way customers could see what there was and what it cost without the semi-commitment of having to enter a forbiddingly formal shop, or speak to a member of staff. This was not just about the potential embarrassment of an unfamiliar environment. In one of the clichés of courtship in the middle twentieth century, the girl—always her not him—gets the boyfriend to stop and admire the rings in the jeweller's window. Hint!

In the decades after the war, further jewellery chains appeared that catered for those without the means of the Mrs Dalloway gentlemen— with one in particular eventually becoming notorious. After Gerald Ratner took over the family firm in 1984, its branches and turnover rapidly multiplied. There were a thousand Ratner's stores in the UK alone by the end of that decade (and a comparable number in the US); the company also by then owned H. Samuel, along with two other chains. In 1991, Ratner was invited to address the annual convention of the Institute of Directors, and the remarks he made at that event about the products sold by Ratner's—'total crap'!—have gone down in business history as the last word in self-destruction. He pointed out that a pair of Ratner's gold earrings cost less than a prawn sandwich from Marks & Spencer, and quipped that the sandwich might well last longer. What he said, seen as patronizing to customers, caused a steep decline in the store's sales and share price. This unintentional anti-ad, easily accessible on YouTube, retains its potency (and comedy) as a marketing deterrent.

Notes

1. Thomas Turner, *The Diary of Thomas Turner 1754–1765*, ed. David Vaisey (Oxford: Oxford University Press, 1984), 255, 288, entries for Monday 23 August and Thursday 16 September 1762.
2. Madame de Lafayette, *La Princesse de Clèves* (1678), ed. Bernard Pingaud (Paris: Folio Classique, 2012), 48. The repeated 'surprised … surprise' is the same (and the same word) in the French.
3. Virginia Woolf, *Mrs Dalloway* (1925), ed. David Bradshaw (Oxford: Oxford University Press, 2000), 95.
4. Woolf, *Mrs Dalloway*, 96.
5. Woolf, *Mrs Dalloway*, 63.
6. Woolf, *Mrs Dalloway*, 96–7.
7. Woolf, *Mrs Dalloway*, 97.
8. Ellis E. Somake and Rolf Hellberg et al., *Shops and Stores Today: Their Design, Planning and Organisation* (London: B.T. Batsford Ltd, 1956), 73.

29

Sweet Shops

S weet shops were a classic type of small local shop, and there were *lots* of them. They were cheap to set up because most of the stock came from manufacturers' reps, who made regular rounds and gave credit; and there was just one (but there *was* one) regular busy buying time each day, which was the hour after children came out of school. The shop might have a turnover of no more than a few pounds a week; but there were not many risks if (as sometimes happened) the owner was not seeking a full living income from the business. In the last part of the nineteenth century a street of just over a hundred terraced houses in the Hanover area of Brighton had eight grocers, five bakers, eight greengrocers—and five confectioners, 'two of which, Mrs. Payne's and E. Keeping's, were next door to one another at numbers 27 and 28!'[1]

So popular was this smallest of small ambitions that at least two books were published in the mid-twentieth century on the specific subject of running a sweet shop. These enthusiastic publications were working hard, though, against a counter-current of opinion singling out the sweet shop as the obvious case of the expendable and redundant back-street shop. A worst-case relegation of this type is a reference in the early 1930s to 'small dirty house shops in the slums, often doing a negligible trade in "gob-stoppers," liquorice bootlaces, etc., every one of which one could wish to see closed down.'[2] After the war, it became possible to mount a specific defence of the sweet shop. 'This section is written for the confectioner who may be surprised to hear that, like the butcher, the baker, and the grocer, he sells FOOD.'[3] So ends the first paragraph of a chapter of *Sweet-Shop Success* that is simply entitled 'A Sweet Shop Is A Food Shop', in the book collectively produced at the end of the 1940s by Cadbury's Bournville training college near Birmingham, and published by Pitman's; it has several named authors, including a Miss M. Genders. Sweets were de-rationed in the same year, 1949, that the book was published, but the writer of this section is keen to emphasize the fact that they had been categorized as a rationed food in the first place. They cite the acknowledged sustaining value of chocolate and other confectionery—on polar expeditions, apparently, as well as for those doing unusual wartime work, 'Men and women of the Civil Defence, night workers, and all those whose jobs made regular meals impossible'. This was also food that came in a usefully 'compact form'.[4]

In *Sweet-Shop Success*, then, the selling of sweets can be certified as being a matter of national importance, and that is one proud justification for the production of a book to promote it (printed, remarkably for the post-war date, on glossy paper, with handsome illustrations and photographs—and a touch of colour, even). After the war, Bournville also ran dedicated residential courses for women seeking to start a sweet shop, twenty-five students at a time. These cost three guineas for a three- or four-week session, with board and lodging included.[5]

The Bournville book follows another published by Pitman's ten years before—just before the war. *The Sweet Shop* ran to more than three hundred pages, and ended in a way not seen in any other book of business instruction: with a page providing a sample confectioner's will; it is shown duly witnessed by a grocer and a gardener, with imaginary names and addresses fully supplied. As this conclusion would suggest, there is copious detail over the course of the book about the likely life events of a sweet shop and its owner. A chapter on 'Interviewing a girl', for instance, advises against taking on one who is 'extravagantly dressed and made-up', for the surprising reason that her appearance is likely to bring customers in. 'She may attract a number of men to the shop, but our experience is that these are not likely to be good customers, as they will probably waste a lot of time talking, and spend little money.'[6] Not only that: the girl, or rather the two-person side-scene that her presence has produced, will disrupt the social balance: 'other customers are put off, and do not like to come in if they feel that they have to interrupt a conversation before being served.'[7]

This detailed invention of a likely future scenario involves an elaborate construction of characters and scenes based on the single starting point of the candidate's presentation of herself. It is a small but telling example of the fascination of shop books during this period with the behaviour of customers and with every kind of human interaction within a shop. General manuals for prospective shop-keepers almost always include a chapter explicitly devoted to psych-ology, so called, with the idea that this is a subject in which they can find both enjoyment and usefulness, making their own daily observa-tions of buying and selling behaviour. The shop becomes a special sort of scene, with actors following predictable roles in the drama, accord-ing to a set of probable types. How these scenes may play out is a knowledge that shopkeepers can acquire for themselves, it is implied; but watching and thinking about them is a source of interest and pleasure in its own right.

In both sweet shop books, either side of the war, this kind of enterprise is represented as being one of the more straightforward ways to have your own shop. Little initial outlay is needed, especially since manufacturers, keen to get you to sell their branded confection-ery, will supply various fixtures and fittings for the storage and display of their own products. The stock, which (unlike most other edible goods at this time) is mainly sold in small branded packages, is easy to stack and show, and requires no preparatory work or selling know-ledge on the part of the vendor. Sweets also have an exceptionally high profit margin: much greater than with cigarettes and tobacco. These are the natural accompaniments to confectionery sales. They have the same advantage of standard branding and packages, with established channels of small-scale supply from wholesalers; and they provide a small but regular turnover as the recognized everyday treats for ordinary people: 'Out of every £ of their pocket money, men and women as a whole are likely to spend five shillings [that is, 25 per cent] on cigarettes or tobacco', says the Bournville book, going on to point out that this represents in total many times more than the expenditure on sweets and chocolate (and also takes no account of all the accessories associated with smoking, from pipes to tobacco pouches to basic matches).[8]

Three other standard add-ons to the confectioner's trade are biscuits, ice cream, and...books. Biscuits were typically kept on trays beneath a glass-fronted display counter, and sold by weight—as were many types of confectionery, dispensed from large jars. Like the other commodities, ice cream could be regularly delivered, arriving in its refrigerated 'bricks' and smaller blocks. Wall's successfully inaugurated a striking combination of ice cream and sausages, two popular branded food products in these mid-century decades. Copied by Richmond's, whose ice cream plant was installed on the roof of their Liverpool sausage factory, this was an ingenious solution to the problem of the summer decline in demand for sausages. Sell a hot-weather food instead![9]

As for the third of the likely supplements, this usually took the form of the shop's own tiny lending library; both sweet shop books have a section on starting one. In *Sweet-Shop Success*, the chapter memorably begins: 'In addition to chocolates, sweets and tobacco, many of your customers enjoy a murder.'[10] (Did Miss Genders write it? We will probably never solve that particular mystery.) There is discussion of the advantages and disadvantages of buying, as opposed to leasing, the library's stock (again, the channels are well established for both kinds of practice), and there are floor plans of practical store layouts. Both books consider and dismiss the idea that a public library, even if close by, is meeting the same needs or potential demand; the reason (as specified in the earlier book; the later one does not wonder) is that those libraries don't stock the kind of books that customers really want to read. The fact that there is a public library next door or within five minutes' walk need not deter you', says *Sweet-Shop Success*, with consummate confidence. Instead, 'Your real competitors are the long-established, well-stocked libraries of the chain-store chemists and booksellers, the 2d per week chain libraries, and the small libraries in the confectioners' and newsagents', shops'—in other words, for the last lot, places not unlike your own.[11] Here is a whole book world of tiny lending libraries down every street that has disappeared completely from the shopscape of the past half century. Boots is the unnamed 'chain store' chemist, with books as familiar an item on some of its shelves as bottles of medicine or perfume on others.

Another kind of attitude to the ubiquitous sweet shop *cum* tobacconist can be seen in a Pelican book published shortly after the war, by the economist Gertrude Williams (Pelicans were part of the Penguin list). An introduction to what it neatly calls the economics of everyday life, this book points to the density of the current provision of small local shops with a topical illustration:

> Now that the smoking habit is so strongly entrenched, smokers will go to great lengths to get their tobacco and cigarettes and during the post-war shortage the confirmed smoker stood in queues or snooped from street to street to get his supply. But would the habit ever have become so firmly fixed if such quests had been necessary from the beginning, instead of being able to buy a packet of cigarettes every few yards along the road?[12]

More than a decade before the first exposure of the health risks of cigarette smoking, the 'habit' is presented as addictive, also solitary and semi-secretive (snooping from street to street at a time of shortage). The easy access questioned here would come to be gradually curtailed by increasingly prohibitive pricing. To this was added a form of de-branding in the 2010s, with cigarettes hidden from general customer view at the point of sale and packets, in an inversion of commercial logic, designed to deter (through images of the effects of diseases caused by smoking). But perhaps the most striking feature of Williams' vignette is that it represents local accessibility as a problem in itself: the corner shop supplies too much, and too easily, of a good or bad thing (there is no direct objection to cigarettes and tobacco as such). In effect, it is an anti-convenience argument: it shouldn't be possible to get these things instantly.

Small, semi-addictive pleasure purchases may also switch in the other moral direction. The WHSmith trade journal, *Shop Talk*, reported in the mid-1950s that the newly launched educational 'I-Spy' books, at sixpence each, had proved unexpectedly popular with children. A Mr H.M. Mules of the Slough branch described the difference this had made on Saturdays, 'that being the day when the children receive their pocket money':

> It has been noticeable during the past few weeks how the attitude of the children has changed. At the beginning of the 'I Spy' campaign they arrived at the branch complete with bags of sweets or sucking lollies, thus indicating that the sweet shop had had the first claim on their pocket money. Now the first port of call appears to be the 'I Spy' corner of SMITH's.[13]

Twenty years before, Penguin books had first been sold at the price of a packet of ten cigarettes (also sixpence). It was the grown-up equivalent of the same kind of little treat, in the same way taking an opportune bookish turn.

Notes

1. Neil Griffiths, *Shops Book: Brighton 1900–1930* (Brighton: QueenSpark Books, c.1978), 9.
2. Lawrence E. Neal, *Retailing and the Public* (London: George Allen & Unwin Ltd, 1932), 189.
3. *Sweet-Shop Success: A Handbook for the Sweet Retailer*, Produced by the Bournville Studio (London: Sir Isaac Pitman & Sons, Ltd., 1949), 36.
4. *Sweet-Shop Success*, 37.
5. Alice Hooper Beck, 'Sweet Shop', *Housewife* (October 1947), 43–4.
6. Charles Vernon, *The Sweet Shop: A Handbook for Retail Confectioners* (London: Sir Isaac Pitman & Sons, Ltd., 1939), 102.

7. Vernon, *The Sweet Shop*, 102.
8. *Sweet-Shop Success*, 175.
9. Peter Mathias, *Retailing Revolution: A History of Multiple Retailing in the Food Trades* (London: Longmans, 1967), 308.
10. *Sweet-Shop Success*, 182.
11. *Sweet-Shop Success*, 182.
12. Gertrude Williams, *The Economics of Everyday Life* (1950; Harmondsworth: Penguin, 1953), 100.
13. 'I-Spy Morning', *Shop Talk*, June 1954, 155.

30

Umbrella Shops

Long before smartphones, umbrellas were the first of the mechanical devices to travel around town with the person. They are a low-tech tool, whose production method and materials vary from the factory-made to the still occasionally handcrafted. With the prospect of a downpour, no one is meant to leave home without one. When rain arrives unexpectedly in the city, there are street sellers with ready supplies. (But ironically, the metaphorical *rainy day* is a far more costly and serious outlook than the real one, demanding regular savings or insurance payments to cover you, not a simple umbrella.)

The umbrella may seem like the least likely niche commodity to have had specialized shops of its own. Yet there is a proud little history here. Shops selling (and also making) umbrellas were an established if not a numerous species two hundred years ago. A London trade directory of 1817 lists four umbrella manufactories in Oxford Street alone. For comparison, there were thirty-three linen drapers (the highest number in any category). And there was one ribbon warehouse ('warehouse' referring, at this time, to a site for retail sales, not just storage).[1]

In the world beyond the shop, outside in the open, umbrellas are designed for the most specific of uses. Unlike other portable devices, they tend to get left behind all the time; they are usually quite big and bulky and easily neglected when not in use. They are forgotten on buses and trains, in public and private houses; in shops of every kind. Lost and not found, they need to be bought again: good for the trade.

Often divertingly different, umbrellas come in every shade and grade of colour and quality; they have come a long way from the black uniformity matching the bowler hats in the pictures of early commuter crowds. A children's encyclopaedia of the 1950s concluded that the image of the umbrella had brightened since those nineteenth-century days when they represented 'the very symbol of respectability': 'Women have umbrellas of different colours to suit their costumes, and a carefully rolled umbrella adds much to the appearance of a well-dressed man when he walks abroad.'[2]

At the flimsier edge of the market, umbrellas are cheap and mass-produced. At the smart end, they are works of art. This is Constance, in Arnold Bennett's novel of 1908, *The Old Wives' Tale*, receiving a beautiful gift from the newly returned sister who has lived all her adult life in Paris:

> It was an umbrella such that a better could not be bought.... The handle was of gold, set with opalines. The tips of the ribs were also of gold. It was this detail which staggered Constance.... Sophia said calmly that the device was quite common. But she did not conceal that the umbrella was strictly of the highest class and that it might be shown to queens without shame. She intimated that the frame (a 'Fox's Paragon'), handle, tips, would outlast many silks. Constance was childish with pleasure.[3]

With a complexity of sourcing almost worthy of twenty-first century manufacturing, it appears that this premium Paris accessory had its main part—'a Fox's Paragon'—made in England, before being put together and sold in France, and then reverse exported as a present, back to its country of origin. It is the finishing Paris 'detail' that staggers Constance and gives the item all its special value for her.

Another fictional umbrella shop has a small but significant role in Emile Zola's novel *Au Bonheur des Dames* (1883). This novel is about the rapid expansion of a grand department store, Au Bonheur des Dames, selling more and more different things, and taking over several streets of an old Paris neighbourhood. It describes the local shops that are displaced and put out of business as the Bonheur encroaches on their territory and sales. Among those that are threatened, Bourras' umbrella shop is one that stands out. Its owner 'carves the handles himself, so that he had become well known in the area as an artist.'[4] He tries to hold out, refusing to sell up, and updating his interior and windows. He even invents a popular new shape of umbrella, but it is immediately copied by the competing new store, which has also opened its own separate umbrella department. Eventually—and inevitably, within the logic of this novel—Bourras has to watch the demolition of his own shop.

In Jacques Démy's gorgeous film of 1964, *Les Parapluies de Cherbourg* (*The Umbrellas of Cherbourg*), the bright little umbrella shop where the heroine has grown up is closed down when her mother moves away; a shot of a lorry unloading new stock at the end indicates that from now on the products for sale will be washing machines. Instead of the light and lovely objects in all the colours of the rainbow, now it is to be a place to acquire solid appliances, the 'white goods' of post-war domestic consumption.

In real life, we find the resilience of a London umbrella shop which, at the start of the 2020s, is still going strong. With its dramatic plate glass windows on the edge of Bloomsbury, James Smith & Sons has been in existence for nearly two centuries (see Figure 12). In 1975, a feature in the *Sunday Times* magazine had a photograph of it—in black and white, not colour, to signify an old-time historicity. The writer (and photographer) of the piece, Andrew Lawson, chose a selection of now ancient London shops that were still in business, like random remainders from a bygone age. He points out in the text that the frequent complaint about crude modernization is not a new one—not a new one in the 1970s, that is. Casting the historical net back to the previous century, he finds the passage in which Charles Dickens complains about the fancy plate glass and mahogany counters that were coming in during the 1830s. Dickens, he says, would have 'detested' James Smith's, which had and has all those features, but which 'to my mind, is one of the gems of London'.[5]

Figure 12. James Smith's umbrella shop, Bloomsbury, London, at the time of the Diamond Jubilee celebrations for Queen Victoria, 1897
Image courtesy of James Smith & Sons Umbrellas

Lawson's article was published almost half a century ago, and so it has now itself become part of the history that it describes. James Smith's umbrella shop, meanwhile, with its workshop downstairs, is still open and doing well. The umbrella shop: permanent pop-up.

Notes

1. *Johnstone's London Commercial Guide*, list reproduced in Alison Adburgham, *Shops and Shopping 1800–1914* (1964; 2nd edn. London: George Allen and Unwin, 1981), 14.
2. 'Umbrellas', *Oxford Junior Encyclopaedia* (London: Geoffrey Cumberlege, Oxford University Press, 1955), Vol. XI, 465.
3. Arnold Bennett, *The Old Wives' Tale* (1908), ed. John Wain (Harmondsworth: Penguin, 1983), 515.
4. Emile Zola, *Au Bonheur des Dames* (1883; Paris: Garnier-Flammarion, 1981), 57.
5. Andrew Lawson, 'Counter Revolution', *Sunday Times Magazine*, 30 March 1975, 39; the photograph of James Smith's is on page 36).

Afterword

Figure 13. Opening day of Sainsbury's first self-service store, Croydon, June 1950
Image courtesy of Sainsbury Archives

This photograph (see Figure 13) was taken on the first day of self-service shopping in Sainsbury's newly converted Croydon store, in 1950. Today it appears as touchingly ancient—from the enormous coat and heavy footwear of the leading lady to the starched white apron of the store manager who greets her. The tins of condensed milk look irredeemably dated, both what they are and the way they are shown, so precisely lined up on that special shelving unit. The picture looks like something out of an archive, and that is just what it is. Yet in its own time this same photograph had an entirely different meaning. It was an image not of bygone times but of a modern future, the shape of shops to come. The focus then was on the wire baskets the women are carrying—on how they had picked those jars off the shelves all by themselves, instead of asking for them over a counter.

The manager's familiar presence on opening day is a transitional reassurance that even here, in this self-service space not yet called a 'supermarket', there is still someone there to show proper appreciation of your custom. But in reality, much had changed. Not only were customers fetching and carrying all the goods themselves, but the process of shopping was now separated into two quite different phases, with their corresponding spaces. In this newly converted Croydon store, as the Sainsbury's trade journal explained to its staff nationwide: 'Customers, after having made their purchases, leave the shop by one of five exit lanes known as "check-outs".'[1] A word with a future, that one. Unlike any other type of shop, the visit to a self-service store has this definite point of exit which is spatially differentiated from the rest of the store and requires a quite different orientation on the part of the customer, who performs certain tasks in a certain order. As in the traditional shop, there is a counter, and an employee on the other side of it. But the cashier's role has nothing to do with getting you the goods or weighing them out, or asking what else you would like. Even so, if the customer is shopping alone, this is likely to be the one moment of interaction with another person in the shop.

Laying out the contents of a basket or trolley, paying, and packing them up again is a peculiar ritual of its own, perhaps involving a quantitative jolt—can it be that much?—as opposed to the open state before, with one thing after another picked up and put into the trolley at will. The checkout has constraints and requirements that do not apply elsewhere in the store. No lingering; and specific actions of first laying out and then packing up again, to be performed while standing within a narrow passageway. Walking up and down the aisles, it is possible to choose or unchoose as often as you like—whereas this is a place to get out of as fast as possible.

From their earliest days, supermarkets have always had trouble with the checkout, that dream-breaker. If the wait is too long, the customer may leave in a state of stress, whatever their mood had been up to that point. American researchers of the 1950s devoted years of study and survey, again and again, to the seemingly intractable problem of the abruptness and sometimes the slowness of the checkout experience. Barcodes arrived on the scene as a kind of miracle. The scanner was first introduced in a Marsh supermarket in Troy, Ohio in 1974. Barcodes not only shortened the time that it took to go through the checkout, they also streamlined the inventory end of the process: no more need for human hands and eyes and attention to count all the tins on the shelves.[2]

With the hindsight of later history, it looks now as if the supermarket was already on the way online long before *that* form of digital technology was delivered in the first years of the twenty-first century. As online retail would later be, this was a store in which the process of deciding what to buy or not buy could take seconds or hours, at the customer's discretion or distraction: in which there was no commitment, until the moment of checkout, to purchasing anything that had been put in the basket. The supermarket's mechanical sounds and scannings are not so far from the pings of the personal device that provides the means to browse and buy, but today we touch only the screen or the keyboard—never the goods themselves.

So now there is that new sort of checkout, in relation to which the one in the supermarket begins in its turn to seem quaintly old-fashioned. In this ongoing shift of shopping history, online retail has been drawing attention away from the sales that take place in bricks and mortar shops—that is, in the kind of shops that you walk in and out of, that used to be called just *shops*. As in the days before self-service, the labour of packing the goods up and taking them home reverts to the (now online) store and its workers; the customer simply awaits. And as in the time of self-service superstores, the high street—*the* high street, but understood as the shops of a thousand different towns and out-of-towns—is once again in question.

'Bricks and mortar'—that gloomy phrase is used with monotonous regularity to state the contrast between the old and the internet ways of shopping. Lumbering and cumbersome like the words that name them, it is as if actual shops were to be looked upon as no more than a heap of building materials, no longer fit for purpose. There is no suggestion even of goods for sale, let alone pleasant surroundings or display. With no mention of windows, 'bricks and mortar' makes it sound as if they are boarded up already—as if to condemn them in advance.

Further linguistic damage is inflicted by the internet taking over so many terms associated with physical shops. Not least, with the *windows* opened to access an online shop (after the 'bricks and mortar' blanking out of the real ones). There are also the online *basket* and *checkout:* just click, no queues, no worries. It is strange that it should be a called a basket even though its screen icon is a trolley. But in any case, it is a basket with magical properties, capable of holding as much as you choose to put in it, and never becoming too heavy to transfer into the equally capacious checkout trolley. We also *visit* an online shop, without irony, even though we have not moved an inch.

In another surreptitious supersession, the large-scale online retailer may also have retail space in the non-virtual world beyond the website. In other words there may be a shop, or multiple shops, as well. But this, so the online language tells us, is just a contingency, with the outlet functioning more like a showroom or open stock-room. It doesn't have to be there—just as, in the same way, non-virtual shops in general can be presented now as superfluous and dispensable. In addition, there will likely be warehouses—bricks and mortar, and not a window to be seen—in which human and not-human bodies do their work, and where no customer has ever set foot.

The bricks and mortar phrase also has the strange effect of suggesting that shops can all be placed in a single category, as if there were no relevant difference between the large supermarket and the small and still counter-service bakery, say. Against such casual relegation of all the non-virtual shops, this book has described some of the very many variations of their types and practices, both at any one time and across different periods and locations. These are not features to lose or let go of, whether in language or in reality.

And nor will we. In his introduction to a report at the end of 2019 on the plight and prospects of the British high street, Sir John Timpson spoke of the overall aim as 'quite simply: making the town centre a place people want to be'.[3] For the past few decades, shops have been suffering from seemingly intractable challenges: first out-of-town stores, then online shopping, taking the trade away. The report gave examples to demonstrate what some enterprising towns had done to bring back a sense of shopping vitality to their centres. Many more initiatives have been gaining attention and approval since Sir John's report, not least in old urban centres such as Nottingham and Stockton-on-Tees.

In January 2020, another report made a comparable case for shops in France, by arguing that the *gilets jaunes* protests of the previous year had had more to do with the social environment of particular localities than with a person's own economic situation within it. If a place is rundown, then so are the people, even if they do have a job. The loss of local amenities was a crucial factor in this, the report said; in particular the presence, or not, of shops.[4] True to French style, the authors even cited an early work by Balzac in praise of the local shopkeeper. You can build a new town from scratch, says the story, complete with houses, church, people, a teacher, and hopefully children to follow—but it will all come to nothing 'so long as this microcosm is not linked up by the strongest of social ties, a grocer'.[5]

In the long pandemic months of 2020 and 2021, the shopping mood in Britain began to change in wholly unexpected ways. Big chains were still shutting down and boarding up, and restrictions on people's movements were spurring online ordering of every kind. But at the same time, lockdowns and working from home also led to a brightening of interest in the social importance of real shops, and a widespread resolve to maintain or restore their role as community resources. Local shops came into their own during the lockdowns as places accessible for 'essential shopping', that wonderfully question-begging phrase. And many of them were also doing home deliveries. In this way, online ordering became detached from its default connection with big companies and large-scale networks; a type of service that used to be found in every neighbourhood had suddenly been revived. At the same time, the shop down the road, if not round the corner, became somewhere to go for a walk and a chat, as well as whatever it was that you happened to need to buy. Life was changing in so many ways undreamt of a year before. And people were going back to the shops.

Notes

1. *J.S. Journal: The Sainsbury House Magazine*, 3:4 (September 1950), 8.
2. On checkout research see Rachel Bowlby, *Carried Away: The Invention of Modern Shopping* (London: Faber, 2000), 243–5.
3. Sir John Timpson, Introduction, *The High Street Report* (2019), 5; this document is a summary of Steve Millington et al., *High Street 2030: Achieving Change* (Institute of Place Management, 2019).
4. See Yann Algan, Clément Malgouyres, and Claudia Senik, 'Territoires, bien-être et politiques publiques', *Les notes du conseil d'analyse économique* 55 (janvier 2020).
5. Honoré de Balzac, *L'Épicier* (1840), *Les Français peints par eux-mêmes: Encyclopédie morale du dix-neuvième siècle*, vol. 1, Médiathèque André Malraux de Lisieux, 2.

ACKNOWLEDGEMENTS

This book is indebted to several public libraries for making available digital and other resources—in one case, for hunting out a survey of local shopping from fifty years ago, eventually found tucked away on a shelf in a back room. Warm thanks to Alison Lucas of Leighton Buzzard Library, and to staff at Croydon Central Library, Shropshire Archives in Shrewsbury, and Heathfield Library in East Sussex. Paul Williams of the Museum of London pointed me towards invaluable materials in the Sainsbury Archive. I would also like to thank David Williams of the Ightham History Project for generously sharing his knowledge of Benjamin Harrison.

For their encouraging responses to draft chapters, and for conversations that helped the book along in all sorts of ways, I want above all to thank Chris Bowlby, Rick Bowlby, Tom Bowlby, Peter Brooks, Anne Cheng, Helena Dollimore, Jonathan Dollimore, Louisa Dollimore, Carol Dyhouse, Claire Lindsay, Kathryn Pogson, Uta Staiger, and David Vaisey.

I thank too those involved in producing and marketing the book at OUP, in particular Katie Bishop, Anna Gell, Amy Guest, Luciana O'Flaherty, Jayaprakash Periyanayagam, and Cathryn Steele.

INDEX